# THEOLOGY AND ACTION

# THEOLOGY AND ACTION

*After Theory in Christian Ethics*

Charles R. Pinches

*William B. Eerdmans Publishing Company*

*Grand Rapids, Michigan / Cambridge, U.K.*

BJ
1251
.P55
2002

Wm. B. Eerdmans Publishing Co.
255 Jefferson Ave. S.E., Grand Rapids, Michigan 49503 /
P.O. Box 163, Cambridge CB3 9PU U.K.

Printed in the United States of America

07 06 05 04 03 02      7 6 5 4 3 2 1


**Library of Congress Cataloging-in-Publication Data**

Pinches, Charles Robert.
    Theology and action: after theory in Christian ethics / Charles R. Pinches.
        p.        cm.
    Includes bibliographical references.
    ISBN 0-8028-4886-9 (pbk.: alk. paper)
    1. Christian ethics.   2. Thomas, Aquinas, Saint, 1225?-1274 — Ethics.
    I. Title.

    BJ1251.P55   2002
    241 — dc21

                                                            2001050814


www.eerdmans.com

*To my parents*

**Charles W. Pinches**

(1913-2000)

*&*

**Helen L. Pinches**

*Ordinary saints*

# Contents

# Preface

Some books have a longer than average gestational life. This one began as far back as twenty-five years when as an undergraduate student at Wheaton College I was introduced to Ludwig Wittgenstein and Wittgensteinians such as G. E. M. Anscombe and J. L. Austin. My teacher then, C. Stephen Evans, would undoubtly have rather been reading Kierkegaard; I remain all the more grateful to him for taking the time to introduce me to these thinkers. Our reading of Gilbert Ryle's book *Dilemmas* made an especially strong impression on me. Ryle shows us something of the independent life even false dilemmas can come to have, especially as we form a language or set of theories around them. The influence of the kind of analysis I learned from reading Wittgenstein or Ryle is evident in the first three chapters of the book.

I had the great good fortune to find a place to study Christian theology and ethics where these philosophical influences could be developed rather than ignored or disparaged, namely the Department of Theology at the University of Notre Dame. This was because of the presence of teachers such as David Burrell, C.S.C., whose love for Wittgenstein and Aquinas (together) I have come to share, but most especially for me in those days because of Stanley Hauerwas, who became my teacher, mentor, and close friend. My debt to him extends far beyond this book but includes it as well. Without his encouragement, it would never have come to be. He has read it through carefully in its entirety and offered helpful criticisms. He has read some portions, in fact, many times; parts of chapters 2 and 6 reflect work done in my dissertation, which he directed. David Solomon was a reader of that dissertation; he helped me read Julius Kovesi and Anscombe better than I could have done alone. I am grateful to him for nourishing my long-standing interest in human action.

Ideas carried in the mind for decades need the chance to spill out. In the past two or three years my students and colleagues at the University of Scranton have listened patiently and thoughtfully as this has come about. I am grateful to members of my department, particularly Scott Bader-Saye and Brian Benestad, for offering criticisms of my writing. While visiting professors on the faculty, both Paul Wadell and Emmanuel Katongole offered helpful suggestions about portions of the book. The University also has generously supported my work, providing me with funds to gain the help of others. My research assistant, Jason Danner, typed many of my scrawled corrections and gave me the benefit of his theologically astute observations along the way. Amy Rowe carefully proofread the entire manuscript, saving me from many embarrassing errors. Marie Gaughan faithfully printed and assembled the manuscript at its many stages of development.

Besides these personal debts, I wish to acknowledge the publishers of two of my essays from which the material of chapters 1 and 2 are drawn: the entry entitled "Action" in *The Encyclopedia of Bioethics*, rev. ed., ed. Warren T. Reich (New York: Macmillan, 1995), pp. 56-63, reprinted by permission; and "Principle Monism and Action Descriptions: Situation and Its Critics Revisited," *Modern Theology* 7 (April 1991): 249-68.

Finally, I want to thank my wife, Robin, for her abiding love and care. Her gifts sustain me daily. Our children, Jody, Nathan, Claire, and Seth, have patiently endured the tests of silly examples that found their way into the book, and many more that did not. Their laughter, mingled with Robin's, have saved me from the curse that can so easily settle upon those of us who imagine we have something significant to say, namely, the curse of taking ourselves too seriously.

# Introduction

It is impossible to speak about the moral life for more than a sentence or two without bringing up the topic of human action, or, more accurately, without focusing on some particular human action as the object of our judgment, after which the topic of human action might or might not be discussed, depending on the company. And to be honest, in some company the lack of such an ensuing discussion might be for the better, for human action is a difficult topic and we can easily get lost. Generally, we understand human actions better when we do them than when we stop to discuss them.

Of course, this is not to say that doing is understanding when it comes to human action. Consider the following quotation from Stuart Hampshire's justly famous *Thought and Action*.

> It is possible that a man might not be doing what he honestly says that he is doing, without it being true that he is not doing what he intended to do. He might make a mistake in describing the achievement at which he is aiming, because he has false opinions about the proper and conventional description of the achievement intended. . . . [A] man may be doing something intentionally in circumstances in which he may be said to have a false opinion about the nature of his intended action, in virtue of the fact that he hon-

estly misdescribes it, or that he would misdescribe it, if the question were raised.[1]

This may sound unnecessarily complicated. Yet with due reflection on Hampshire's points, I suggest they bear up. Just because Joe says this is what he is up to doesn't mean that's actually what Joe is up to. And this is not to say that Joe is lying. He probably actually believes what he says about his action. He's just not gotten it right. (If a context is needed, we might consider some alternative descriptions for Joe's action, whatever it was: "Joe, you were exaggerating"; "Joe, it's plain that you were only trying to impress her"; "Joe, you were hogging the ball"; etc.)

How might Joe have gotten himself into the position of having what Hampshire calls "false opinions" about what he is doing? One clear way is simply that he is self-deceived.[2] He may have a stake in perpetuating certain false beliefs about himself simply because he would rather they were true. Accepting the truth of certain descriptions of his actions might negate these false beliefs, and so he holds tight to another set of action descriptions that will allow him to retain his self-deception.

Yet this is not the only way Joe might get it wrong about his action. He may be the mildest sort of man, with minimal self-delusions, but nonetheless have gotten quite turned around in his actions and his well-meaning and honestly proffered descriptions of them if he has been raised on a false set of descriptions of the world, if he has been taught to speak a language that falls consistently short of reality.

---

1. Stuart Hampshire, *Thought and Action* (Notre Dame, Ind.: University of Notre Dame Press, 1982), p. 95.

2. I say little in the book directly about the importance of certain psychological states as they affect our capacity to act well as well as to describe well what we have done. Evidently, though, it is a key matter. As Aquinas plainly understood, no full account of the human/moral life can be given without the development of a complex and intricate human psychology. Of course, for the Christian Aquinas, this will involve giving due emphasis to sin, something less openly discussed in our own time.

This point about sin and psychology cannot but also imply that there is such a thing as a Christian psychology. However, it need not imply that only Christians can do psychology well. Indeed, for a subtle account of self-deception, see Herbert Fingarette's *Self-Deception* (Berkeley: University of California Press, 2000).

Through no real fault of his own, Joe will have trouble knowing what he is doing, let alone telling others accurately about it.

Jean Bethke Elshtain has recently expressed the worry that our time is one in which true descriptions have slid into the shadows. She believes there is no more important thing for us all to do than insist on proper naming.

> The first concrete project for citizens who live in hope is to insist that we name things accurately and appropriately. Why is this so vital? One extraordinary sign of our times is a process of radical alteration in language, understanding and meaning. . . . [W]e are painfully aware of what happened when totalitarian regimes had the power to control language and to cover mass murder with the rhetoric of "improvement of the race" and even "mercy and compassion." We are much less attuned to the ways in which our own language, hence our own understanding of the world, may be contorted by drawing us away from, rather than closer to, that which we are depicting.[3]

While I suspect things are a little more complicated than she makes them seem, I share Elshtain's worry. In one sense this book might be thought of as an attempt to heed her call. How can we get to a place whence we can better describe our lives, our actions, and the world in which they are played out?

One place we clearly cannot go to do this is to a god's-eye view of the world. We cannot float above the contingencies and particularities of our world, grasping hold of some eternal truth that can give us a way to freeze-frame them all, or reduce our actions to one kind of good or evil on the basis of some one great clarifying principle. In his aptly titled *Theology after Wittgenstein*, Fergus Kerr suggests that this is a lesson we should have learned from Wittgenstein.

> However deeply inclined we may be to suppose that the stability there is in our way of life, and thus our structures of knowledge and so on, must be grounded in (say) the unchanging realities that underlie the flux of experiences, perhaps certain non-observable enti-

---

3. Jean Bethke Elshtain, *Who Are We? Critical Reflections and Hopeful Possibilities* (Grand Rapids: Eerdmans, 2000), pp. 127-28.

ties occupying a realm that escapes the ravages of change and vicissitudes of history, Wittgenstein wants us to acknowledge that the stability there is, such as it is, is already given in the customs and practices of everyday intercourse. The given cannot be explored or explained any more deeply because it is the foundation of every kind of exploration and explanation. If you like: the given cannot be discovered except by showing how it makes possible all that we do and suffer. I discover myself, not in some pre-linguistic inner space of self-presence, but in the network of multifarious social and historical relationships in which I am willy-nilly involved.[4]

In the pages of this book I will suggest that this lesson has not been especially well learned. Indeed, much that has been written about human actions after Wittgenstein proceeds as if before him. It is my hope, however, that we can treat human actions otherwise, after Wittgenstein, after certain other thinkers dependent upon his work such as Hampshire, or G. E. M. Anscombe or Julius Kovesi, as well as after others less explicitly dependent on Wittgenstein but who have understood the sea change moral thought must now pass through after the controlling presumptions of the Enlightenment have been abandoned, thinkers such as Alasdair MacIntyre, Stanley Hauerwas, or, for that matter, John Paul II.

What this means specifically is that, following Kerr, I shall be interested in what is "given in the customs and practices of everyday intercourse," as well as in linking particular things discovered there with how they make "possible all that we do and suffer." As will be apparent in the first three chapters and again in the sixth and eighth, I hold that before we can give these things their due, we must be disabused of a certain persistent urge to theory, particularly moral theory but also "action theory," as it has been sculpted out of analytic philosophy in the past few decades. I treat action theory in chapter 1, and then move in chapters 2 and 3 to certain presumptions about morality that bear connection not only to the standard moral theorizing of the Enlightenment but also to a physicalism that is detectable in the philosophical action theory discussed in chapter 1. I am particularly concerned with the thinking done in theological circles. In chapter 2 I

---

4. Fergus Kerr, *Theology after Wittgenstein* (New York: Basil Blackwell, 1986), p. 69.

cover Protestantism in the era of "situation ethics," whose presumptions about how to think about morality and therefore about human action, I allege, extend far beyond the on-the-spot thinking of Joseph Fletcher. In chapter 3 I consider the more recent debate in Catholicism about human action after *Veritatis Splendor*, alleging again that the same presumptions are at work, especially in the work of the proportionalists.

Most of the work of the first three chapters of the book is negative. The question that will nag the reader throughout them will be, where else can we turn if we are to adequately take into account, do, and describe human actions? Given the point made by Kerr, it is plain that we cannot but start in the midst of human life, in the practices of everyday discourse. But how is constructive work to be done in such a context?

From Claude Levi-Strauss, and also Jacques Derrida, Jeffrey Stout borrows an image to describe how moral inquiry should be conceived, that of the *bricoleur*. "The *bricoleur* . . . does odd jobs, drawing on a collection of assorted odds and ends available for use and kept on hand on the chance that they might someday prove useful." Stout continues: "All great works of creative ethical thought (and some not so great) . . . involve moral *bricolage*. They start off by taking stock of problems that need solving and available conceptual resources for solving them. They proceed by taking apart, putting together, reordering, weighting, weeding out, and filling in."[5]

Stout's image is not unhelpful. Moral reflection is about the moral life, which is varied and unpredictable. Moral situations are particular situations, as are the people who live them out with grace and courage or bitterness and envy. Hence, when we set about to reflect on the moral life, like the *bricoleur*, we need a variety of tools or materials to think well about its particular characteristics. Indeed, constructive work in ethics cannot proceed, as perhaps was once thought, by quantum leaps with the discovery of a new principle or theory that will gather all that was once puzzling into a new orderly pattern. We will need to consider one question at a time, knowing that the answer to one question may suggest another question that may in its turn call for a different sort of answer altogether.

5. Jeffrey Stout, *Ethics after Babel* (Boston: Beacon Press, 1988), pp. 74-75.

The constructive work on morality and human action in this book proceeds roughly according to this pattern. In chapter 4 I consider the relation between moral actions and human actions, concluding with Aquinas that they are the same. Questions of how particular human actions are named take up chapter 5. No naming formula is offered, but, again with Aquinas, I conclude that something like his species distinctions are key, and we rightly use them to repudiate redescriptions of particular actions in other terms. In chapter 6 I look more closely at moral notions, attending to the various ways they are formed and used in descriptions of particular human actions. Chapter 7 begins with the observation that frequently enough we wish to point out certain cases of someone's not acting, and then goes on to consider the relation between actions and failures to act. Aquinas is once again helpful, especially as he discusses the relation between sins of commission and sins of omission. Finally, in chapter 8 I take up the question of whether the attention to particular action descriptions, depending as it does on the language a people speak, is inherently conservative. Here some of the theological themes that have peppered the book become more explicit and are gathered together well enough for us to see a way to go on. In a way, all the interesting work yet remains after chapter 8, for particular human actions or virtues and vices and the complicated relations between them will need to be discussed, one at a time.

Bricolage is in one sense, then, an apt description of the work of this book, and more broadly, of the sort of work we will need to do as moral inquiry once again becomes rich, embodied, and particular. However, despite its virtues, I think bricolage cannot finally be our guiding metaphor, particularly for further work in theological ethics. To begin to see why not, we need to glance ahead in Stout's text to see whom he calls a *bricoleur*.

> Take Aquinas, whom we too often remember, misleadingly, as the author of a great system of natural law. This makes him too much like the precursor of the Esperantists. His real accomplishment was to bring together into a single whole a wide assortment of fragments — Platonic, Stoic, Pauline, Jewish, Islamic, Augustinian, and Aristotelian. . . . My point is that viewing Aquinas as a sort of *bricoleur*, a strong moralist engaging in a kind of selective retrieval and

reconfiguration of available moral languages for his own use, helps make sense of what he was doing.[6]

It is indeed a mistake, I believe, to see Aquinas as the author of a great system of natural law. Aquinas was not a theoretician like Kant, for instance — whom Stout would class as an "Esperantist," by which he means someone who hopes to set out the ground rules of a universal language of morals "in abstraction from the vagaries of particular traditions," a universal language that "rules the deep structure of morality as such."[7] On the other hand, neither is it particularly helpful to call Aquinas a *bricoleur.* Unlike the *bricoleur,* Aquinas is not an odd-jobber, dealing with one problem today and another tomorrow; nor does he set about to shore up this or that affirmation of some particular moral truth such as Stout's declaration that slavery is wrong is true.[8] While it is true that when the *Summa* is finished we do indeed have standing before us a remarkably detailed and intricate structure, and while it is also true that Aquinas is interested in making particular moral judgments about, say, slavery, if we are to understand the work of Aquinas and its significance for ongoing discussion in theological ethics, we must see that Aquinas is about neither system building nor fixing particular problems by combining bits and pieces of traditions or thinkers. Rather Aquinas is fundamentally interested in discerning reality.

A better image to describe Aquinas is that of the forester. A forester attends to leaf and bark, notices height and span. On the basis of such particulars he makes judgments about a tree's species, generally adding a thoughtful assessment of a particular specimen's relative health. Moreover, he not only knows how to identify particular species but can also discern the pattern of a forest. He knows which species grow together, which compete. What is for most of us simply a collection of trees has for him a structure, not imposed by theory on the forest but discernible to his trained eye in the forest itself as it grows or ages. Forests are different, not only in the varieties of species in them but in the types of interactions that go on between species. The good forester will not only note these differences, he will also rec-

6. Stout, p. 76.
7. Stout, p. 5.
8. See Stout, pp. 21-31.

ognize their different goods. As well (and finally), the forester will know not only about the trees of the forest but also about the basic elements that support its life — how we must have soil and water and climate if we are to have any trees at all.

With regard to our own study of human actions, which follows Aquinas, we must see that while Aquinas certainly helps in the identification of particular acts in species and variation, he also discerns more than this. Like soil to a forest, human action is not one of a number of things that are to be found in the human moral life; rather it is essential to its very existence. If we use Aquinas as guide, we are well advised to begin any inquiry into the moral life with an investigation of human action. The *bricoleur* does not typically concern himself with what is essential and basic in this sense. He moves from one job to the next, guided mainly by what presents itself; he does not, like Aquinas, mark out the ground. This is not to say that to proceed in an investigation of the moral life we need a foundational theory of action — indeed, as I try to show, this is just what we do not need. Again, while a structure may come to be as the *Summa* unfolds, Aquinas does not set out with a plan to build this structure, so his work in human action is not rightly conceived as "laying the foundation," particularly as modern moral theorists have imagined a theoretical foundation always to be the first step in constructing a morality. As forester discerning an existing forest (the forester is dependent in his work on the prior existence of the forest, whereas plainly the builder is not dependent on the prior existence of the building — indeed, if it already exists he is out of a job), Aquinas might have begun elsewhere than with human actions, perhaps with the virtues, or the passions, and worked his way back round to action.[9] But wherever one begins in thinking about mo-

---

9. Aristotle describes moral virtue in Book II of the *Nicomachean Ethics*, before he moves on to discuss matters relating to action in Book III — the same matters with which Aquinas begins I-II of the *Summa*. I do think Aquinas's ordering makes the greater sense, yet Aristotle's also does not really confuse us. I do not want to say that ordering makes no difference. Rather, the point is that beginning with virtue would not be like starting on the construction of a house with the second story (without the foundation or the first floor). One could do it, just as one could begin investigating a forest by attending to climate rather than soil. But of course — and this is the point — full investigation, full knowledge, of the forest could not be had without attending to each of these essential factors, of which, on the analogy, human action is one.

rality, if anything more than the particular moral judgments of the *bricoleur* are to be ventured, then the nature and meaning of human action must be explored.

In sum, Aquinas is better understood as a forester than as a *bricoleur* because he sets out not to construct, but rather to discern what is there, and as he discerns he discovers not just individual phenomena to note and perhaps to tinker with, but structures and relations that cannot but remain if we are to go on being human beings. Perhaps this book, which in its constructive chapters returns repeatedly to Aquinas's work, is closer to bricolage than to forestry. I move from point to point, and, while in two or three of its chapters I set about to offer an account of key parts of Aquinas's view of human action, nowhere do I try to lay forth his full view, let alone examine the many scholarly disputes about its key features.[10] However, the repeated return to Aqui-

---

10. There are far more thorough and detailed treatments of Aquinas's account of action available, some of the best quite recent. Ralph McInerny's *Aquinas on Human Action: A Theory of Practice* (Washington, D.C.: Catholic University Press, 1992) is engaging and accessible and at the same time written by a noted Aquinas expert, which I evidently am not. One of the most detailed and careful treatments available is Stephen Brock's *Action and Conduct: Thomas Aquinas and the Theory of Action* (Edinburgh: T. & T. Clark, 1998). Brock is interested, as I am in the first chapter of this book, in setting Aquinas's account over against that of certain of the action theorists, although he typically assumes the validity of the questions the action theorists ask, which I do not.

Beyond the fact that I am not fully equipped to do Aquinas scholarship, I have another reason for refraining from engaging in it. To extend the metaphors in the text, Aquinas scholarship in effect takes up residence in the great mansion that comes to be as Aquinas does his work. I am grateful to those who live there. However, my concern in this book is to investigate human action rather than Aquinas's view of it, to which it must be added that, so far as I can tell, there is no one so consistently on the mark about human action than Aquinas, and hence it only makes sense to return to his work.

Three other studies in human action have something like this shape; i.e., they borrow consistently from Aquinas as they set out to investigate human action. These are Robert Sokolowski's *Moral Action: A Phenomenological Study* (Bloomington: Indiana University Press, 1985), Alan Donagan's *Choice: The Essential Element in Human Action* (New York: Methuen Press, 1988) together with his *Human Ends and Human Actions: An Exploration of St. Thomas' Treatment* (Milwaukee: Marquette University Press, 1985), and Jean Porter's *Moral Action and Christian Ethics* (New York: Cambridge University Press, 1995). I engage Porter in chapter 6 — I believe she passes by a key feature of Aquinas's account, namely, that all human actions are moral actions. Sokolowski's treatment is, I believe, more helpful than Porter's, and particularly than Donagan's (upon whom Porter partly depends), which remains tied up with his concern to connect Kant and Aquinas reveals how I also hope to do more than bricolage. This hope is rooted in the rather thin possibility that by trailing after the greatest forester of the human life ever to mark a tree, something will rub off. But there is something more, a greater hope. This is that, like Aquinas, I hold that, though fallen, we are God's own creatures, intricately and marvelously made, and so the investigation of our life, the human/moral life, does not merely reveal interesting particular features of it, but something as well of the nature of the reality that rests in the God who created and redeemed us.

---

nas, a project in which I have no interest whatsoever. Sokolowski is particularly attentive to the relation of human action to human relationships. As he says, "Any human performance is capable of engaging [the] dimension of defining or confirming the agent's place in the web of human relationships" (p. 48). Actions, he points out, are like transactions between people; they are, as it were, "folded into people" (p. 61). These are lovely insights that draw human action into the complex shape of the moral life, where it belongs. However, Sokolowski's phenomenological interests, whereby he analyzes what goes on in a human act in terms of what turn out to be something like stages, such as "appraisal," "anticipation," and "performance," result in the creation of a specialized vocabulary that it seems better to avoid. I am not particularly interested in detailed analyses of what happens to us phenomenologically as we act, not the least because, as I argue in chapter 7 by drawing actions and omissions into the same essential category, this may be absolutely nothing at all.

10

# 1. Actions in Context

*Why All Action Theories Are Bound to Fail*

## 1. Homeless Behavior

I awoke one morning to a surprise. A fox had found its way into our backyard. Our neighborhood is semirural, so it is likely foxes come into it periodically. But I had not seen one in the backyard before, and so I was immediately attentive.

What do I know about foxes? Not very much. I can, however, recognize one, so on this occasion I did not need to spend much time deliberating about what sort of creature this was in the backyard. Rather, the question that rushed to mind — unarticulated, but no less strong — was: "What is a fox doing in broad daylight in our backyard?"

As I watched with rapt attention, the fox began to behave in what seemed a strange way. It began prancing about in a sort of circular pattern, lunging forward and upward as if to snap at something just beyond its reach. It dipped its head, rubbing it sideways against its right foreleg, then bringing it up again. Suddenly it ran forward, then stopped in midstride, crouching back on its haunches. In a flash the fox was up again, snapping at the air, now shaking its head side to side as it did so. I could not tell if it made any sound, for there was a great crowd of crows in the trees cawing with urgency; moreover, it was cold, and I kept the window shut. It looked to me, however, as if the fox were whining in pain. The strange display continued for what seemed like a long time, although I'm sure it was not more than a minute or two. Finally the fox began to move gradually in a direction, across into the neighbor's yard and toward the street.

It was then that I decided to leave the window and head for the phone. For I had by now come to believe that the fox was rabid and someone — I wasn't sure who — needed to be told. It was early, and there was as yet no human presence in view, but I was concerned that soon someone would be venturing out.

I do not know if my interpretation of the fox's actions, that it was suffering from rabies, was correct. In a few minutes the fox was gone from the neighbor's yard, and the policeman — the only person I could raise on Saturday morning, and whose response to my story was one of the mildest sort of interest — never saw it at all. The interpretation that the fox was rabid, however, provides a way of bringing together a number of things that happened that morning: the fox's prancing, the appearance that it was in pain or distress of some kind, even its presence in daylight in our backyard. Of course, my ignorance of foxes and fox behavior may have caused me to miss something important. Perhaps the fox was responding to the squawking crows . . . maybe the little leaps in the air were just the sort of thing foxes do to threaten away annoying birds.[1] Of course, you can tell I am only guessing. To go any further we would need to consult someone who knows more about foxes and how they typically are affected by rabies.

We have gone far enough with the fox to begin to consider our main subject: action, human action. Whether or not foxes can be said to act, there certainly is such a thing as "what foxes do." They trot, for instance, in a quite distinctive, foxy way. Like most carnivores, they hunt for their food, and for this they use their excellent sense of smell. When a fox sniffs the ground and trots along at a quick and determined pace, we can say that it is hunting. The fox in my backyard, I have no doubt, was not doing this, or anything else I could from my

---

1. Farley Mowat describes similar kinds of behaviors in a wolf he observed. In this case the wolf was attempting to mesmerize ducks so that it might catch them. As Mowat points out, we tend to interpret behavior of wolves (or foxes) in relation to our own fears, rather than really attending to the sorts of creatures they actually are. In a similar way it is quite imaginable that "the fox has rabies" presented itself to me precisely because of these fears, and was completely inaccurate. See *Never Cry Wolf* (Toronto: Seal Books, 1984).

limited knowledge call by name. I could not, in other words, understand its behavior in relation to any available description of what foxes do, and so I began to think about rabies, which is, of course, something foxes get and which causes them to behave strangely.

In her article "Moral Beliefs," Phillipa Foot imagines observing a man clasping his hands three times in an hour.[2] What could it mean, she asks, for us to say that this was a good action for the man to perform? Not unlike the fox, the behavior this man displays immediately puzzles us — evidently Foot has this in mind. Place the man, for the moment, in my backyard in the morning. There he stands, quietly, periodically clasping his hands, three times in an hour. Were I watching out the window, I would be as puzzled by what he was doing as I was by the fox — indeed, more puzzled. What could he possibly be up to?

The man's behavior so observed is what I should like to call "homeless." By homeless behaviors I mean, simply, a series of movements passed through or postures struck by some human person (or even some fox), ones that appear to arise internally from within the person (i.e., not from some external force like the wind), but for which we can find no name or apparent meaning. Homeless behaviors are behaviors about which it is meaningful to ask: What on earth could that person be doing?

As apparently internally caused, homeless behaviors are candidates for the designation "action."[3] Yet since their meaning and significance is obscured, we cannot yet rightly call them actions. For, as I shall maintain in various ways throughout this chapter, all actions require a home. That actions require a home is, I believe, an obvious

2. Phillipa Foot, "Moral Beliefs," in *Virtues and Vices* (Oxford: Basil Blackwell, 1978), p. 118.

3. Aristotle marks out the territory of "voluntary actions" in terms of the fact that "the principle that moves the instrumental parts of the body in such actions is in him [the person], and the things of which the moving principle is in a man himself are in his power to do or not to do" (*Nicomachean Ethics* 1110a16, trans. David Ross [New York: Oxford University Press, 1980]). If we observe the hand clasping of Foot's man, we will lead with the assumption that what he is doing is an action, which will entail, as Aristotle here suggests, that it proceeds from a principle from within him rather than from outside him, which itself implies that he is not compelled by some external force to do it. However, just because the action puzzles us so, we have no idea what it means and will hold in reserve any robust determination that it is an action, as is shown by the fact that we will go looking for external causes such as mental illness or hypnotism.

fact. However, it has turned out to be not so obvious for various philosophers and theologians. So it is something we shall need to work to show. The showing, as Wittgenstein might suggest, is a kind of therapy. We need therapy to break well-ingrained patterns of thought and analysis.

In this vein, let us think a bit more about the hand-clasping man in my backyard. I have given the impression that he is, like the fox, a stranger. If I tell you without introduction that I was awakened one morning, looked out my window, and saw there the hand-clasping man, you will assume this is a highly irregular occurrence. Sometimes we play tricks on one another by leaving regularity or normalcy out of an action description: "A beautiful woman just invited me to come to bed with her !" — leaving out that the woman is my wife. Part of what it means for an action to have a home is that it can be located by specific answers to such questions as *who, what, in what setting,* etc. By deliberately withholding some of what we know of these matters in our description, we can make what is familiar sound strange. Homelessness for the hand-clasping man's behavior would turn out to be a trick (and therefore not actual) if it were true that the man was my father, who suffered with arthritis in his hands and diligently followed an exercise routine each morning in the backyard.

Seemingly mild phrases have, in this context, considerable power. "In my backyard" creates in a hearer a great deal of expectation about what actions or occurrences might be described as happening there. "I saw a fox this morning in a field" and "I saw a fox this morning in my backyard" will elicit quite different responses from those to whom they are spoken, as we can see quickly by considering a next step: "I saw a fox this morning in my house!" So we might change the venue. Suppose the hand-clasping man is a stranger on a public beach where I am sunbathing. This helps draw the description closer to the orbit of our lives. As a field is where we expect to see foxes, so the beach is the sort of place where we sometimes expect to see human strangers doing quite different sorts of things. As well, it is the sort of place where we observe things, and where the context does not force on us strong preconceptions about what people are up to. This is to our purposes, for we need to see what happens on those relatively rare occasions when we have the time to notice homeless human behavior — to observe it long enough to become puzzled by it. (If the man stood on the street corner clasping his hands, we would walk by him with little notice, assuming he was simply waiting for a bus or something of the sort.)

So we are imagining we see a man on the beach clasping his hands three times in an hour. He is a stranger who means little to us. Note, however, that neither the relative neutrality of the setting nor the man's being a stranger keeps us from being puzzled by his hand-clasping behavior. To the contrary, it grasps our attention as other behavior on the beach does not precisely because it is odd. As with the fox, we look automatically for some home for this odd behavior. This reveals something important, namely, that, as in foxes, there is some identifiable set of behaviors that we expect from human beings. If we see a man standing on the beach holding a pole with a line attached extending into the water, we know immediately what he is doing: he is fishing. As foxes hunt, so some people fish. Fishing is one of *the sorts of things human beings do*. However, clasping one's hands three times an hour is not, which is another way of saying that, once observed, it cannot but stand for us (at least initially, before any further explanation is found) as a homeless behavior. As such we will not rest easy with it. Indeed, almost without reflection or choice we will begin to ask ourselves questions that might help in finding the behavior a home: What sorts of things do people do on the beach, and is there a way this odd bit of behavior can be placed in relation to one of them? For instance, is this man attempting to get a certain sort of tan? Or is he practicing some sort of meditative technique? Might this be some kind of religious ritual, a certain form of prayer perhaps?

When we look like this for a home for a behavior, we are attempting to fit it within a way of life. As Alasdair MacIntyre has noted, human behavior always needs to be placed in the context of a history or a "narrative."

> [I]n successfully identifying and understanding what someone else is doing we always move towards placing a particular episode in the context of a set of narrative histories, histories both of the individuals concerned and the settings in which they act and suffer. . . . [W]e render the actions of others intelligible in this way because action itself has a basically historical character. It is because we all live out narratives in our lives and because we understand our own

15

lives in terms of the narratives that we live out that the form of narrative is appropriate for understanding the actions of others.[4]

As MacIntyre would hold, odd behaviors like Foot's man clasping his hands are those which do not fit clearly into any recognizable human narratives. They are really unintelligible. We are simply at a loss to know what sorts of actions they are — or even if they are actions at all.

In his use of the category of narrative, MacIntyre is careful to stress that he does not have in mind the unique and independent story of each person. Indeed, despite the fact that we like to imagine ourselves as our own self-creators, there is no such thing as my story separate from everyone else's. For "we are never more (and sometimes less) than the co-authors of our own narratives. Only in fantasy do we live what story we please."[5] Finding a home for a behavior, then, cannot amount merely to locating it in the characteristics of a particular person. It is of little help, for instance, to say that, well, that's just what old Jake likes to do: he likes to go to the beach and clasp his hands three times in an hour. Such a response puzzles us not only about Jake's behavior, but about Jake himself. Rather, for the description of an action to help us, it must locate that action within the context of a people, a culture, among whom certain actions are meaningfully performed.

This is not to deny the power of an individual person's explanations of his actions. As opposed to foxes, we expect human persons to behave distinctively as individuals within a particular people within the human species. Indeed, a logical step to take with the hand-clasping man on the beach is simply to hail him and ask him what he is up to. If we do, we give the man an opportunity to tell us something about himself as an individual human being. Yet again we must note that not any answer will do. As Foot notes, if someone wants to tell us that hand clasping is good to do, he shall "first have to answer the question 'How do you mean?'"[6] In this same way, there are some things that the man might say that will help us locate his behavior, such as "warding away demons" or "isometrics for my weakened hands." Others, such as "eating ice cream," will only deepen our dismay.

4. Alasdair MacIntyre, *After Virtue* (Notre Dame, Ind.: University of Notre Dame Press, 1981), p. 197.

5. MacIntyre, p. 199.

6. Foot, p. 118.

This establishes something important about human actions rightly described. While what an actor says about her own action cannot but count, no one supposes that the full power of naming or of explaining an action resides only with the one who does it. Generally we presume the actor is in the best position to name her own action or explain its home, yet she can fail in this. For instance, if a teenager on the beach has just smashed a powerful serve at the opposing team and then sees fit to proclaim: "I'm not playing volleyball, I'm playing chess," or "I'm not playing volleyball, I'm trying to impress the girls," we are right to respond, in the first case, "Nonsense! That's volleyball!" or in the second, "While you may very well be trying to impress the girls by your fine play, you are undeniably playing volleyball."

MacIntyre makes a similar point when he notes that while some explanations do locate for us the narrative home for a particular odd behavior, others do not. In a humorous example, he imagines that a stranger waiting in line for a bus suddenly turns to him and says, "The name of the common wild duck is *Histrionicus histrionicus histrionicus.*" By itself the sentence is meaningful, even true. Moreover, a stranger making a comment to MacIntyre at the bus stop is not by itself puzzling. The problem, and the humor, arises when the content of the comment is about the scientific name for ducks and not something like "This rainy weather is getting tiresome." As MacIntyre goes on to say, the action can be rendered intelligible in certain ways, such as when the stranger explains that he mistook MacIntyre for someone who had earlier asked him if he knew the scientific name for the common wild duck. This explanation provides a narrative home for the man's action, and it becomes to us fully intelligible. But there are clearly limits to what sorts of explanations can work in this context. As MacIntyre notes, "suppose that the man at the bus stop explains his act of utterance by saying 'I was answering a question.' I reply: 'But I never asked you any question to which that could have been the answer.' He says 'Oh, I know *that*.' Once again his action becomes unintelligible."[7] The point, in other words, is that the odd behaviors which we have been discussing are not odd simply because we have no direct access to the particular intentions of the one who does them. They are rather odd because they lack any place in a way of life or nar-

7. MacIntyre, p. 196.

**17**

rative that we can understand or even imagine a human being living. They lack any human home.

## 2. Modern Analytic Action Theory

MacIntyre tells us that his comments on action are written *over against* a discussion of human action dominated in the past half-century by analytic philosophers. Under the title "action theory," British and American philosophers have spent a great deal of time discussing "action" as if it were something that could be analyzed quite apart from any human home. This discussion has been focused upon discrete events or movements that can be described virtually without reference to the narrative context in which a particular living being performs them — almost as if it could make sense to say, merely, that there was a snapping at the air in my backyard on the morning the fox visited.

MacIntyre holds that the analysts have set about to analyze "actions as such" when, in fact, what he calls "intelligible action" is the more fundamental concept.

> It is important to be clear how different the standpoint presupposed by the argument so far is from that of those analytic philosophers who have constructed accounts of human actions which make central the notion of "a" human action. A course of events is then seen as a complex sequence of individual actions, and a natural question is: How do we individuate human actions? . . . If in the middle of my lecture on Kant's ethics I suddenly broke six eggs into a bowl and added flour and sugar, proceeding all the while with my Kantian exegesis, I have not, simply in virtue of the fact that I was following a sequence prescribed by Fanny Farmer, performed an intelligible action.
>
> To this it might be related that I certainly performed an action or a set of actions, if not an intelligible action. But to this I want to reply that the concept of an intelligible action is a more fundamental concept than that of an action as such. Unintelligible actions are failed candidates for the status of intelligible action; and to lump unintelligible actions and intelligible actions together in a single class of actions and then to characterize action in terms of what

items of both sets have in common is to make the mistake of ignoring this.[8]

Here MacIntyre introduces yet another odd bit of behavior. His purpose is to draw our attention to a fundamental mistake in the standard discourse about actions in analytic philosophy. As he holds, analytic philosophers have treated actions as if they were individual discrete entities: "a" human action. "Action" has been understood as a class term, like the term "mammal." In order to discover what an action is, one gathers a variety of discrete "actions," like leaves raked in a pile. A formulaic expression is adopted for this purpose: "Person P doing action $x$ at time $t$." For example, "P clasping his hands at $t$," or "S squeezing the trigger at $t$," or "M breaking eggs at $t$." Once they are gathered, it is presumed by the analysts, we should be able to characterize "action" in terms of what features the entities expressed in the formula share, as we might characterize mammals by such a common feature as that they suckle their young.

This classificatory approach is operative in Donald Davidson's widely accepted view that actions are a species of events. It is not necessary here to deny the truth of such an assertion. Rather, the point to see is simply that an analysis of human action that begins with "events" will be drawn along a certain trajectory that invariably will treat what MacIntyre calls intelligible action in the same way it will treat unintelligible action. Or, put more concretely, it will analyze "M breaking eggs at $t$" without any further reference to the strange fact that he did this in the midst of his lecture on Kant rather than, say, in his kitchen while preparing breakfast.[9] By drawing out his under-

8. MacIntyre, pp. 194-95.

9. When speaking of breaking eggs, perhaps MacIntyre has in mind an example Davidson uses liberally in his article "The Logical Form of Action Sentences," in *Essays on Actions and Events* (New York: Oxford University Press, 1980). This is: "Jones buttered the toast in the bathroom with a knife at midnight." (See the discussion, pp. 105-8.) Davidson actually plays with this "action" by first describing it as "it": Jones did it slowly, deliberately, in the bathroom, with a knife, at midnight — a description which tricks us into thinking the "it" is something horrible like a murder. This plays with our expectations — and as I hold, a great deal can be learned from these expectations about, for instance, how actions have meaning, and require a home. Yet, as the title of the article indicates, Davidson then moves to a discussion of grammar — which of course also involves our expectations of meaning, but more narrowly. Here is where analytic philos-

standing of actions in relation to events, Davidson and other analytic philosophers actually remove them one step further from the human context in which they require MacIntyre's intelligibility. Whatever we take an event to be, it will clearly stand less rather than more in need of intelligibility than an action. For instance, "the book's hitting the floor at $t$" (an imagined event description) will plainly lend itself less to contextual inquiry than will the imagined action description of "P throwing the book on the floor at $t$."

Of course, there is logic to the analysis of action in terms of events. Like good scientists, analytical philosophers are looking for something more basic, something more minute and independent, in terms of which actions can be understood or analyzed, namely, events. But the net effect of the move is in fact to draw the action theory discussion further away from the human homes we have been suggesting all human actions require.

First, in this step back from actions, analysts must now begin to puzzle about what *events* are, about what makes one event identical to another event, and so on. While this discussion of events may yet remain in a given philosopher's mind as a detour along the way to understanding action, it will be thought a necessary detour, which becomes long and demands a great deal of analysis and discussion.[10]

Second, when turning back to their primary topic, action, having established a baseline for discussing it in terms of the discrete entities called "events," these philosophers feel compelled to give an account of what features *added to* an event make for a human action. In almost any theory, these features have to do with the fact that the events that are also actions were brought about in some way by human beings —

---

ophy conveniently listens to Wittgenstein with only one ear. It attends to grammar without noticing that grammar presumes a way of life — in which breaking eggs in the middle of a lecture on Kant or clasping one's hands three times in an hour or buttering toast in the bathroom at midnight, even if expressed in fine grammatical form, can have no sense to us as an action, unless it can be found a human home.

10. Michael Zimmerman, for example, begins his book on action with a long series of arguments which work to show that events are "abstract entities." He describes this work as follows: "A theory of events may be drawn up for a variety of reasons, but my purpose here is strictly limited, my motive ulterior. It is the provision of a comprehensive and enlightening theory of human action that is my main goal, and the theory of events which I shall draw up is intended only to provide a basis for such a theory of actions. I take it that actions are events" (*An Essay on Human Action* [New York: Peter Lang, 1984], p. 3).

not in any way whatsoever, but by human design or intention. And so, as the analysis proceeds, we will need to speak in some detail about what this human involvement amounts to.

In action theory a fair bit of disagreement has arisen at this point. Precisely how are we to understand the human element that, added to an event, makes for an action? Approached from the bottom up, from event to action, it will be difficult to identify and describe exactly how it is that an event becomes an action when something like human intention is added in. As some hold, the human involvement with the event occurs in conjunction with another event in the one who acts. So Davidson speaks of "mental events,"[11] what occur in the mind of the agent in relation to her acting. Or, as others such as Carl Ginet hold, actions are to be distinguished from nonaction events by our human experience of them, that they include a certain "actish phenomenal character,"[12] something we all experience in acting but cannot clearly describe.

It is important to see that MacIntyre's (and my own) disagreement with action theory *precedes* these disagreements in action theory about how events are turned into actions by some human participation. To be explicit, we hold that the debates of action theory are based on a common false assumption. This assumption is that to get to "what an action is" we can begin by expressing candidates for action in the formulaic "P doing $x$ at $t$." The preceding discussion of homeless behavior displays this. The man clasping his hands or MacIntyre breaking the eggs fits nicely in the formula. Yet we have no idea what sense either makes.

In short, the procedure the analysts have adopted provides no way of distinguishing between what I have called homeless behaviors and human acts. Indeed, it appears not at all interested in the distinction. Instead it is carried by the presumption that the analysis of what actions are must center on the discrete units expressed in the formula. As such it disregards the homes that we have seen are necessary if any particular action is to make sense or even be identified as an action. To understand "M breaking eggs at $t$," we shall need to know the "sto-

---

11. See Davidson's essay with that title in *Essays on Actions and Events*, pp. 207-28.

12. See Ginet's *On Action* (New York: Cambridge University Press, 1990), pp. 11-22.

ries" that make this intelligible as an action M did, not only regarding how the particular person M has come to the point, just now, of breaking eggs, but also the broader story of why humans break eggs, why we bake cakes (if that is what is going on), in what contexts we typically do such baking and why this is fitting. Action theory, however, pays these stories no mind.

MacIntyre's way of putting this point is that action theorists have failed to attend to the crucial distinction between intelligible and unintelligible action. As he holds, "the concept of an action is secondary to that of an intelligible action." (Or, to say anything about action, any analysis of what it is, must begin with our presuming an action's intelligibility.)[13] In the terms we have been using, analytic philosophers

---

13. I qualify MacIntyre on this point simply because I am not sure that the notion "unintelligible action" is intelligible. This is because to say that someone acted implies that his action makes some kind of sense, i.e., that it has a home in relation to his own projects (his story) or to the larger practices made available for his participation by the communities and stories from which his life springs — even if we do not at one or the other point understand these relations completely. As such, the term "intelligible action" is redundant. This is also why I entitled the first section of this chapter "homeless behavior" rather than "unintelligible action." Of course, the determination that something a human being did — which makes it a candidate for being a human action — is unintelligible takes time precisely because we need to look for a context or home in which it might fit. (In this regard, it is very hard to formulate any universally valid rules that specify, for example, that when a human being does $x$, it is intelligible in such and such a way, or that it is unintelligible. I had the pleasure recently, however, of running across an attempt at such a rule. When Brer Rabbit spies Mr. Man working with some wood, a hammer, and saw, he attributes design to his building something — and he is right, for Mr. Man turns out to be making a trap for Brer Rabbit. As he describes Brer Rabbit's interest and concern in Mr. Man's activities, Uncle Remus comments, "Don't nobody be building nothing just 'cause it's a sunny day." Julius Lester, *Uncle Remus: The Complete Tales* (New York: Phyllis Fogelman Books, 1999), p. 107.) Or, put more stuffily, if someone builds something for the sole reason that it is a sunny day, his behavior is unintelligible. This is related to the fact that human beings are such inventive creatures, and our behavior, like our words, is always subject to interpretation. In this way a judgment that behavior $x$ that P did is plainly unintelligible (and so not a human action) must always remain open to disproof. MacIntyre's "intelligible action" can therefore have sense just insofar as we imagine saying: "P did $x$, but at present I can make no sense of it." Whatever it was P did might in this context be termed an "unintelligible action" — which in turn could give meaning to MacIntyre's locution "intelligible action." To have proper sense, however, I believe the term requires just this kind of qualification, which MacIntyre does not give. As such, his use of it is misleading.

have proceeded as if actions are homeless, discrete entities that, by means of a formula, can be extracted from human life into a kind of laboratory in which they are analyzed and characterized. As I hold, with the extraction the "actions" become odd, homeless behaviors. If the analysts have been successful in disguising this fact, it is only because they have presumed homes for their actions even after their procedure has denied these homes' significance.

## 3. Action Trees without Roots

From the tilled soil of action theory has grown an odd plant: what philosophers have named an "action tree." Jesus noted that we know a tree by its fruits. With respect to theories, the fruits are the questions or problems engendered. As I shall try to show briefly in this section, action trees have produced far more puzzling questions than they have answered, adding to the fog that has covered most philosophical discussion of human action since the early twentieth century.

I have suggested that almost all action theorists have accepted Davidson's starting point: actions are a species of events. Why is this? That is, why have these philosophers been so quickly drawn to "events" as the place to begin when speaking of action? The answer is mainly to be discovered in the fact that events are thought by analytic philosophers to exist irreducibly. As such, events can serve to moor actions ontologically. Since there is nothing they can be further analyzed in terms of, they can be thought to be the original matter, the atoms with which a world is built.

Epistemologically speaking, this model is Western scientific: the world is best known when broken into its tiniest pieces. It is true that this model is coming increasingly into question. Yet if we are to discover the logic of action theory, including the sorts of questions it ends up posing, we must for the moment accept it. Events, now understood as the tiny ontic units from which a coherent analytic view of action can arise, have a curious feature: they exist only at a particular instant and at no other time. The event "the book's falling on the floor" that just occurred in my office existed once in that instant the book dropped but now is no longer, and never will be again. Particularly if we wish to come round to speaking of actions as a species of events, this cannot but cause some trouble. For it means I can never do the same thing twice. If my wife calls on the phone and asks what I'm doing just now, and I respond that I'm doing the same thing I was doing yesterday, I'm working on my book on action, I will be, strictly strictly, uttering a falsehood, for each action (*qua* event) is its own individual entity.

This is a poor match with ordinary language, for we speak routinely about "doing the same thing as before." If the work of action theory is to go on, a way will need to be found to reconnect events and actions back to ordinary language. One philosopher, Roderick Chisholm, has suggested that this should cause us to revise what we think actions and events are: rather than as instantaneous occurrences or temporal states, we should understand actions and events as proposition-like entities. As such they can recur. So, the single event "the sun's rising" (expressed in this proposition-like form) happened today and yesterday, and will happen again tomorrow.[14]

Chisholm's suggestion, however, has not gotten much of a following among action theorists. A more common way to deal with the repeatability question is to draw a distinction, as Alvin Goldman has, between "act types" and "act tokens."[15] An act token is a particular act performed by a particular person at a particular time — what exists instantaneously, and never again. An act type, however, is more like an event as Chisholm thinks of it, a recurring entity that can be done by different persons in different circumstances.

Once made, however, the distinction has turned out to be a way to skirt the problem. For in the main drift of action theory discussion, "act tokens," the unrepeatable entities expressed in the form event *e* or action *a* at time *t*, have received scrutiny while "act types" have been merely catalogued and shelved. With this return to the tiny, unrepeatable events, a new problem surfaces, one that occupies considerable space in the ongoing discussion. How, it is asked, is one action (now conceived as the particular thing done at time *t*, the act token) to be individuated? Or, how is the particular thing done at *t* to be isolated and identified in distinction from other things done, or other de-

---

14. Roderick Chisholm, *Person and Object: A Metaphysical Study* (La Salle, Ill.: Open Court, 1976).

15. Alvin Goldman, *A Theory of Human Action* (Englewood Cliffs, N.J.: Prentice Hall, 1970), pp. 10-19.

scriptions applied to, the occurrence at time *t*? This problem directly accounts for the sprouting up of the action trees. Here is an example of one taken (with slight revision) from the writing of Carl Ginet.[16]

Let us begin with the description "S's taking target practice at time *t*." Reconfigured, it could yield the following list of action descriptions:

1. S's willing to move her finger at *t*
2. S's moving her finger at *t*
3. S's pulling the trigger at *t*
4. S's firing a gun at *t*
5. S's shooting at the bull's-eye at *t*
6. S's violating an ordinance prohibiting firearm use at *t*

As we have already observed, the formula "P doing *x* at *t*" is that standard by which the action theorists have gathered actions into a set. If actions, expressed by the formula, are discrete entities, then each different true expression of the formula should point to a different particular action in the set. What action trees reveal, however, is that for any expression "P doing *x* at *t*," there are many additional expressions, following precisely the same form, that seem also to be about what P did as P did *x*. So we come upon a difficulty: How can we distinguish between S's taking target practice and S's shooting the bull's-eye? We might imagine that they are temporally distinct, i.e., *t* is different in each description. Yet this will not do. For plainly S did not take target practice *and then* commence to shoot the bull's-eye, or vice versa. Rather S's shooting the bull's-eye was the same thing as S's taking target practice.

Or was it? This has become a major sticking point in a debate about the individuation of action that has continued for some decades in the intellectual cul-de-sac called action theory.[17] Some philoso-

16. Ginet, p. 73.
17. Much of the work of action theory took place in the sixties and seventies. Since I believe action theory is an intellectual cul-de-sac, it is my hope that those who have gone into it will eventually find their way out, a good bit because there is increasingly less to say. Nevertheless, discussion continues, even if at a slower pace. See, for instance, Hugh McCann's relatively recent *The Works of Agency* (Ithaca, N.Y.: Cornell University Press, 1998), particularly the two opening sections entitled "The Ontology of Action" and "The Foundations of Action," pp. 17-126.

phers, such as Davidson, have said that, yes, these are in fact the same action, under different descriptions.[18] Others, notably Alvin Goldman, have argued that dissimilarities between each description prohibit them from being understood as of the same action. (For example, among the numbered parts of the action tree above we can say that description 2 caused 4, but evidently 6 did not.) To Goldman and others, it seems better to adopt a pluralist approach that construes each of the above designations as of distinct acts. Since this leaves unexplained the obvious close relation between them, various alternatives, which reconnect the discrete acts, have been offered by "pluralists." Among these is Judith Jarvis Thomson's attempt to re-collect the various actions as parts of one larger whole or Goldman's notion that they are related in a special BY relation (e.g., S shot at the bull's-eye BY pulling the trigger).[19]

I suggest that something has gone awry in this discussion. Put in previous terms, actions require homes. Aside from description 1 above, which is actually rather mysterious and not very clearly related to 2-6, and description 2, which is interesting only after descriptions 3-6 follow, all the descriptions place "what S did" in a home. Or, following MacIntyre, each takes what S did up into a narrative or set of narratives.

Suppose we remove a description such as 2 in the action tree from the rarefied air of the action theory debate. While waiting at the bus stop, I say to someone: "S moved her finger." Even if this person knew S, his appropriate response would be "And . . . ?" By itself the description lacks sense, like the description "a man clasped his hands." It is even difficult to tell if it is an action. With description 3 added, we begin to form a picture. So, S fired a gun! (In effect, description 4 merely confirms what we assume after hearing 3, namely, that the trigger was of a gun, that the gun was loaded and did not jam, etc.) Almost anywhere and at any time, bus stop or parlor, a report that S fired a gun holds our interest. For most of us the firing of a gun is uncommon; moreover, it is potentially highly important since, after all, when peo-

18. See Davidson, "The Individuation of Action," in *Essays on Actions and Events,* pp. 163-80.

19. For a discussion of the BY relation, see Goldman, pp. 20ff. Thomson's views are to be discovered in her *Acts and Other Events* (Ithaca, N.Y.: Cornell University Press, 1977).

ple fire guns, living beings are sometimes killed. Following the descriptions in the tree, number 5 calms our fears. S was shooting not at a person but at a target — and S hit the bull's-eye! Perhaps S is a practiced marksman. But as description 6 tells us, it so happened that S shot the gun in a place or at a time that the law prohibited. Here a different story intersects the one we have been so far rehearsing about how some people practice shooting guns so they can shoot with accuracy. This second story involves the sorts of things societies regulate, such as the use of lethal weapons.

While these descriptions are sufficient to render S's moving finger intelligible (so "S's moving her finger at *t*" is no longer completely homeless), they hardly exhaust the range of stories into which S's action may fit. Consider, for instance, these additional descriptions: "S's letting out her aggressions," "S's earning her summer camp riflery badge," "S's impressing her counselor." These and so many other imaginable descriptions place S's action in the context of our human lives — and it is within, and only within, such narratives that human action has genuine meaning.

It is now possible to say, as in this chapter's subtitle, why all action theories are bound to fail. As we have been suggesting, action theory has been guided by a pressing interest to extract particular actions from the rich mix of narratives that characterize human life, so that "actions" could be identified as entities in themselves, separate from the mix. In this way the trouble that action theorists have gotten into with action trees and the individuation of action is entirely predictable. Since their procedure began with the extraction, sooner or later the reinsertion will prove difficult. The difficulty is with the governing idea that the true identity of an action can be found out by removing it, by means of the formula "P doing *x* at *t*," from its various homes in human life. Actions require these homes.

Action trees are a fitting symbol of the ways the action theorists have mistakenly construed human actions. Generally, the result of action theory is not increased understanding of actions as we humans do them in our world, but rather the sprouting of a new sort of world in which action narratives no longer weave and interweave in a complex web of practices, traditions, human purposes, and the like. In this new world each act has its own space that does not intersect with any other space, like atoms in a molecule or bricks in a wall. To create this

27

new world, Goldman and others must first chop the real human world into discrete entities. Once cut from their homes in human life, actions can be made to appear as such discrete entities. Yet once again, as such they are no longer recognizable as human actions at all. Indeed, they might just as well be bits of homeless behavior, like the man clasping his hands.

## 4. Under Anscombe's Descriptions

The work on human action done by G. E. M. Anscombe is frequently referenced in action theory literature. A recognized pioneer in the discussion of action and intention, during the time of her active engagement with action theory she was also a mysterious figure. It was difficult to determine to what degree Anscombe's work related to the more particular debates in action theory about, for instance, "act identity" or the aforementioned distinction between "act tokens" and "act types."

After most of her substantive writing on topics related to action had been published and discussed, Anscombe published a rather remarkable article in *Nous* entitled "Under a Description."[20] In it she offered a series of replies to a variety of criticisms of her ideas about human action, particularly her notion of "under a description." Her replies are direct, pithy, sometimes comical and at other times merciless. Taken as a whole, they constitute a kind of exposé of a great deal of what otherwise has been written in action theory literature. I believe the perspective behind these replies coheres with the one I have been advancing.

The discovery of this critical perspective in Anscombe involves some explication of various comments in her article. Such explication also allows us, with the help of a few penetrating phrases from her work, to crystallize the criticisms so far advanced of action theory into a few key metaphors.

Anscombe numbers her responses to various criticisms of her

---

20. "Under a Description" was published in *Nous* 13 (1979). It appears as well in G. E. M. Anscombe, *Metaphysics and the Philosophy of Mind: Collected Philosophical Papers Volume II* (Minneapolis: University of Minnesota Press, 1981), pp. 208-19. Citations subsequently will refer to this reprinting.

work. Typical of her writing, the responses are remarkably condensed, lending eloquence, but also sometimes obscurity, with their clipped brevity. I suspect this was purposeful: the sharp staccato of the responses accents the divergence in background and concern that Anscombe correctly perceives between herself and her critics. Building upon these brief remarks, elaborating when appropriate, I shall try in what follows to make the radical divergence clear.

We begin with a response (replicated here in its entirety) to an objection Anscombe simply numbers (3).

> I have on occasion stared dumbly when asked: "If one action can have many descriptions, what is *the* action, which has all these descriptions?" The question seemed to be supposed to mean something, but I could not get hold of it. It ought to have struck me at once that here we were in "bare particular" country: *what* is the subject, which has all these predicates? The proper answer to "What is the action, which has all these descriptions?" is to give one of the descriptions. Any one, it does not matter which; or perhaps it would be best to offer a choice, saying "Take whichever you prefer."[21]

How are we to understand this response, the question that occasioned it, and the gap between the question and the response? I believe Anscombe provides an important hint when she speaks of her eventual recognition that the question puts us, once again, in "bare particular country." As I have suggested, action trees rise from a different kind of soil altogether than that in which we live our daily lives. They grow, we might say, in another country than that humans inhabit. The ontological concern running through action theory to catalogue a reality in which each part is distinct and irreducible, with no replication and no interwoven stories or practices, is the same as a concern to leave the country of human habitation for another land, a country of bare particulars.

Metaphorically, "edifice" fits this world better than the more organic "tree." In bare particular country, reality is man-made, and each bit of construction material subsequently retains its shape and marks its place. If human life is addressed within this constructed world, in

21. Anscombe, p. 209.

**29**

the edifices that theories have constructed, it always lies only at the very top level and can be peeled back at will to expose the true distinct and particular realities upon which that life is imagined to rest. If, for instance, there is a particular brick in some building in bare particular country that happens to be so positioned that a door always bangs into it when opened too far, and the inhabitants of the building come to call this brick "the banger," we would imagine, according to the rules of bare particular country, that *the* object that we sometimes describe as "the banger" is really simply a brick. "Banger" is just a name that can be stripped back to get at the real thing. This is the kind of picture of the world that lies behind the question that so puzzles Anscombe about action. It presumes, simply, that beneath all the various ways one might *refer* to an action lies the *action itself* in its basic, stripped-down form.

If this is the interlocutor's picture, as Anscombe evidently believes it is, then he cannot but be frustrated with her response, as I suspect she means him to be. ("Take whichever you prefer.") For such an interlocutor wants one description that is the action precisely so he can have an irreducible entity, a building block, that is only itself, and overlaps with no other. To rephrase Anscombe's reply to this objecter: I know what you hope to find, but you can't have it for it isn't there. And to get anywhere at all about actions, you are going to have to learn that there are no "bare particulars" to be found and begin looking for something else altogether.

In response to the criticism she numbers (4), Anscombe adds a caveat that makes plain that she does not mean by "take whichever you prefer" in number 3 that we are free to make up whatever description we choose about an action.[22] No, for any action there is a set of

---

22. Anscombe notes that her phrase "under a description" has been changed in some authors to "done under the description," as if something was done and then placed under a description, or as if the description and the thing done were two quite separable things. When understood in this way, she quite understands why some people would object to her use of the phrase — but of course, it is not at all how she meant it, nor how, on the face of it, it should have been understood. "This [the use of phrases such as 'done under a description'] indeed opens one's eyes to what some people may have found objectionable about the expression ['under a description']. What can be meant, for example, by saying that something happened under one description but not under another? No natural sense suggests itself for 'happening' or 'being done' or 'be-

true descriptions and another set, a huge one, of descriptions that are untrue. Anscombe's "Whichever you prefer" does not refer us to the untrue descriptions, only the true ones. To return to an earlier example, the teenager on the beach *is* trying to impress the girls, and he *is* playing volleyball, and he *is* serving the ball very well indeed, and so on, but he *is not* playing chess. We rightly respond, then, to the question of what is *really* going on here, or *really* being done, not by looking for some one root thing, the only thing, that went on (at time *t*), but by asking if it is true that such and such was being done or was occurring at that time.

Later in the article Anscombe addresses the matter of how to individuate human actions. As mentioned earlier, for analysts who hope to find bare particulars, the concern to individuate actions has led to something resembling an infinite multiplication of actions such that for any one thing done, such as shooting the bull's-eye, there are a plethora of descriptions (as in Ginet's action tree), each of which can be thought to count as a different particular action. For instance, Alvin Goldman holds that virtually every new way of describing what was done, insofar as it is not identical to a previous way, has to be counted as a new action. So when someone playing chess checkmates his opponent by moving his queen, we should say he (action 1) checkmates his opponent by (action 2) moving his queen. Anscombe replies with diffidence to Goldman's approach, not so much denying that he is correct in counting this number 1 and that number 2, but by seeing no point in the counting, adding by way of warning: "someone who says the player performed two acts though only one move, must proceed carefully, neither confounding the acts nor dividing the move."[23] Then she adds these comments about counting:

> Some people don't like recognizing events or actions as individuals. There is, they point out, no answer to the question "How many actions did you do this morning?" or "How many events have taken place in this room in the last hour?" This, however, merely shows that neither "action" nor "event" is much use as a count-noun, but

---

ing performed' together with the phrase 'under the description *d.*' At best, the phrase seems redundant — one might say: What happens happens under every description that is true of it" (p. 209).

23. Anscombe, p. 212.

there are many count-nouns that apply to actions and events, e.g. "Death," "kiss," "explosion." Just the same holds for *material objects,* or *things.* "How many things are there in the room?" is unanswerable unless contextually specified. A difficulty about how events or actions might be uncountable, while deaths which are events, and kisses which are actions, are countable, is paralleled by the corresponding difficulty about material objects or things, which may be uncountable, while pies and bicycles and men, which are material objects, may be perfectly countable. Both difficulties are spurious. Being countable or uncountable is, as Frege would tell us, not a property of objects, and there is not some curious character of "being an act" or "being an event" which justifies the erection of unheard of principles of individuation which would never be applied to sword-thrusts or dinners.[24]

Why is it that actions I did this morning can't be counted? Is it that there are too many to count? Surely there are very many indeed, but we should not be misled into thinking this is Anscombe's point. Rather, the point is that, as with "things," we cannot know what it would mean to count them as specified only as that, only as "actions" or "things." So if someone asks "How many things are in this room?" it is not merely that there are so many that it would be burdensome to go around counting them. No, it is that the designation "thing" doesn't take us to any location from which we can begin counting. Or, put another way, if we set about to count the "things," we would straightaway run into the trouble of whether or not to count this or that as one of the things this person was asking us to count. ("Is this book one thing, or do you mean also to count the pages? Or the words on the page? Or the letters? . . .") This is not to say (again) that a word like "thing" or "action" is so terribly ambiguous as to have no real meaning. In the right context it can be used with quite clear meaning. Moreover, as Anscombe shows, particular actions such as kisses can be counted, as can things like pies or books. But these must be specified before it makes any sense to start up counting.

What this tells us is that there is no use in setting out, as the analysts do, a general method by means of which actions per se can be in-

24. Anscombe, p. 213.

dividuated. As Anscombe says, "In conclusion: I may seem to have let myself off too easy, not giving any account of the 'individuation' of actions or events. But it is not possible to do that, if it means fixing criteria for what is a single action or event."[25]

Anscombe's points about individuation and countability connect to our main contention regarding actions and their homes. The general designation "action" can help us when we are already involved in a discussion of one, such as kissing. Or, if a context calls for it, we may meaningfully go looking to see if an action was performed, as when a person dies we set about to discover if his death was accidental or brought about by some human action. Actions are done by human beings, they have meaning and sense within their human homes; but meaning and sense evaporate when it is imagined that actions are singular entities, bare particulars, that can be extracted from the rich context of human life.

When we speak of a particular action, like kissing, we know it as such precisely because we know about how kissing fits into human life. (Note that there is not just one place it fits, but many.) Despite its oddity, we can even field a query about "how many kissing actions John performed this morning" as we could not field a similar one about "how many actions John performed this morning." As MacIntyre would say, we know the sets of narratives in which "John giving Jill one hundred kisses" is intelligible and so go on from there. By contrast, "P doing $x$ at $t$" offers no narrative at all, only a philosophical phantasm.

As I have tried to show in this chapter, and as Anscombe believes about her critics, action theorists have ignored these essential features of action. Why have they done this? Perhaps it is because they want to do something else than consider actions as they are in our human world, precisely because that world is resistant to the formulas action theorists formulate. Despite evident conceptual difficulties, these theorists have persisted in extracting "actions" from their homes in human practices, purposes, and narratives. As I have argued, their project was bound to fail. For all human actions require a home.

25. Anscombe, p. 216.

# 2. Situation Ethics and Action Descriptions

*The Persistence of Monism in Protestant Ethics*

## 1. Introduction

Action theorists in analytic philosophy are not much concerned with the morality or immorality of human action. Or perhaps better put, whatever concern action theorists may have about morality, they bracket, for their interest is to describe what actions are in general, and questions of whether an action is morally right or wrong arise in particular cases. Consequently, moral concern about action is at best a supplement to the discussion of the identity of a human action.

This direction might be reversed. If we follow the assumption that action theory and morality are two quite different territories of inquiry, we could begin with a primary concern about "morality" and then come upon problems of action unawares. I suspect this is the more common pattern. For all of us in daily life find ourselves making judgments we call moral about what someone does: his acts. If we set about to investigate these judgments, we find ourselves rather suddenly in the midst of a great forest of human actions to which our judgments relate. It is then that we begin to ask more about what human actions are and how they should be described.

This pattern is readily detected in a popular movement in Protestantism in the mid-1960s called "situation ethics." Its champion, Joseph Fletcher, the author of the widely read book bearing the movement's name, was an Anglican priest. The movement's chief critic was Paul Ramsey, the renowned Methodist theologian and moralist. Indeed, Ramsey and Fletcher became locked in a debate that is important for our purposes since it was primarily about human actions and how they are rightly described.

If asked who won this debate, some will say Ramsey, for his arguments evidently had more bite, and in the circle of professional Christian ethicists his memory is the more hallowed. Yet others will say Fletcher had the greater effect since the thought patterns of situation ethics, if not its name, have received a warmer welcome in the popular Western imagination than the covenant thinking of Ramsey. As I shall try to show, however, the victory (or loss) is rightly thought of as shared. For, while Ramsey perceived where Fletcher's thinking was erroneous, the error itself was something he shared insofar as he was, like Fletcher, what I shall call a "principle monist." Perhaps Fletcher was in the end the subtler thinker, for he more clearly perceived what principle monism entailed, namely, that all moral action be redescribed in terms of one guiding and overarching moral principle.

## 2. Situationism and the Problem of Action Descriptions

Situationism can be summarily defined as the view that the moral rightness or wrongness of an action is altogether dependent upon the situation. As Joseph Fletcher puts it, "in Christian situation ethics nothing is worth anything in and of itself. It gains or acquires value only because it happens to help persons (thus being good) or to hurt persons (thus being bad). . . . Good and evil are extrinsic to the thing or the action. It all depends on the situation. What is right in one case, e.g., lending cash to a father who needs it for his hungry family, may be wrong in another case, e.g., lending cash to a father with hungry children when he is known to be a compulsive gambler or alcoholic."[1]

The claim to highlight in this quotation is that "good and evil are

1. Joseph Fletcher, *Situation Ethics: The New Morality* (Philadelphia: Westminster, 1966), p. 59.

*extrinsic* to the thing or the action." What Fletcher seems to mean by it is that no action (or object) can in itself be called good. Rather, goodness is the sort of thing that is withheld from or added to an action when it is done in one or the other situation. So it is neither right nor wrong to lend cash to a father with hungry children; rather it *becomes* right or wrong in the particular situations described.

Let us call Fletcher's position on this point "extrinsicalism," in contrast to the position to which he sees himself opposed and which he names "intrinsicalism." According to Fletcher, intrinsicalism is an error that underlies a whole way of thinking about ethics, a root problem. "The real error . . . is the intrinsic theory under which, logically, a thing is either good or evil. But good and evil are not properties, they are predicates or attributes. And *therefore* what is sometimes good may at other times be evil, and what is sometimes wrong may sometimes be right when it serves a good enough end — depending on the situation."[2] For clarity, let us consider how Fletcher's extrinsicalism might work out in the example he gives about lending cash to the father whose children are hungry. If we take "lending money to a father with hungry children" as an action which might be proposed as good, Fletcher would tell us it is not, at least not intrinsically. Instead, to insure its goodness something must be *added to it,* such as that the father is not a gambler or alcoholic.

While this might seem sensible, difficulties arise. For suppose we simply now include this condition in a newly described action: "lending money to a nongambler, nonalcoholic father whose children are hungry." Since Fletcher has argued that it is precisely the lack of this qualifying condition — i.e., that the father is neither alcoholic nor gambler — which shows that the original action, described as "lending money to a father with hungry children," is not intrinsically right, why not suppose that the new action in the emended description is intrinsically right? (If Fletcher insists that there might be other qualifying conditions, an additional emendation could be made in the action description to include these.)[3] But by definition extrinsicalism ex-

---

2. Fletcher, *Situation Ethics,* p. 123.

3. Paul Ramsey himself has made something like this argument in his long article "The Case of the Curious Exception," in *Norm and Context in Christian Ethics,* ed. Gene Outka and Paul Ramsey (New York: Scribner, 1968), pp. 67-135.

cludes this possibility: no actions are good (or evil) in themselves. Logically, then, we must assume that Fletcher holds that "lending money to a father with hungry children" is the *true* action, the thing, while "lending money to a gambling, alcoholic father with hungry children" is the action *plus* an extra element, the bit about gambling and alcohol.

But why is this true? If the condition that the father is a gambler and alcoholic is extrinsic to the action, why isn't the fact that the man is a father or that his children are hungry also an external condition? On what grounds do we know being a father is intrinsically part of the action and being, say, a nongambler is extrinsic to it? Or if being a father is not intrinsic to the action, what is? Lending money? If so, why include money? Why not merely lending anything at all, perhaps a car or a pair of shoes? These are questions Fletcher never addresses. His view is one that, on the one hand, assumes that we all know precisely what the parameters of a human action are but which, on the other hand, plays with these parameters as though putty in the hand.

One way of responding to Fletcher's extrinsicalism is to point out, as did Herbert McCabe, that actions, like the words used to describe them, have a relatively fixed place in the network of signs and symbols which is the medium of our communication.

> Human action has significance in itself prior to any significance that may be given to it by what a man may have in mind when he does it. . . . Human acts have significance not the way stones have temperature but the way words have meaning. I cannot change the temperature of the stone just by taking thought, but neither can I change the meaning of a word just by taking thought, for it belongs to the language not to me. Nor can I change the value of my behavior by taking thought, for its value is its meaning in the total system of communications which is the human world.[4]

Fletcher's extrinsicalism presumes that actions and action descriptions are in and of themselves morally neutral: as if they are simple brute facts about the world to which we must add our moral assessment. What it fails to understand is that many action descriptions — and often the very terms that make them up — carry a moral assess-

4. Herbert McCabe, "The Validity of Absolutes," *Commonweal* 83 (1966): 434.

ment. Indeed, these descriptions, coupled with our capacity to choose which of them we want from a multitude of possibilities, are precisely what allow us to be sensitive, as Fletcher advocates, to the moral particulars of a given situation.

In his essay "A Defense of Intrinsicalism against Situation Ethics," Aurel Kolnai asks us to consider the descriptions "committing parricide" or "committing fratricide." In Fletcher's view, the descriptions themselves will have to be morally insignificant for, as he might put it, the rightness or wrongness of parricide or fratricide is dependent entirely upon the situation. But Kolnai points out that these descriptions themselves already carry moral condemnation and, interestingly, already have responded to a certain set of details of particular situations. As he says,

> The description of actions is . . . essentially variable and a difficult matter: some typically relevant "circumstances" may change the nomenclature under which the action can fall, others may not; but even in the latter case circumstances are relevant because, and in so far as, they subsume the action performed or contemplated also under another morally significant category of actions. It is morally worse to murder one's own father or brother than to murder a stranger, and we may designate the first two kinds of murder by the special names "parricide" and "fratricide."[5]

If Kolnai and McCabe are correct about actions and the language of their description, we can anticipate that Fletcher's extrinsicalism will lock him in constant battle with commonly used action descriptions throughout his ethics. According to Paul Ramsey, this is just what occurs. In his long article "The Case of Joseph Fletcher and Joseph Fletcher's Cases,"[6] Ramsey details repeated abuse on Fletcher's part of moral language and action descriptions. He accuses Fletcher of (1) feeding on the moral meanings of terms such as "murder" or "adultery" employed in action descriptions — something he cannot

5. Aurel Kolnai, "A Defense of Intrinsicalism against Situation Ethics," in *Situationism and the New Morality*, ed. Robert L. Cunningham (New York: Appleton-Century-Crofts, 1970), pp. 266-67.

6. Paul Ramsey, "The Case of Joseph Fletcher and Joseph Fletcher's Cases," in *Norm and Context in Christian Ethics*, pp. 145-225.

consistently do given his extrinsicalism — while simultaneously (2) embarking on a program of redescription whose logical outcome is nothing less than the radical reorganizing of these terms and, consequently, of moral meanings in general.

Ramsey's first accusation can be illustrated as follows. "Murder," a moral term, by design does not cover all cases of intentional killing, as is shown by the fact that we do not use it to refer to killing in war. Indeed, the action, murder, is an immoral killing, at the least. Since Fletcher's scheme will resist this, i.e., resist an action's being "in itself" wrong, he will need to displace "murder" to some degree, claiming that it is not always wrong — it depends on the situation. Yet to do this he chooses examples that do not clearly fall under the designation "murder" at all, such as Dietrich Bonhoeffer's role in the attempt to assassinate Hitler, but calls them so nonetheless.[7] While some of us might share with Fletcher the intuition that Bonhoeffer's attempt to kill Hitler was not wrong, it does not follow from this that we believe murder is sometimes right. Far more likely we would simply hold that Bonhoeffer's attempt, had it been successful, would not have been a case of murder. This need not be thought of as sophistry. To the contrary, it arises simply from the subtlety of the designation murder — a term all of us learned to use long before becoming aware of what "morality" or "the situation" meant — which leads us to become skeptical of its use in this context. (We need not decide that Bonhoeffer's plan is *wrongly* understood as a murder plot; we need merely to have some serious questions about whether it is rightly so understood.) So it is partly by means of our understanding of murder that we entertain Fletcher's suggestion that Bonhoeffer's plan to "murder" Hitler was not wrong. As Ramsey says, "Fletcher must keep in place the ancient landmarks [e.g., 'murder'] in order to destroy them."[8]

Ramsey's second accusation refers most directly to Fletcher's frequent use of extraordinarily broad terms such as "acts of loving kindness" in his descriptions of actions.[9] Due to their generality, these terms are more easily filled up with content from a general moral the-

7. See Ramsey, "Case of Joseph Fletcher," p. 202, and Fletcher, *Situation Ethics*, p. 33.

8. Ramsey, "Case of Joseph Fletcher," p. 204.

9. Ramsey calls these terms "genera." See Ramsey, "Case of Joseph Fletcher," p. 67.

ory than more act-specific terms like "murder" or "adultery." Strategic use of such broad terms in redescriptions can serve to override the more specific terms which are far less open-ended. If I *redescribe* an act of adultery as an act of loving kindness and drop the former designation, I have won the moral debate before it has begun — for who could object to someone's doing an act of loving kindness? As Ramsey puts this, "Fletcher has redescribed the action under scrutiny so extensively that the justification of it becomes superfluous."[10]

Ramsey's criticisms of Fletcher's abuse of action descriptions are astute. Perhaps *too* astute. For as I shall try to show, Fletcher's abuses stem from characteristic errors in matters pertaining to action descriptions present not only in Fletcher's work but in the work of many philosophers and theologians, including Ramsey himself. As Ramsey sensed in his first accusation above, our moral compass is directed by our complex understanding of moral terms, the "ancient landmarks" by which we map out our moral lives. These landmarks, as Fletcher shows in spite of himself, crop up invariably in our moral discourse, with or without justification from a moral theory. Moral theorists like Fletcher may at some point take note of these terms and subject them to scrutiny, in some cases attempting to reorient them in relation to their theory. As Ramsey points out in his second accusation, Fletcher, a self-declared utilitarian,[11] "is carrying through a program of redescribing human actions in terms of all their circumstances and all their consequences in the course of justifying what is done."[12] Yet there is a sense in which, as a moral theorist, this is precisely what Fletcher should do. And insofar as Ramsey also assents to a certain kind of moral theorizing, perhaps it is what he should be doing as well.

## 3. Principle Monism Unveiled

To sum up the argument as it has so far progressed in this chapter, Joseph Fletcher's extrinsicalism plays fast and loose with human ac-

10. Ramsey, "Case of Joseph Fletcher," p. 200.

11. Consider this quotation from Fletcher, "What's in a Rule," in *Norm and Context in Christian Ethics*, p. 332: "Let us say plainly that agape is utility; love is well-being; the Christian who does not individualize or sentimentalize love *is* a utilitarian."

12. Ramsey, "Case of Joseph Fletcher," p. 199.

tions, as many of his critics saw, including Paul Ramsey. Yet we shall need to ask *why*. As I have begun to suggest, Fletcher's abuse of action descriptions traces below the shallow topsoil of extrinsicalism to deeper rootings in what I shall call *"ethical principle monism."* Further, in this deeper soil are planted many other systems or theories of ethics, some championed by ethicists who otherwise appear to have nothing at all in common with situationism, such as Paul Ramsey. I do not mean that Ramsey is equally guilty with Fletcher of misusing moral action descriptions. As we have already seen, Ramsey is in places quite sensitive to the complexities of action descriptions and thoroughly aware of the significance of moral terms like "murder" or "parricide." This, however, is not due to Ramsey's consistency with his moral theory but *in spite of* it. Indeed, Fletcher does us the odd favor of being consistent with principle monism, so we can see clearly its untenability in light of what it implies about action descriptions and moral terms.

To see how Fletcher's situationism is rooted in principle monism rather than strictly in the extrinsicalism he professes, we might note that Fletcher can abandon extrinsicalism without seriously damaging his project. Suppose, for example, he admits there is at least one exceptionless moral rule, "Never begin a nuclear war," for example.[13] Following the pattern of analysis laid out in utilitarianism, Fletcher gives himself room to claim without contradiction that some states of affairs are so replete with disutility or lack of love that we cannot imagine circumstances in which they could be justifiably brought about by human action. If Fletcher did this, then he could be thought of as an intrinsicalist just to the extent that he could say it is always (in any situation) wrong to start a nuclear war. But this admission

---

13. Jonathan Schell's *The Fate of the Earth* (New York: Avon Books, 1982) strikes me as putting forward this position in the way I am imagining Fletcher might. On the matter of exceptionless moral rules, see Ramsey's *Deeds and Rules* (New York: Scribner, 1967), pp. 123-44, and "The Case of the Curious Exception." See also Donald Evans's "Love, Situations, and Rules," in *Norm and Context in Christian Ethics*, pp. 367-414, and "Paul Ramsey on Exceptionless Moral Rules," in *Love and Society: Essays in the Ethics of Paul Ramsey*, JRE Studies in Religious Ethics 1 (Missoula, Mont.: Scholars Press, 1974), pp. 67-88. While the points made by these two thinkers are interesting and often helpful in displaying the various ways in which rules function, I am not sure that establishing that there are or are not exceptionless moral rules is finally very important.

would not hinder Fletcher from analyzing all other actions, such as "murder," "parricide," "stealing," and so on, as morally neutral in themselves, as merely becoming wrong in the situation to the degree that they lead to states of affairs which do not maximize love or utility. Strictly, one could be an "intrinsicalist" and continue to abuse action descriptions in the same manner that Fletcher abuses them.

This is where principle monism factors in. To define it more clearly, ethical principle monists hold that there is one supreme principle upon which the whole of morality can be founded. By this they need not mean there is only one valid ethical principle. In fact, the monist might hold that the supreme principle yields any number of other valid moral principles. Yet these other principles must stand in a dependent relation to the supreme principle from which they are derived. They are subsidiaries, carrying in themselves no independent moral weight.

In principle monism two characteristics are salient. First, principle monists take their principle to be *constitutive* of morality. What is moral is what coheres with the principle, what is immoral is what diverges from it. If some situation can be found in which the principle does not apply at all, then it is rightly understood as nonmoral.[14] Second, they employ an essentially deductive procedure in ethics. Most monists hold that there exist other valid moral rules than the fundamental monistic principle — even Fletcher acknowledges a need in his situationism for "rules of thumb." In a principle monism, however, these additional rules must be produced, or at least ratified, by the supreme principle prior to their being put into effect. Since this is part of the logic of their system, principle monists are bound to adhere to a

14. Edmund Pincoffs has made this point with a slightly different focus. His concern is that the so-called moral problems which have increasingly played a dominant role in philosophical ethics are problems only for those who hold to certain monistic moral theories *and* that those who hold to these theories cannot sensibly have moral problems which fail to be problems on the basis of the theory. "The difficulty with the standard theories . . . is that one cannot make sense, independently of the theory adopted, of the claim that a given worry is a moral problem: that, from the point of view of the advocate of the theory, the only worries that are moral problems are those that arise for persons who accept the theory. All other supposed moral problems are merely illusory: they are not moral problems at all" (*Quandaries and Virtues: Against Reductivism in Ethics* [Lawrence: University of Kansas Press, 1986], p. 45).

certain sequential procedure in their thinking about ethics. The supreme principle must first be stated and affirmed as true and then applied to concrete situations, producing in its application the subsidiary rules. The subsidiary rules, in other words, essentially are deduced from the supreme principle when an additional minor premise is supplied by the particulars of a new and previously uncharted situation.

Principle monisms can diverge on both the content of the supreme principle and the logical relation of the subsidiary rules to the supreme principle. So monisms can appear radically different. Paul Ramsey is as much a principle monist as Joseph Fletcher, Immanuel Kant as much as Jeremy Bentham. The latter pair illustrates a difference in content, Kant's categorical imperative being significantly different from Bentham's principle of utility. But both function in their respective systems of ethics in approximately the same way: they are supreme and foundational principles, constitutive of what morality is.

Kant and Bentham differ as well concerning the logical relation of the supreme principle to subsidiary rules, but this difference is better illustrated by Fletcher and Ramsey, since the two Christian ethicists are in basic agreement about the content of the supreme principle — or at least the language in which it is expressed, namely, that *agape* is the supreme end of morality. Yet Ramsey and Fletcher disagree about whether or not *agape* entails specific subsidiary rules. Ramsey is concerned that the meaning of *agape* be tied down. Hence his claim that there are some things which *agape* always prohibits, direct killing, for example. Fletcher, *qua* extrinsicalist, sees no need for such a claim. However, Ramsey, *qua* monist, cannot but agree with Fletcher that the reason direct killing is wrong is because it violates the supreme *agape* principle[15] — for this is the only sort of reason one can finally have morally. On this point Ramsey shows himself a brother under the skin to Fletcher. Both agree that the agapic principle (however it is formulated) is constitutive of morality. What is wrong is necessarily a violation of the agapic principle, and it is wrong precisely be-

15. In a discussion of direct killing in the context of the morality of war, Ramsey says: "[The Christian] governs himself by love and develops the rule of double effect and the distinction between direct and indirect killing, as logical and necessary limits of action that is permitted . . ." (*War and the Christian Conscience* [Durham, N.C.: Duke University Press, 1961], p. 178).

cause of this. That they disagree over whether *agape* implies specific rules such as "never directly kill" is an important fact, one that cannot be forgotten as their moral views are compared. But as I have been arguing, it does not affect their mutual classification as *agape* principle monists.

## 4. Is Paul Ramsey a Principle Monist?[16]

Principle monism stood as a theoretical presumption for most mid-twentieth-century Protestant Christian ethics. Despite patterns in his practical work that suggested another vision, Ramsey was no exception to this general trend. He, like Fletcher, was a principle monist. The two men's agreement on monism is a key part of the argument of this chapter. Given their other disagreements, particularly those regarding human action, the agreement is striking. It suggests that Monism had made its way so deep within the fabric of inquiry in Christian ethics as to go unnoticed by its proponents. It held the thought of these two apparent enemies together in ways neither recognized.

Joseph Fletcher did not disguise his utilitarianism. From utilitarianism, monism follows as a matter of course since the greatest happiness principle reigns — that is its basic point. Ramsey was opposed to utilitarianism. However, he was a principle monist. Consider as a display of Ramsey's monistic views the following four quotations:

> [1] Christian ethics proposes that the basic norm and the distinctive character of the Christian is Christian love *(agape)*. If other ethics rest upon a concept of moral duty *(deontology)* or upon a goal to be achieved *(teleology)*, Christian ethics finds its basis in *agape*.[17]

16. It important to emphasize that the following section is about certain *portions* of Ramsey's writing, not all of it. Indeed, as I have mentioned, Ramsey is sometimes quite sensitive to the matters of action description I have raised; from these parts of his writing we in fact still have a good bit to learn. A brief discussion in his last work, *Speak Up for Just War or Pacifism* (University Park: Pennsylvania State University Press, 1988), pp. 104-5, is worth reading in this regard, as well as the excellent article already cited, "The Case of the Curious Exception."

17. Ramsey, *Deeds and Rules*, p. 2.

[2] Paul was so thoroughly emancipated from his Jewish background as not to appeal to Torah. . . . His exhortations generally have authority only as love's directions. . . . Christian love will not be limited by any previously existing regulation drawn from what society or "surely nature itself" teaches, it will not conform to preconceptions about right and wrong or conventional codes of conduct with which authorities on good and evil happen to be prepossessed.

Nevertheless, such love, far from being directionless, lays down its own directions, internal self-regulations conformable only to the needs of the neighbor.[18]

[3] The central ethical notion or "category" in Christian ethics is "obedient love." . . . This concept, basic to any understanding of the Christian outlook with the demands it places on moral action, gives us the clue essential to understanding certain other ideas, such as "justice," "right" or "obligation," "duties to oneself," "vocation," "virtues" of moral character, "sinfulness" and the "image of God," which in turn are of crucial importance in elaborating a theory of Christian ethics.[19]

[4] [A]pplications of the rule of "double effect" in traditional Christian morality, like the rule itself, can be shown to be a deposit or creation of the Christian love ethic itself. . . .

If today the Christian affirms that the right of conduct of war can never include the strategic bombing of whole civilian populations . . . the reason is not that he adopts (and "seasons" with love) a rigorous alien natural law principle drawn from some source outside of Christian morals, but that he finds himself still required to do only what love requires and permitted to do only what love allows to be right. An ethic of Christian love has no alternative but to renew and re-create its own articulation in the rule or principle which surrounds non-combatants with moral immunity from direct attack.[20]

18. Paul Ramsey, *Basic Christian Ethics* (Chicago: University of Chicago Press, 1950), p. 78.
19. Ramsey, *Basic Christian Ethics*, p. xi.
20. Ramsey, *Christian Conscience*, pp. xix-xx.

Drawn from three sources written over a span of seventeen years, these quotations display the essential characteristics of principle monism. In [1] we see that Ramsey conceives of Christian ethics resting upon a "basic norm" or a concept in a way parallel to other normative moral theories. While Ramsey may elsewhere be critical of these other theories, he is not critical of their monistic structure. Indeed, he lifts the monistic theoretical structure from normative philosophical ethics, sliding it underneath Christian ethics as well.

In [2], relying upon what he understands to be the thought of the apostle Paul, Ramsey speaks of the power over morality the new concept of love is to have. Love, in a way, rewrites morality, paying little attention to nature or convention. Granted, and as is displayed in [3] and [4], the new ethic which love creates includes concrete directives, such as those against direct killing, or provides the "clue" to further concepts such as justice, vocation, sinfulness, and the like. In this Ramsey is rightly distinguished from Fletcher's utilitarianism since his new love morality contains specific and binding subsidiary rules. But insofar as love for Ramsey first erases the moral slate — as in [2] — and proceeds to "re-create its own articulation" — as in [4] — he is no less monistic.

This is not to say that Ramsey's conviction that, contra Fletcher, Christian morality must include binding concrete rules and principles is insignificant. For when he engages in a normative analysis of cases, he has a wealth of more specific concepts upon which to draw — for example, those he thinks follow from love in [3] or [4]. It is Ramsey's allegiance to these various particular normative concepts that saves his ethics from the quicksand of situationism. But this allegiance is not a product of Ramsey's monism; it is in spite of it.

From this juncture, in a full study of Ramsey's ethics, a number of questions might be pursued: What is the relation between Ramsey's theory about Christian ethics and his actual work within it? Is he a monist in theory but not in practice? And what of the relation of ideas such as justice, right, or vocation in [3] to Ramsey's supreme principle of love? Is he consistent in actual fact with the monistic pattern to which he assents in [2], that requires that the supreme principle pick out these other concepts to serve it? Or rather, do these moral notions in his ethics have an independent life from love, functioning as alternative authorities to its monistic omnipotence? Ramsey's corpus of writing is large enough and substantial enough to make these questions complex as well as worthy of further study. To be clear, I do not mean to dismiss Ramsey's work because he professes principle monism. Rather our present agenda is, first, to show the logical relation between monism and the abuse of action descriptions, and second, to demonstrate the ironic fact that Paul Ramsey, who attacks Fletcher's abuse of language with such force, himself holds the same set of theoretical assumptions in which that abuse is rooted, namely, those of principle monism.

In considering Ramsey's own attitude toward monism, one final piece of writing is important. This is Ramsey's "Letter to James Gustafson."[21] It is particularly important for our purposes both because it comes late in Ramsey's life, after he has had decades to moderate the *"agape* alone" monism of *Basic Christian Ethics,* and because in the article Ramsey responds specifically to Gustafson's characterization of his work in Christian ethics as monistic.

Besides monistic, Gustafson calls Ramsey's work many things, among them agapic, deontological, and rigorist.[22] Ramsey's reaction to these is mixed together in some five pages, from which his response to the monism charge can be culled. Ramsey begins by noting that he wishes to revise his key terms: love ought to be understood in terms of covenant. Since we have been calling him a love monist, this point is interesting but not crucial; one can be a covenant monist just as well as a love monist. But to elaborate, Ramsey advances two more points: First he says, "there is little or no significant difference between listing obedience, gratitude, hope, faith, humility, etc., *alongside* love and an understanding of love rich in diverse aspects or elements bearing the same-named virtues."[23] Second, he claims that "[f]ar from monism, I am really rampantly pluralistic and 'unsystematic' in doing ethics."[24]

With the first point Ramsey seems to suggest: monist, nonmonist . . . it makes little practical difference so long as one recognizes and

21. Paul Ramsey, "A Letter to James Gustafson," *Journal of Religious Ethics* 13, no. 1 (1985): 71-100; hereafter referred to as "Letter."

22. James Gustafson, *Ethics from a Theocentric Perspective: Ethics and Theology* (Chicago: University of Chicago Press, 1984), pp. 84-93.

23. Ramsey, "Letter," p. 75.

24. Ramsey, "Letter," p. 77.

applies certain crucial concepts in Christian ethics, i.e., obedience, gratitude, hope, etc. This point can be hailed as an advance. Yet at the same time we must ask in which way it cuts. The normative approach Ramsey implies in it is evidently pluralistic: a *variety* of moral concepts have come into play. But this shifts the burden of explanation to any-one who might maintain that the variety of terms and concepts can be understood in the light of one overarching concept. That is, if what we need is obedience, gratitude, hope, and so on, why say any more than that? Why must these be grounded in *agape* or some other monistic concept? So why appeal to it, as Ramsey repeatedly does throughout his work?

Formulating a response to Ramsey's second point is more difficult since we must know more clearly just what he thinks are the "ram-pantly pluralistic" aspects of his thought. Two clues are offered. First, he points out that he never closes the door on the matter of whether or not there are exceptionless moral rules. Second, he claims that he has in the past favored a combination of "methodologies," and is therefore far from monistic.

With the discussion of exceptionless moral rules, another matter with which Gustafson is concerned has intruded, namely, whether Ramsey is a deontologist. If his rules are telic, then the implication is that they are not exceptionless. Here Ramsey wishes, I think, to be thought of in neither exclusively teleological or deontological terms, so he leaves the question open. This is well and good, but ultimately irrelevant to Ramsey's classification as a monist. There are both deontological monists (e.g., Kant) and teleological monists (e.g., Bentham and Fletcher), and there is no reason to suppose that we cannot have monists who are neither or both.

But let us ask, in what way does Ramsey think of himself as com-bining methodologies? He refers us back to his "Two Concepts of Rules in Christian Ethics,"[25] in which he borrowed for his agapism categories normally used in discussions of the status of rules in utili-tarianism. "If one is going to push 'pure agapism,' I said, there are four options: pure act agapism, pure summary-rule agapism, pure rule agapism, or some combination of these approaches, or their varied use according to which best serves to throw light on our pathways. I

---

25. In Ramsey, *Deeds and Rules*, pp. 132-44.

rather favored the latter, as best leading us to what love requires. Or one could be a 'mixed agapist.' Or a 'nonagapist' who uses some other root metaphor or theological principle."[26]

This quotation is revealing. Initially it skirts the monism charge, but then it ends with a statement which indicates that monistic assumptions persist in Ramsey's idea of how ethical theorizing works. By citing different forms of agapism Ramsey misses the point that any sort of agapism, insofar as it confesses the supreme governance of love, will be monistic. So act agapism, summary-rule agapism, pure rule agapism, some combination of rule and agapism — all are monisms in virtue of their being *agapisms*. It is not until Ramsey mentions "nonagapism" that he has gone beyond this. But immediately — and revealingly — he *assumes* that any version of nonagapism will use some "root metaphor or theological principle." In other words, he assumes Christian ethics to be rooted in one metaphor or principle. And so monism persists. It is evident both in *Basic Christian Ethics,* published in 1950, and in this characterization of his life's work published in 1985, just three years before his death.

Why were monistic assumptions so entrenched in Ramsey's thought, despite his evident wisdom and intellectual power? I suspect the answer lies with the tradition of thought Ramsey inherited with other Protestant contemporaries as they set about to work in the newly identified field of Christian ethics. While it would require a whole book to elucidate, the suspicion is that principle monism is absolute in twentieth-century Protestant Christian ethics, from Søren Kierkegaard to Paul Lehmann, just as it assumed that a ground for all Christian ethics must be found in the concept of *agape.* (Even if unintentionally, Gene Outka's *Agape: An Ethical Analysis*[27] actually traces this assumption quite clearly, as it moves historically through major Protestant thought in the past two hundred years on ethics and love.) In short, Ramsey was raised on monism. And while he had the good sense to see that Fletcher, who also was raised on the same diet, had a habit of abusing action descriptions, he could not see that this had everything to do with the monism both professed.

---

26. Ramsey, "Letter," p. 77.

27. Gene Outka, *Agape: An Ethical Analysis* (New Haven: Yale University Press, 1972).

## 5. Competing Moral Authorities:
## Principle Monism and Action Descriptions

A good deal more will be said in this book regarding descriptions of human action and how they are given appropriate and thorough recognition. The argument so far in this chapter, however, has confined itself to three specific points. To begin, we have pointed out that actions and action descriptions were a crucial concern in the situation ethics debate of the 1960s, and that a key charge against situationism was its alleged abuse of human action descriptions. Second, we have suggested that this abuse is rooted in the ethical principle monism presumed by situationists like Joseph Fletcher. Third, we have tried to show that the presumption of monism was in fact widespread, encompassing even one of situationism's most penetrating critics, namely, Paul Ramsey. We have said little, however, of the actual nature of the abuse or, for that matter, why it should be considered abuse at all. As an initial foray into these matters, let us begin with the most basic arguments about how monism and action descriptions interact, and why this interaction must be thought problematic.

In what follows I shall argue that principle monism necessarily *swallows up* moral action descriptions, wresting from them any independent moral force. Depending upon the specific type of monism, these moral descriptions may or may not be spit back out by the principle as valid; yet if and when they are, their validity rests in the monistic principle rather than the description. This is a bad thing for three reasons at least: (1) it is unworkable; (2) it commits itself logically to the possibility that what might be called the "data" of ethics might be entirely eliminated by the monistic principle; and (3) it is essentially reductive and denies, for no good reason, the diversity and variety of the moral life.

What we have previously called the *constitutive* character of the supreme principle in a monism can be understood as *omnipotence* within the moral system. It has the exclusive power to determine that any action being contemplated is in some situation moral, immoral, or "nonmoral": it is moral if it coheres with the principle, immoral if it diverges from it, and nonmoral if the principle is not involved. The supreme principle is thus the sole arbiter of moral significance or relevance. In utilitarianism, for example, only consequences regarding "happiness" or pain and pleasure are relevant; all other considerations are simply set aside.

On the analysis given earlier, the omnipotence of the moral principle cannot but be challenged by action descriptions, particularly those that clearly carry moral judgments such as descriptions like murder, fratricide, or adultery. When we call something a murder, we are saying (in part) that the action to which we are referring is morally significant; indeed, it is morally wrong. We use the description just to distinguish the action from other actions to which it is not clear that such a definite moral judgment applies. In short, the description "murder" of itself has moral power — yet, in principle monism, supreme moral power rests in the principle. The powers, then, must face one another down.

In a monism the results of this face-down are predetermined: any conflict *must* be settled in favor of the supreme principle. For if moral descriptions and/or terms are given *independent* power to grant or pick out moral significance, then the monism dissolves. A consistent monism can solve the power struggle in one of only two possible ways: either moral terms are trampled and some effort is made to remove them (one finds this in Fletcher and utilitarianism), or they are allowed to remain, having received the stamp of approval by the supreme principle. (This calmer approach can be attributed to Ramsey.) In either case, moral terms must be (at least theoretically) investigated, judged, and in some cases condemned by the supreme principle.

One might ask if moral terms do not need in some cases to be rethought, revised, or even abandoned. Yet principle monism does more then revise; theoretically it demands a reconsideration and possible reworking of our *entire moral vocabulary*. This is because the logic of principle monism requires that there be no competitors to the supreme moral principle. Hence, all moral terms will need to be checked by the principle. Yet moral terms and descriptions are so ubiquitous in our vocabulary and in our presumed view of the world that this would be impossible. Not only would the monist need to check a term like "murder," he would also need to check far less weighty — although no less "moral" — terms like "litter," "punctual," or "thoughtless."

But there is more than a practical difficulty in this. For it is properly asked how the principle monist knows his principle to be correct. Undoubtedly his first answer will be that it is a right and proper distillation of our "moral experience." But what is moral experience if it is not what we know as we use these moral descriptions? We know the world as containing "liars," "adulterers," "considerate persons," and "honest persons." Moral terms and descriptions are a presumed and necessary part of anything we might call moral experience. Consequently, it is difficult to imagine how the monist's justification of his principle could work. Since the abolishment of these terms must always be for the monist a theoretical possibility, they cannot serve at the same time as the ground for the justification of his monistic moral principle.

I suppose it is open to the monist to deny that he is interested in the coherence of his principle with the moral experience or traditions encased in our terms and descriptions. He may say his principle is a "divine command," or "self-evident," or "intuitive." If we set aside for a moment how far this suggestion is from how we live and speak, and grant its logical possibility, we might still ask why such a person needs *one* principle rather than many. That is, what is gained by saying that God has ordained the monistic principle of love rather than that he has ordained "no murder," "no stealing," "no adultery," etc.? Why, after all, is it better to have one foundational consideration or principle in ethics rather than many?

Our attraction to monism likely relates to our hope for a stronger justification for our particular moral beliefs. We imagine "that we should love" (for example) can provide a deeper justification for "that we should not murder" or "that we should not be cruel." But it is not at all clear that cruelty or murder *need* this sort of justification, and it is even less clear that the principles which are supposed to provide it, principles which are the product of moral theories such as those of Ramsey or Fletcher or Bentham or Kant, are better "justified" than the particular beliefs about murder or cruelty themselves. As Edmund Pincoffs has put this point, "If it is a truism that cruelty is wrong, then the proposition does not require justification. Where is justification to end but in truisms? But then, how are we to understand the relation between justificatory ethical theories [Pincoffs's term for my 'principle monisms'] and these truisms?"[28]

Another reason we find monism attractive is our condern for uni-

28. Pincoffs, p. 54.

formity; a monistic principle could be thought to provide one scale on which all our particular actions could be weighed. We hope to be able to say, for example, that of two actions we are contemplating, action *a* is utility-maximizing or love-filled to the degree *x*, and action *b* is utility-maximizing or love-filled to the degree *x* plus *n*. So *b* is to be preferred. Underneath this hope lies a belief about comparability that, as Bernard Williams has pointed out, "rests on an assumption about rationality, to the effect that two considerations cannot be rationally weighed against each other unless there is a common consideration in terms of which they can be compared." But, Williams goes on to say, this "assumption is at once very powerful and utterly baseless. Quite apart from the ethical, aesthetic considerations can be weighed against economic ones (for instance) without being an application of them, and without their both being an example of a third kind of consideration."[29]

In the end we can simply say that there is no strong reason to reduce the very many terms and descriptions of human beings and their actions to one moral principle. These descriptions and terms are numerous and, as such, responsive to the very many particularities of how an action is done, to whom, with what intent, and so on. It is these particularities that make up the complex fabric of our varied moral lives. Insofar as monism, any monism, imposes the authority of one moral principle over this complex variety, it cannot but cheat our lives and draw our attention away from what really matters within them.

## 6. On Developing a Nonmonistic Christian Ethics

The concern of this book is to move toward a theological ethics that responds to and integrates an adequate account of human action and action description. Thus far our work has been principally negative. In chapter 1 we saw how actions can be, and have been, grossly misunderstood when separated from their homes in our human lives, and in this chapter, how moral theories can be, and have been, constructed

9. Bernard Williams, *Ethics and the Limits of Philosophy* (Cambridge: Harvard University Press, 1985), p. 17.

so as to run roughshod over the significance of action descriptions. The criticism will continue in the next chapter, for we have yet to consider the debate that is most current and relevant for how actions are understood in Christian theological ethics, namely, the contemporary Catholic debate — where once again we encounter significant misunderstanding.

In the midst of this primarily negative enterprise, it is worth pausing briefly to imagine what positive directions the critique might open to us. If, for example, principle monism is eliminated because of its structural disregard for action descriptions, what might be an alternative? Can we have pluralism in Christian ethics? That is, can we give up the search thinkers like Ramsey and Fletcher, in their time, evidently presumed must be undertaken for some "root metaphor or principle" by which a Christian ethics could be justified?

Despite the practical difficulties we have noted, one might yet hold that any attempt to sketch a pluralistic alternative to monism will necessarily diminish the potency of a Christian ethic since it will require a conservatism concerning existing linguistic and other commonly agreed-upon moral structures. A pluralism cannot press for a justification of all our moral notions and/or practices in Jesus' command that we "love one another as I have loved you" — a command that might be thought a monistic principle capable of standing above us, bringing critical judgment upon the traditionalism and conventionalism of our inherited moral language.[30]

In reply to this objection, the first thing to note is that whether or not Christians or others think we need to place ourselves in a position from which all our moral beliefs and practices can be evaluated, in fact this is just the sort of thing we *cannot* do. As I have been suggesting, we cannot *suspend* our moral terms, for they are the furniture of the

---

30. In fact, as Christians celebrate its presentation to the disciples by Jesus on Thursday of Holy Week, the love commandment depends upon a story. To borrow a term from the first chapter, its *home* is in the narrative that has, by John 15 (where it is recorded) already been plainly given to the disciples as what they must live. They know love because they have known Jesus, whom of course they will come to know more deeply in the succeeding hours and days of suffering, death, and resurrection. The love commandment is therefore not at all like the putatively "universal" principles searched after by Kant or Mill in the nineteenth century. For to know what the command means, one must know the story of Jesus as told in the Gospels and by the church.

moral world about which we reflect when we do ethics. It does not follow from this, however, that we are consigned to uncritical acceptance of every existing moral notion. For criticism of some of our moral notions in terms of others is possible and appropriate. As others have argued, this in fact is a much better description of how reason-giving and belief justification actually work, particularly in ethics. To quote Bernard Williams, "some beliefs can be questioned, justified, or adjusted while others are kept constant, but there is no process by which they can all be questioned at once, or justified in terms of almost nothing. In Neurath's famous image, we repair the ship while we are on the sea."[31]

In this context the prospect of doing *specifically Christian* ethics may look bleak since appeals to an ethics that is founded, as Ramsey supposes in quotation 1 above, on an entirely distinct Christian supreme principle simply cannot work. Yet two further points show that this is not so. First, to extend Neurath's imagery, Christians need not think of themselves as sailing the same ship or even navigating the same sea as persons who do not share their convictions or their vocabulary. We need not think that ethical reflection, which probes and criticizes some accepted moral notions and/or specific action descriptions in terms of other shared notions or commitments (instead of founding them all on one principle), is, in all cases and as exercised in all communities, the same process. Christians embrace and regularly use a number of notions that are not used by others, such as forgiveness, sin, God's gifts (Eucharist), gentleness, humility, self-sacrifice, hope, and the like. Furthermore, Christians may sometimes refuse to use — or use only in an emended form — notions that are otherwise standard in others' talk about morality, e.g., "rights," "power," "self-survival," or even "justice."[32] And finally, as Christians we often discover that even when we employ terms widely used outside our community and tradition, we do not always mean what others seem to

31. Williams, p. 113.

32. Stanley Hauerwas has argued that liberalism has so subverted the notion of justice that it is better left alone by Christians, since "in the interest of working for justice, contemporary Christians allow their imaginations to be captured by the concepts of justice determined by a liberal society and as a result contribute to the development of a society that makes substantive accounts of justice less and less likely" ("Should Christians Talk So Much about Justice?" *Books and Religion* [May/June 1986]: 14).

mean. In fact, the analysis of just what we Christians mean by our moral terms is itself an important part of Christian ethics. Ramsey suggests this to Gustafson in his "letter." "[S]ometimes it will be found more illuminating to deepen 'moral notions,' to explore more deeply the meaning of moral offense-terms. For example, your [Gustafson's] splendid chapter on suicide is, I believe, flawed because you take that to be any *act of self-destruction* rather than exploring first the *meaning* of the forbidden suicide."[33]

Taking this cue from Ramsey, consider the following quotation from R. F. Holland. In it he is engaged in discovering just what the Christian (or "religious person") might mean when he employs the moral term "suicide."

> The sanctity of life is an idea that a religious person might want to introduce in connection with suicide, but if he left the matter there he would be representing suicide as objectionable in the same way and to the same degree as murder. It is only when he thinks of life as a gift that the difference starts to emerge. For the murderer does not destroy a gift that was given to *him;* he destroys something which was given to someone else but which happens to have got in his way. This argues his crime to be from the standpoint of ordinary ethics worse than that of suicide, of whom at least it may be said that it was his own affair. On the other hand the suicide, unlike the murderer, is — religiously speaking — necessarily an ingrate; and the ingratitude here is of no ordinary kind, for it is towards his Creator, the giver of life, to whom everything is wed.[34]

What Holland does here is consider how an action, suicide, might be differently conceived according as that action is received within some way of seeing and living in the world. Christians hold a variety of beliefs about God, humankind, and the world, and one of these is that our lives come to us as a gift from God. This means that within a Christian's very notion and description of suicide will be embedded the concern that suicide demonstrates some form of ingratitude. This will make a considerable difference, not only in how we judge the moral seriousness of a particular suicide but also in

33. Ramsey, "Letter," p. 77.
34. R. F. Holland, *Against Empiricism* (Totowa, N.J.: Barnes & Noble, 1980), p. 153.

what we think suicides are. Arguments will develop, both within and between communities, about how suicide should be understood. The retention of the description "suicide," laced with a peculiar sort of meaning in relation to ingratitude, may become quite radical. Indeed, it has been borne out historically that calling something by its true name can sometimes be extremely dangerous. In our own age, for instance, resistance to ideology or other totalizing forces, those that are by nature highly monistic and bent on replacing older language with a new theory-generated set of terms, may be the key radical political task.

We should not suppose, then, that Christians who resist principle monism in ethics do little more than protect the status quo. And to mark one further point, Christians may also wish to note (as Ramsey in his response to Gustafson had come to suspect) that any sort of monism tends to be reductive of the various and multiform stories they wish to tell of God's choosing Israel, sending his Son Jesus, and being continually present with the church. We need not suppose that one principle, such as that which enjoins *agape,* can sum this story up, becoming its sole representative in the so-called moral realm. As Stanley Hauerwas has said,

> even if love is freed from its sentimental perversions, it is still not an adequate principle, policy, or summary metaphor to capture the thrust of the Gospel for the Christian's moral behavior. Love is dependent on our prior perceptions of the truth of reality that can finally be approached only through the richness of the language and stories which form what we know. The Christian is thus better advised to resist the temptation to reduce the Gospel to a single formula or summary image for the moral life. Christian ethics and the moral life are as rich and various as the story we hold and the life we must live to be true to it.[35]

Christians, in other words, are not "people who love" or "people whose principles of morality are founded on *agape*"; they are people who are guided by the story told in the Bible and retold in various forms throughout the span of the church. This story and their continued reflection upon it is encased in a variety of descriptions of the

35. Stanley Hauerwas, *Vision and Virtue* (Notre Dame, Ind.: Fides, 1974), p. 120.

world and of human actions that are not shared by other communities. This difference cannot but affect how the world is understood, how the moral life is lived, and how critical reflection about both is carried out.

# 3. *Veritatis Splendor* and Proportionalism

*Contemporary Catholic Disagreement about Action*

## 1. Debating the Splendor of Truth

While long anticipated, Pope John Paul II's encyclical *Veritatis Splendor*[1] nonetheless fell like a bombshell in the midst of contemporary Catholic moral theology. The act of its issuance quickly became a case in point of one of its key subjects, namely, how rightly to understand human action: What was John Paul II *really* doing as he issued this powerful letter to his fellow Catholic bishops? What were his intentions, and how are we to interpret the significance of his actions? Was he, as Bernard Haring mournfully cried out in the early days after its issuance, trying "to endorse total assent and submission to all utterances of the Pope"?[2] Or was he, as Maciej Zieba maintained, mounting "a defense of freedom," arguing "vigorously that only truth gives sense and meaning to human freedom; and because of this, human beings have an inner duty to search for the truth"?[3] And who, af-

---

1. The encyclical letter *Veritatis Splendor* is reprinted in English translation in many places, including in *Considering "Veritatis Splendor,"* ed. John Wilkins (Cleveland: Pilgrim, 1994). In subsequent citations I use the numbered divisions included in the official text.

2. Bernard Haring, "A Distrust That Wounds," in *Considering "Veritatis Splendor,"* p. 9.

3. Maciej Zieba, "Truth and Freedom in the Thought of Pope John Paul II," in *Considering "Veritatis Splendor,"* pp. 38-39.

ter all, is in a position to determine just what it was that John Paul II did when he issued his encyclical?

As one lay Catholic reader suggests, the answer to this last question may be: not the moral theologians. "Professional theologians may in some ways be its [the encyclical's] worst audience. They will inevitably read it with anxiety," for they are so ready to engage with its particular arguments. Yet "this anxiety perhaps blinds a little to the vision of the encyclical; a vision which those of us who live more fully in the secular world can see is both refreshing and inspiring."[4] The moral theologians, in other words, being so anxious to read their names in the encyclical, may have missed its full force.

For the purposes of this book, however, I should like to narrow the inquiry about *Veritatis Splendor (VS)*. As I mentioned, human action and how it is rightly described is one of its most central topics, and following the concerns of this book, I shall take this as my focus in interacting with the encyclical.

Perhaps the best known of John Paul II's positions in the encyclical is his defense of the idea that there are intrinsically evil acts. Indeed, he writes his letter to warn his fellow bishops against modern theories of ethics that suggest otherwise. Richard McCormick, a Jesuit theologian, wrote to rebut the pope, not so much on the matter of whether there are intrinsically evil acts (although how this is to be understood remains in question) but about whether the pope has gotten "proportionalism" right.[5] After McCormick's response another interlocutor, Martin Rhonheimer, joined the fray to rebuff McCormick, as if on be-

---

4. Oliver O'Donovan, "A Summons to Reality," in *Considering "Veritatis Splendor,"* pp. 51-52.

5. The precise definition of "proportionalism" will, of course, be under dispute, not only because of the debate that swirls around it but also because of the terms proportionalists typically use to lay out their position, such as "premoral evil," "ontic evil," or "fundamental reality." Philip Keane, S.S., offers a characterization that is about as clear as the subject matter admits: "First, this approach [proportionalism] seeks to reflect more completely on an action by bringing to consciousness the premorally (or non morally or ontically) good and evil features of the action. Second, this approach, without dismissing other criteria, uses proportionate reason as the decisive criterion in moving from the premoral level to the level of objective moral goodness or evil." "The Objective Moral Order: Reflections on Recent Research," in *Introduction to Christian Ethics: A Reader,* ed. Ronald P. Hamil and Kenneth R. Himes, OFM (New York: Paulist, 1989), p. 459.

half of the pope. I should like particularly to concentrate on this three-cornered exchange; virtually the whole of it is about human action.

Shortly after the encyclical was issued, McCormick published a brief response in a Catholic monthly, the *Tablet*, under the title "Killing the Patient."[6] We will return to this response nearer the end of this chapter. In another, later article McCormick offers a long and meandering survey of various responses to *VS* mixed in with his own assessment. This was published in *Theological Studies* under the title "Some Early Reactions to *Veritatis Splendor*."[7] The article is, to apply the term McCormick uses to describe the encyclical, rather "predictable": McCormick appreciates his allies and takes some jabs at his opponents. The article takes on life near its end when he turns to a discussion of action, one he is brought to as he opposes Russell Hittenger's defense of *VS* in *Crisis*.[8] The discussion of action continues as he responds to Ralph McInerny, to Joseph Fuchs and Peter Knauer (two theologians with whom he is allied), and finally to Martin Rhonheimer.

McCormick believes he has found in Hittenger a "physicalism" about human acts. That is to say, he believes that Hittenger thinks acts can and should be named according to the physical movements performed in them. According to "physicalism" — a term that is used almost always pejoratively — what one *intends* to do in the activity is extrinsic to the act one performs. McCormick characterizes his disagreement with Hittenger as follows: "For Hittenger, intention means one thing and one thing only: *something in addition to an action already constituted*." For McCormick, however, "intention makes the act what it is."[9]

As McCormick understands it, what Hittenger is referring to when he worries about "intentions" and how they might move to and fro, changing or legitimating acts at will, are in fact rightly referred to as

6. Richard McCormick, "Killing the Patient," in *Considering "Veritatis Splendor,"* pp. 14-20.

7. Richard A. McCormick, "Some Early Reactions to *Veritatis Splendor*," *Theological Studies* 55 (1994), reprinted in Charles Curran and Richard McCormick, S.J., eds., *John Paul II and Moral Theology: Readings in Moral Theology, No. 10* (New York: Paulist, 1998), pp. 5-34.

8. Russell Hittenger, "The Pope and the Theorists," *Crisis* 11 (1993): 31-36.

9. McCormick, "Some Early Reactions," p. 18.

"motives" for action. Since for McCormick "intention makes an act what it is," a change in intention will bring about a change in act. There is no reason, then, for Hittenger to fret — nor the pope, for that matter. For motives (which Hittenger mistakes for intentions) do not have direct power over an action. As McCormick puts it, motives supervene; their addition or subtraction to an act does not change its name or its being. In making this point McCormick actually enlists the support of the encyclical. He cites a passage in which something called "ulterior intentions" are referred to and then states, quite boldly, that "intentions that are ulterior to the object of an act . . . are motives."[10]

It is always helpful to have an example, and McCormick is kind enough to provide one. Against Hittenger he distinguishes "self-stimulation" (masturbation) for self-pleasuring from "self-stimulation for sperm testing," claiming these are two different acts since their intention is different. On the other hand, "killing" and "killing for world peace" are descriptions that point to the same action, killing, although the second specifies a motive (not an intention) for the killing, while the first does not.

There is some plausibility in these examples, I think, but they evidently depend on some fine distinctions. Is there a clear way to distinguish motive from intention? While McCormick apparently believes there is, he seems to decide this is not the place to puzzle the point through and moves along to another matter. However, his implication is plain. McCormick suggests that the encyclical is generally captured by the type of error he thinks Hittenger makes. This is, once again, "physicalism," whereby the naming of an action is done entirely in terms of its physical movements. Physicalism always shortchanges intention. In contradistinction, and as McCormick would have it, "me murdering Jeff" specifies an action that is determined by my morally unjust intention that Jeff be put to death.

We might go on to say that it follows that murder, since it necessarily involves this unjust intention, is an "intrinsically evil act." However, according to McCormick, this solves almost nothing. For the crucial question will come down to whether or not the description "murder" applies in my case — something that cannot be determined unless we know more about me and my intentions. If the pope supposes that "murder"

10. McCormick, "Some Early Reactions," p. 19.

can be specified according to a predetermined pattern of bodily movements, as for example we can specify a plié in ballet, then he has a wrong idea about human actions. In effect, he would be a physicalist, and physicalists necessarily misunderstand the nature of human action.

We shall, in our next section, consider if the pope is rightly thought to be a physicalist about action. Yet as we do we shall need to mark a quite surprising development. Martin Rhonheimer published an article in the *Thomist* entitled "'Intrinsically Evil Acts' and the Moral Viewpoint: Clarifying a Central Teaching of *Veritatis Splendor,*"[11] to which McCormick responds in the article we have begun considering. In Rhonheimer's subsequent response to McCormick's response, "Intentional Actions and the Meaning of Object: A Reply to Richard McCormick,"[12] he turns the tables. For as he holds, it is not the pope but rather McCormick and other proportionalists who are the real physicalists!

## 2. Will the Real Physicalism Please Stand Up

What are we to make of these opposing charges? Let us begin by looking more closely at *Veritatis Splendor* to see how the pope might imagine the physicalist view to relate to the errors he feels so compelled to warn against. As an initial working definition, let us say that "physicalism" is the view that human acts can and should be defined in terms of the physical movements that make them up. Identification of human acts would follow, then, for the physicalist, along the same lines as the way an observer might identify certain moves in ballet: That was a pirouette, that other a plié, etc. The idea is that if a person was observed to go through a certain series of movements as specified by a given act description, then the person who performed the movements can be said with confidence to have done that act.

The basic objection against physicalism is that it sets aside the crucial participation of the human will in the act. McCormick has called

---

11. Martin Rhonheimer, "'Intrinsically Evil Acts' and the Moral Viewpoint: Clarifying a Central Teaching of *Veritatis Splendor,*" *Thomist* (1994).

12. Martin Rhonheimer, "Intentional Actions and the Meaning of Object: A Reply to Richard McCormick," *Thomist* (1995).

this "intention," but we should not assume that is the only thing it can be called. *VS* talks in different terms, speaking of, for example, the importance of the "perspective of the acting person" (78) or of the "participation of the will" in the action. This by itself is important. While some might call him a physicalist, plainly John Paul II does not mean to be one; indeed, when he employs the phrases just noted, he means to avoid it. Indeed, he seems to believe that traditional Catholic teaching is not susceptible to the charge, frequently leveled by the proportionalists,[13] that it is physicalist about human action.

Not only does John Paul II wish to avoid physicalism himself, as we go deeper into the encyclical we find that he thinks ideas or attitudes that contribute to something like physicalism are at the root of many of our modern moral and political difficulties. Specifically, he believes that in much contemporary thinking, freedom (associated with will and therefore with intention) has been severed from nature (associated with body and therefore with the bodily participation in a particular act). Consider in this regard the following quotations.

> Our own age is marked, though in a different sense, by a similar tension [to that of Trent]. The penchant for empirical observation, the procedures of scientific objectification, technological progress and certain forms of liberalism have led to these two terms being set in opposition, as if a dialectic, if not an absolute conflict, between freedom and nature were characteristic of the structure of human history.

For the pope, the division between freedom and nature has left nature bereft of soul, and consequently has affirmed a freedom that is only about itself.

> In such an understanding, nature would include in the first place the human body, its makeup and its processes: against this physical data would be opposed whatever is "constructed," in other words "culture," seen as the product and result of freedom. Human na-

---

13. Lisa Cahill, for instance, in response to *Veritatis Splendor*, makes this generalization about church teaching: "Church teaching holds that 'love' is a foundational meaning of sex, but tends to revert to a sacralization of physical process whenever sex is the moral issue" ("Accent on the Masculine," in *Considering "Veritatis Splendor,"* p. 57).

ture, understood in this way, could be reduced to and treated as a readily available biological or social material. This ultimately means making freedom self-defining and a phenomenon creative of itself and its values. Indeed, when all is said and done man would not even have a nature; he would be his own personal life-project. Man would be nothing more than his own freedom.

These two quotations are drawn from number 46 of the encyclical, these last words bringing that section to a close. Number 47 begins as follows:

In this context, objections of physicalism and naturalism have been leveled against the traditional conception of the natural law, which is accused of presenting as moral laws what are in themselves mere biological laws. Consequently, in too superficial a way, a permanent and unchanging character would be attributed to certain kinds of behavior, and, on the basis of this, an attempt would be made to formulate universally valid moral norms.

Note that the pope explicitly acknowledges the objection of physicalism. Obviously he believes it does not stick. But there is more here. For it is not just that the charges of physicalism and naturalism do not tell against the traditional Catholicism the pope represents. It is that the charges themselves arise out of a confused modern view. This surely is the meaning of the phrase "in this context" which begins number 47. Simply, it refers us back to the discussion in 46 of the bifurcation of freedom and nature. The pope appears to be suggesting that the modern reduction of nature to a mechanistic sphere, a sphere of the biological apart from freedom, actually produces accusations of physicalism against the church's teaching. This is where we might begin to place Rhonheimer's surprising charge against the proportionalists, that *they* are the physicalists.

Let us suppose, at this point without evidence, that it is true that the proportionalists are physicalists under the skin. Consider the pope's position if he is called to defend traditional church teaching against the charge of physicalism when that charge is leveled from within the presumptions of physicalism itself. How can he proceed? Since the "physicalism" charge is made by physicalists-under-the-skin, any direct response will be in danger of falling into physicalism, since it needs to be made in terms the subterranean physicalists can understand and accept. In such a context a better strategy is to criticize the assumptions underlying the charges and to change the terms of the debate. A careful read of certain passages of the encyclical gives the impression that this may be exactly what the pope is attempting to do.

In the section just cited, number 47, after noting the physicalist charges, the pope turns back quickly to the consuming matter of the body and freedom.

> A freedom which claims to be absolute ends up treating the human body as a raw datum, devoid of meaning and moral values until freedom has shaped it in accordance with its design. Consequently, human nature and the body appear as *presuppositions or preambles*, materially *necessary* for freedom to make its choice, yet extrinsic to the person, the subject and the human act. Their functions would not be able to constitute reference points for moral decisions, because the finalities of these inclinations would be merely *"physical"* goods, called by some "pre-moral." To refer to them, in order to find in them rational indications with regard to the order of morality, would be to expose oneself to the accusation of physicalism or biologism.

If we translate the pope into a rough-and-ready vernacular, the sort used by sparring philosophers over drinks, one might imagine John Paul II saying to those who charge him with physicalism: Look, on your terms I'll always end up looking like a physicalist because you begin with an understanding of nature that treats the human body as raw datum, something freedom (and therefore morality) is built atop. So when I start attending to the body when I talk about human acts, I'll look to you like I'm fishing around in the merely physical for a complete description of those acts. In fact, though, what I mean to do is deny that there is such a thing as the "merely physical," particularly when human beings are involved. Rather, the human being is a unity "whose rational soul is *per se et essentialiter* the form of his body" (48).

Many have questioned — I believe with some justification — the choice of "intrinsically evil acts" as the hill the encyclical has chosen to die over.[14] However, our discussion here suggests that, whether or

14. Herbert McCabe, for instance, suggests that by accenting acts that violate

not the choice was fortunate, there are deeper matters bubbling under the charges and countercharges of physicalism. What, after all, does the sort of thinking typically proffered by proportionalists about actions imply about the human body and its relation to soul? Martin Rhonheimer believes there is considerable trouble on this point. As he holds, proportionalism supports (and is supported by) a picture of a human being who hovers over the "physical world," manipulating it in his acts to bring about certain outcomes.

We shall turn shortly to Rhonheimer's charges of physicalism against the proportionalists. Yet before we leave the text of the encyclical, let us look about in it further to see if and how it might be thought to embody physicalist presumptions. If physicalism involves that description of human action entirely in terms of the physical movements involved in it, then we can check through *VS* to see if this happens. That is, does the pope on any occasion speak of a human action as if it were nothing but the physical movements involved in it?

Generally the pope avoids physicalism, although certain of his descriptions could be clearer. Some trouble arises, I believe, around the use (or the avoidance) of the term "intention." One wonders if the pope uses the term sparingly because it is a byword of the proportionalists he opposes. For example, John Paul II opens section 74 with the following question: "But on what does the moral assessment of man's free acts depend? What is it that ensures this ordering of human acts to God? Is it the *intention* of the acting subject, the *circumstances* — and the particular consequences — of his action, or the *object* itself of his act?" The question is meant to establish the terms of the debate about action, for the three options mentioned are each considered in their turn, concluding with the object, which John Paul II believes is the correct answer to the opening questions. Indeed, since the encyclical targets the views of the proportionalists and the consequentialists (these are directly addressed in 75 and 76), and since the pope associates these with an elevation of "intention" and circumstance (consequence) over "object," then it is evident that the question is a bit of a setup.

---

*caritas* rather than exploring what, more positively, a human community based in friendship might look like, the pope cuts off roots of access to the virtues, particularly in Aquinas, since "[y]ou cannot fit the virtues into a legal structure without reducing them to dispositions to follow the rules" ("Manuals and Rule Books," in *Considering "Veritatis Splendor,"* p. 68).

Setting up the terms in so stark a form is unfortunate. One might wish to agree with the pope that there is such a thing as the object of an action, and that it is this that crucially defines what the action is. At the same time one might also want to say that, for instance, certain sorts of "intentions" (what sorts will be important) are crucial for determining what the object is. As I hope to show by considering the position of Aquinas in the next two chapters, it is possible to hold such a view while avoiding the errors of proportionalism.

Pursuing this contrast between the position of the proportionalists and that of his encyclical, the pope goes on to say:

> In order to offer rational criteria for a right decision, the theories mentioned above take account of the intention and consequences of human action. Certainly there is need to take into account both the intention — as Jesus forcefully insisted in clear disagreement with the scribes and Pharisees, who prescribed in great detail certain outward practices without paying attention to the heart — and the good obtained and the evils avoided as a result of a particular act. Responsibility demands as much. But the consideration of these consequences, and also intentions, is not sufficient for judging the moral quality of a concrete choice. (77)

The phrase used in the quotation from section 74 quoted above was "the intention of the acting subject." It is not sophistry to distinguish this phrase from "the intention . . . of a particular act" as used here in 77. This would be the difference between saying "my intention in asking him to supper is . . ." and "the intention in the act of inviting someone to supper (which I am just now doing) is. . . ." However, I do not see that the pope avails himself of this distinction. In these two quotations the phrases appear to be used interchangeably. Once again, perhaps this is because the pope means to leave the language of intention behind with the proportionalists.

In this light it is worth noting that the term "direct intention" of an act, long used in discussions of the principle of double effect, is not to be found in VS. The notion behind the term seems historically to have been that more than one level of intentionality can be applied to many actions: something like the intention in the act itself (i.e., direct intention) and the set of intentions the agent happens to bring to the act in a particular circumstance. While there are some difficulties with the presumption of levels (as I hope to show), there is also a good deal of sense to it. Indeed, the distinction plays a role throughout our debate, with both sides adopting (but not always consistently using) a linguist convention to note it. For instance, the encyclical speaks of *ulterior* intentions: "There are the acts which, in the Church's moral tradition, have been termed 'intrinsically evil' *(intrinsece malum):* they are such *always and per se,* in other words, on account of their very object, and quite apart from the *ulterior intentions* of the one acting and the circumstances" (80, emphasis added).

As noted, Richard McCormick fixes on this passage and, in response, redesignates these ulterior intentions as "motives" brought to the act by the agent. In a technical discussion we might benefit from following the rule that the intention in the act itself, the "direct intention," be called simply "the intention," and any other intentions the agent might bring to the action be called motives. The rule, however, would wreak havoc with our ordinary usage, for we use the terms "intention" and "motive" almost interchangeably. (E.g., a politician might say "my motive for . . ." or "my intention in . . . calling you here was to ask for your support in November." I suspect no one would notice a difference.)

In the end, however, the somewhat slippery use of "intention" in *VS* does not cause it to fall in any clear way into physicalism. In no passage does the pope imply that the object of the act is rightly and completely described in terms of a series of bodily movements. In fact, the pope employs a variety of phrases such as "the deliberate consent to certain kinds of behavior" or the "involvement of the will in the concrete choices which it makes" (75) which keep human will and human behavior intertwined. Critically, it seems that while the involvement of the will in human action is presumed, when the encyclical turns to discussing "intrinsically evil acts," it does not reiterate or explicate how and why these acts cannot be understood in physicalist terms, that is, why any intrinsically evil act is not merely a bodily movement but also involves an act of the human will. We might hope for an explication of these acts in terms that demonstrate how they are not merely physical movements and also show how they are, in an important sense, fixed in such a way that certain sorts of "intentions" or "motives" cannot shove them aside. We do not receive this. But it

**69**

does not follow that "intrinsically evil acts" are rightly understood as merely physical movements; indeed, insofar as they are human acts, they *cannot* be understood in this way.

I believe this is safe to conclude that physicalism does not underlie the encyclical in any clear way, although there are points where it could be clearer in its language to distinguish its views from a physicalist misunderstanding. But what about the countercharge? Can physicalism be found amid the proportionalists?

To discover how this might be, we need to turn to Rhonheimer's discussion. His first task is to defend the encyclical's treatment of the "object" against the critic's charges of physicalism. In doing this he deepens the concept of the object by reconnecting it with the language of intention. A way into Rhonheimer's position is to consider an exchange McCormick sets up with the pope about intention, which we have already marked.

> The verdict here [about there being intrinsically evil acts] concerns "*choice* of certain kinds of behavior." In *VS*, n. 80, "intrinsic evil" is referred to the object, and this again means: to kinds of behavior, insofar as they are objects of choice. What is called "intrinsically evil," therefore, is concrete choice, describable in behavioral terms, that cannot be reduced to simple "behavior," however, because every choice includes an intention of the will, and a corresponding judgment of reason. That is also the reason why the encyclical speaks here about *ulterior* intentions, and not about intention as such: because "object" and intention are not mutually exclusive terms. There is some intentionality required so that an object of a human act can be constituted.

McCormick affirmed in his article that proportionalism makes precisely this point, inputting to *Veritatis Splendor*, and to critics of proportionalism generally, a different view, one rather easy for him to criticize. In this way he avoids the real issue and conceals the weakness of proportionalism and consequentialism. This weakness, however, is that a consequentialist refuses to speak about "actions" or about intention involved in the choice of concrete actions; he or she only talks about intentions as related to foreseeable consequences, thereby describing, and continuously redescribing, "actions" from the standpoint of a value-balancing observer; in this way he arrives at what he calls the "expanded notion of the object." When McCormick says, "intention tells us what is going on," he is perfectly right. But he neglects to ask: How are intentions shaped? Upon what do they depend? And, finally, What is, not intention and intentionality, but intentional *action?*[15]

This last piece of the quotation reminds us of the ironic fact that Rhonheimer means to charge McCormick and his fellow proportionalists with the physicalism they attribute to the pope. But the charge is subtle. It begins with an essential agreement with McCormick's phrase that "intention tells us what is going on." What Rhonheimer means to do, however, is to consider intention in the specific sense in which it is related to a particular action, as opposed to the broader sense in which the term might be used to refer to the intentions of an agent or to "intentionality." This is why the notion of the object of an action can never be abandoned. In quoting the oft-used phrase of proportionalism, namely, that we need an "expanded notion of the object," Rhonheimer points in the direction of his own view — and he would say the pope's — that the net effect of the proportionalists' "expansion of the object" is to make the one who acts, the agent, a "value-balancing observer." That is to say, *proportionalism encourages the agent to think of her action not as her action, but rather as an event she might bring about.* By "expanding the object" of an action to include any number of things in addition to the specific intention to which the object of the action is already tied (e.g., "killing" with the intention to bring about someone's death), proportionalists turn the agent into a calculator of outcomes who regards each situation from a distance, manipulating it (intentionally) with his "actions" rather than acting (intentionally) within it.

It follows for Rhonheimer that the proportionalists are physicalists just insofar as they come to see "my action" less as what I do and more as an event or span of time in which certain things occur or are brought about by me. In one sense this is a sort of angelism, for it puts the agent above the world in which she acts. But, as the pope would hold about the consequences of severing body from soul, its result is also a physicalism about the world in which we act: it is inert, merely physi-

15. Rhonheimer, "Intentional Actions," pp. 284-85.

cal. We come to this inert world with our actions, moving it from one state of affairs to another. The following quotation sums up this point, showing how the proportionalists' criticisms of the encyclical's view of human action actually arise from a physicalism (or naturalism) of which they, the proportionalist critics, are entirely blind.

> [A]dherents to these "teleological" approaches do not seem to have recognized the real source of their misunderstanding, which consists in overlooking the fact that practical reason is embedded in the intentional process of human acting, being a part of it. That is why, I think, these new approaches remain addicted to a surprising, even extreme, naturalism. Particular actions implicitly are considered by them as analogous to "events" and their outcomes as states of affairs. They implicitly presuppose, on the level of particular actions, a causal-eventistic concept of action (action as causing a state of affairs). I said "implicitly," because adherents of "teleological ethics" do not explicitly defend such a corresponding action theory (they actually deal very little with questions of action theory). That is why they are compelled to reclaim the aspect of intentionality — the aspect of willingly taking a position with regard to "good" and "evil" — on the level of fundamental options and attitudes, on the level of *Gesinnung*. So, consequentialists fail to see that, independently from *further* intentions required to optimize consequences or goods on the level of caused states of affairs, an action can be qualified as *morally evil*. . . . The problem is bypassed, even veiled, by describing chosen actions from the observer's viewpoint, thus leaving out of consideration precisely the act of choice. Probably the most famous example of such an argumentative reductionism is Caiaphas's advice to the Sanhedrin: "It is better for you that a single man dies for the people than that the whole people perishes." As a judgment about a simple event of a state of affairs and its desirability this obviously is quite true. But it is well known that Jesus did not simply die but was killed.[16]

Rhonheimer's phrase "causal-eventistic concept of action," I would suggest, names the same view of human action we discovered in chapter 1 among the analytical action theorists. There the standard

16. Rhonheimer, "Intrinsically Evil Acts," pp. 27-28.

view of human action also rested upon an uncritical assumption that the world is essentially inert, the object of scientific investigation and theorizing rather than the place where you and I live and act. (This is what Anscombe called "bare particular country."). In a similar way the monism of chapter 2 imagined that the only correct way to speak of and evaluate the morality of human action was to gather our judgments about human action, moral action, under one principle. All these views, which are part of the same large view, fail to see that human beings act in a human world. This is not a world separate from the world of human bodies and, indeed, all the physical stuff of God's creation, but rather one inextricably intertwined with it since, as the pope reiterates in the encyclical, human beings are created by God as a unity of body and soul. This unity can never be broken if any full sense is to be made of human action.

## 3. Proportionalism's Picture of the World of Human Action

To say that proportionalism is upheld by a disguised physicalism about human action amounts to a serious criticism. As such, it needs support. Are there passages in the writings of Catholic proportionalists that demonstrate this connection?

Martin Rhonheimer shows in his defense of *Veritatis Splendor* how the work of one influential Catholic moralist demonstrates what we have called physicalism about human action. He looks closely at Josef Fuchs's influential article, "The Absoluteness of Moral Terms."[17] While Fuchs begins with the correct point that, *qua* action, all human action must be intentional, Rhonheimer points out that he quickly abstracts "killing" from this requirement, since he supposes it implies nothing about the intentions of the agent. "Killing," then, becomes for Fuchs a morally neutral description, similar, one might imagine, to any other event describable in the most neutral of terms, such as the "falling of a leaf" or "the flying of a projectile." Judgment about the morality of human actions, for Fuchs, can come only after intention is

---

17. Fuchs's article, published initially in *Gregorianum* 52 (1971): 415-57, has been frequently reprinted.

*added to* these eventistic descriptions (this, actually, is not unlike how McCormick describes Hittenger's picture), and these descriptions will have to do with the why of the action. "I killed because . . ." is open to moral appraisal while "I killed" is not yet, since it is understood to do no different work from the phrase "a person's death was brought about." This understanding draws our eye from the key intention in the action killing (its object), i.e., my choosing to bring about someone's death, and focuses instead on the "totality" of things I might have been concerned with as I killed.

Looking elsewhere, and particularly among the responses from Catholic moral theologians critical of the pope's view of action in *VS*, it is quite easy to find language that substantiates Rhonheimer's reversal of the physicalism charge — physicalism now having the implication that an action is what occurs when an agent brings an intention to the inert, physical world so as to effect some sort of change in it. As such, we can expect physicalists to begin with the supposition that actions are morally neutral, and then become morally good or bad as they are applied (one is tempted to say "used") in a particular circumstance.

Consider the following quotation from Lisa Sowle Cahill's response to *VS*'s list of "intrinsically evil acts." "Murder, adultery, stealing, genocide, torture, prostitution, slavery, 'subhuman living conditions,' 'arbitrary imprisonment' and 'degrading conditions of work' have few if any defenders among Catholic theologians. The point of course is that these terms and phrases do not, as the encyclical implies, define acts in the abstract, but acts (like intercourse or homicide) together with the conditions or circumstances in which they become immoral."[18] One can imagine the pope responding: Who

---

18. Cahill, p. 58. As I point out, the notion of "acts in the abstract" is supplied by Cahill and not to be found in the writings of John Paul II. Yet Cahill represents a well-established part of the proportionalist literature; indeed, proportionalism very much needs the idea of "acts in the abstract" to make sense. Consider in this regard the following quotation from Josef Fuchs's highly influential *Personal Responsibility and Christian Morality:* "[C]an behavioral moral norms be universal at all, in the sense of being applicable always, everywhere and without exception, so that the action encompassed by them could never be objectively justified? . . . Viewed theoretically, there seems to be no possibility of behavioral norms of this kind for human action in the inner-worldly realm. The reason is that an action cannot be judged morally at all, considered purely in

mentioned anything about "acts in the abstract"? Cahill has supplied this phrase; it is not in the encyclical. But this is telling, for Cahill seems to be operating with the idea that there are such things as "acts in the abstract" to which moral properties or evaluations are added as they are done by a particular person at a particular time and place, etc. So there are certain acts, or (one wonders if Cahill is thinking) certain bodily movements like "intercourse" or "homicide" (homicide is an especially peculiar choice on Cahill's part since a homicide is the deliberate killing of one person by another), to which certain extra things, conditions, circumstances, etc., are added to get us to cases in which we can say that doing this homicide or having that intercourse was wrong.

McCormick also seems to work within a similar picture of human acts in his responses to *VS*. Quite helpfully, he does this within a passage where he defines proportionalism for us.

> Common to all proportionalists, however, is the insistence that causing certain disvalues (nonmoral, pre-moral evils such as sterilization, deception in speech, wounding and violence) in our conduct does not by that very fact make the action morally wrong, as certain traditional formulations supposed. These evils are said to be premoral when considered abstractly, that is, in isolation from their morally relevant circumstances. But they are evils. Thus theologians sometimes say that they are morally relevant, but not morally decisive. They are morally relevant because they ought to be avoided as far as possible. The action in which they occur becomes morally wrong when, all things considered, there is not a proportionate reason in the act of justifying the disvalue.[19]

I should like to highlight three phrases in this quotation: "causing certain disvalues in our conduct"; "considered abstractly, in isolation

---

itself, but only together with all the circumstances and intentions. Consequently, a behavioral norm, universally valid in the full sense, would presuppose that those who arrive at it could know or foresee adequately all the possible combinations of the action concerned with circumstances and intentions, with (premoral) values and nonvalues" (from *Introduction to Christian Ethics: A Reader,* ed. Ronald Hamel and Kenneth Himes [New York: Paulist, 1989], p. 504).

19. McCormick, "Killing the Patient," p. 17.

from their morally relevant circumstances"; and "the action in which they occur." These exemplify, I believe, proportionalism's world. To describe it in other terms, this world is one comprised of states of affairs that follow one another in succession. Human beings enter this world with their actions, changing it from one state of affairs to the next. Quite simply, we manipulate the inert world with our actions. On this picture, the state of affairs just prior to a particular action contains a variety of things, some of which we can call bad: these are the "disvalues." In the manipulation/action these disvalues are increased or decreased, or perhaps even brought about. They are "caused in our conduct." Considered "abstractly," the disvalues just are; the action/manipulation places them in relation to a set of circumstances by which they can be judged morally relevant, i.e., relevant for our reaching an assessment of whether the action/manipulation was the right one. Perhaps the actor increased one of the disvalues in his action when he didn't need to. For example, in his action/manipulation he caused too much violence or deception to occur.

We have already considered what is wrong with this picture of the world and of human action. Appearing here in a definition of proportionalism offered by one of its key spokespersons, it is hard to see how the pope has gotten the implications of proportionalism wrong. Proportionalism's picture of the world is clearly physicalist, about action, and so also about human beings. To reiterate, it supposes there is a physical world (including, of course, physical human bodies) to which human minds come with their intentions and actions to effect some change. The body is instrument, the mind is intention. They are, quite plainly, not a unity "whose rational soul is *per se et essentialiter* the form of his body." The pope's charge of physicalism sticks, all the more strongly when the proportionalists try to deflect it.

It is worth considering another way proportionalists have tried to defend their view of human action, and to expose the errors in John Paul II's understanding of their position. This is what might be called the "murder is a moral term" response. The above quotation from Lisa Sowle Cahill implies this response, and McCormick takes it up as well. More carefully than either of these thinkers, James Gaffney has developed the response with some subtlety, although finally, I think, with no greater success. In brief, Gaffney argues that the pope's concern about there being intrinsically evil acts is uninteresting since quite plainly there are, precisely because we have such words as "murder" in our vocabulary that prespecify that the acts to which they point are morally wrong. If one wishes, then, to say there is at least one intrinsically evil act, namely, murder, he will get no quarrel from the proportionalists. But, says Gaffney, that murder is an intrinsically evil act is neither earthshaking nor, for that matter, very helpful morally. Interesting and challenging moral considerations arise only after we ask whether a particular act is rightly called a murder; i.e., is this particular act of killing morally wrong or not?

> Most negative moral norms are originally and familiarly formulated in ways that admit, and indeed demand numerous exceptions. Thus the biblical prohibition, "Thou shalt not kill," is obviously understood within the Bible itself to admit several kinds of exceptions, including cases of self-defense, legitimate warfare, and capital punishment. Biblical commentators sometimes recommend the rendering "Thou shalt not commit murder." And thus reformulated, the prohibition might well seem to be unexceptionable. But that is only because the word "murder" *means* illicit homicide — without shedding any light on the practical question of just what kinds of homicide are illicit.[20]

Yet Gaffney here makes a mistake that is as much about language as about action. First of all, it seems plainly false that the term "murder" sheds no light on what kinds of homicides are illicit. Murder involves the purposeful taking of innocent human life; understanding that will take you a long way in determining which acts of one human being killing another are wrong. But more importantly, the idea that Gaffney seems to have in mind about how "moral terms" like "murder" work is that their exclusive function is to ferry our moral judgments to some place in the world.

Let us sketch out the picture of human action and morality that stands behind this view. A world lies before us, a morally neutral world including any number of things, physical objects and the like, but also, and importantly, human actions. One key task we human beings have as we approach this world is to make judgments about

20. James Gaffney, "The Pope on Proportionalism," in *John Paul II and Moral Theology*, pp. 55-56.

things in this world, including this or that particular act. As we work out these judgments, we then apply them to the act as follows: description of act *plus* the moral judgment "wrong" or "right." So, for instance, gouging out the eyes of other people's pet rabbits for fun (description) . . . is wrong (moral judgment). As Gaffney seems to imagine, after doing this for some time we develop shortcuts, and these become embedded in our language. A term like "murder" is just such a shortcut: killing + wrong, or wrong killing. So instead of having to say "the killing of person P by person Q in so-and-so circumstances . . . was wrong," we can say instead, "Q murdered P." The term "murder" carries the moral judgment "wrong" to the killing act we judge to be so.

Note that, understood in Gaffney's way, moral terms have two parts: the thing done and the judgment that it is good or bad. This means that judgment, the second part, is not connected in any clear way to the first part. Indeed, we do the connecting with our moral judgment. This leads to an understanding of how moral descriptions work that can be generalized and therefore formalized. "Murder" is like "stealing" is like "adultery": wrong killing, wrong taking, wrong copulating, wrong $x$-ing (you fill in the $x$).

It is as if there were an expanse of human actions/movements, a great sea of human acts, all of them "morally neutral" — which is why we can use the variable with no loss. We might say of these acts that some are $x$-ings, others $y$-ings, $z$-ings, and so on. By themselves $x$-ings, $y$-ings, and $z$-ings involve no moral judgment whatsoever; once done (this is important for proportionalists since they wait to rule on a particular act until it is filled out in all its "totality"), the act calls out for some human judgment about whether it is right, wrong, or neither. Like anglers on a vast and indifferent sea of acts, we come round with our faculty for moral judgment and select some of the $x$-ings, pulling them up into our moral boat. The boat, it might be presumed, already includes some wrong $y$-ings, perhaps lying about in the bow along with wrong $a$-ings and $b$-ings. Apparently for no reason, or at least no reason that interests the proportionalists, when we pull the wrong $x$-ings aboard, it comes into our mind (or it once came into someone's mind before us) to tie a rope about them and make a proclamation: "Let it be known that these wrong $x$-ings (now substitute "killings") will henceforth be known as murders!"

This is, of course, an absurd picture. It derives its power, however, from the basic working notion of proportionalism, which the pope rightly calls a kind of physicalism. This is once again the idea that there is a "premoral" world — in effect, a neutral physical world in which are to be discovered a variety of act/movements that have, in themselves, no moral significance. To this world human beings come, as minds, as having intentions and a capacity for moral judgment, and, with their moral or immoral acts, make this world a morally better or worse place.

As I have been attempting to show with a variety of snapshots, this world of the proportionalists is a distortion, particularly of human action and action descriptions. Painted with a finer brush than I stroke, Oliver O'Donovan has drawn out the picture as follows.

> What connects them all [the four schools of morality *VS* warns against in its second chapter] is a failure to provide a developed account of the field of moral action, that is to say, of the created world with all its infinite variety of human goods and ends, into which any act that we design has to be projected, within which any act is justified. The view of human action common to these theories, one might say, is like that which one would find in the Book of Job if it were shorn of God's final speeches. The world appears as an empty stage for human merit to parade on, formless, undetermined, infinitely plastic, like the universe before God's first creative word. Action, in consequence, is shaped to the service of the agent-mind or agent-will, rather than to the service of the world. It loses its world-determined meaning *as* action — so that in some theories it comes to look like an expressive gesture revealing the secrets of the heart, in others like an instrumental technique manipulating the world to some end, and in still others virtually irrelevant to moral evaluation. The underlying connexion is the paradoxically "unworldly" character (in this specialist sense) of twentieth-century ethics: that is, its tendency to refuse the world that is given it in favour of some other world which it invents.[21]

In this quotation O'Donovan is drawing together all four of the moral theories the pope rejects in chapter 2 of *VS*, of which propor-

---

21. Oliver O'Donovan, "A Summons to Reality," in *Considering "Veritatis Splendor,"* pp. 43-44.

tionalism is one. (The others are a certain antinomianism, an exaggeration of and misunderstanding of conscience, and the fundamental option.) What O'Donovan alleges in the final statement of the quotation is that a deep and pervasive confusion about "the field" of human action hounds almost all modern theorizing about ethics. I believe the statement is as accurate as it is broad in scope. Of course, so stated, O'Donovan's thesis is sweeping enough to prevent exhaustive display. What one must do instead (and this has been the work not only of this chapter but of the previous two as well) is follow out particular strands of discussion of action in the twentieth century to see where they take us. Three quite different strands of discussion have now thrice led to what is effectively the same end. While still short of proving O'Donovan's poignant remark, I believe we are at a place where its plausibility is established. For further progress we shall need to look for a genuine alternative, one that, as O'Donovan puts it, is about the real world rather than a world invented to fulfill the purposes of some moral or scientific theory. In the next two chapters we will begin to investigate such an alternative as found in the magisterial work of Saint Thomas Aquinas.

Before moving to a systematic treatment of Aquinas on human action, I should like to conclude this chapter with a brief discussion that can serve as a bridge from the modern discussion of action to the older and far richer one in Aquinas. All the thinkers discussed in this chapter are Roman Catholics, and hence in one way or another linked to Aquinas and to his account of human action. Importantly, then, and unlike the previous discussions reviewed in chapters 1 and 2, terms from Aquinas's discussion resurface in the current Catholic debate about action. Perhaps the most important of these is the term the "object" of an action. Not surprisingly, both the pope (with Rhonheimer) and proportionalists like McCormick lay claim to the term. Also not surprisingly, it is the proportionalists who are the greater abusers of Aquinas's meaning.[22] As part of the criticism of this chapter, and in

22. It should be plain that in the contemporary debate about action between the pope and the proportionalists or between Rhonheimer and McCormick, I believe one side is far closer to getting human action right. Moreover, since the work of these first three chapters is to clear away very bad but also very common modern views of human action before moving to consider the far truer account rooted in Aquinas, it is important to find the most serious mistakes and expose them. This is why the proportionalist view

preparation for further and more positive discussion of the "object" in the next two chapters, we need to say something about how the proportionalist use of Aquinas's term is flawed.

## 4. On the Object of an Action

It is quite common for proportionalists to call for "further study" of how the object of an action is to be understood. Put in another way, the concern seems to be that we need to investigate what makes an action what it is, since classically that is how the "object" has been understood, particularly in Thomistic thought. Such a call to study is appropriate, and it will inform our own subsequent reflections in this book. One difficulty, however, in engaging in critical dialogue with proportionalism is that, while the call to study the "object" is common, detailed investigations are scarce.

In his response to *VS*, McCormick does comment on how he believes the proportionalist view of the object of an action will differ from the pope's or from Martin Rhonheimer's. His comments are brief, focusing on an imagined exchange between Knauer and Rhonheimer on a certain action.

> Rhonheimer would say that "the choice to kill a person" . . . is a sufficient description of the object. In contrast to this, Knauer insists that the reason for the act must be included. Thus the very object

---

of human action has been the principal target of this chapter. However, this should not be taken as a blanket assent to all John Paul II and Martin Rhonheimer have said about human action. Some of the ways John Paul II puts his points about action are unfortunate, and also, his account is quite incomplete, pulling up rather quickly with the proclamation of the list of "intrinsically evil acts." In addition, I have chosen to leave aside any discussion of the pope's (as Karol Wojtyla) 1969 book, appearing in English as *The Acting Person* (Boston: D. Reidel, 1979), translated by Andrzej Potocki. This is a good deal because I find the personalism of that book, particularly with its leftover Heideggerian emphasis upon "authenticity," too dense to link in any clear way with the treatment I am attempting to give. Writing *The Acting Person* may very well have shaped Karol Wojtyla into the person God called to be pope in this age when human action is so under attack. However, the book itself has little power to shape its readers to see why this attack is so serious, and also to see with clarity how else we might think about human action in a way that responds forcefully to the attack.

*(Handlungsziel)* of a transplant from a living donor is the saving of another person. Equivalently he is saying that this ratio is what makes it a certain kind of action. Fuchs is saying the same thing when he insists that all elements in the act constitute the object of choice.[23]

One of the difficulties in responding to what McCormick says here is that he fails to specify what "the object" is of. There is no "object" in the abstract; rather there are objects of particular actions such as a killing, and these "objects" are essential in determining what act was done. This means that as soon as McCormick says that "killing" is not the correct object, we no longer know what action is being referred to. That is, the choice to kill is the correct description of the object of the action killing (Rhonheimer), but if the choice to kill is not the correct description of some action (the same action that, apparently, according to McCormick, Rhonheimer mistakenly thought was a killing), then we shall have to know what the action involved for us to find out what is rightly called its object.

This may sound like sophistry, but it has a serious point. Any call to "expand the object," a call one hears often from proportionalists, is meaningless when issued in general. We want to know: Which particular action do you want the object expanded for? And as we expand the object, whichever one it is, how far should it be allowed to grow? This last question seems particularly important, for as we expand, surely we will have to know when to stop. The proportionalists, who consider themselves moral theorists, ought to have some method by which we can determine when an expanding object has grown to the right size, neither too big nor too little.

Surprisingly, however, nothing methodical is ever proposed. Instead, as these lines from McCormick illustrate, typically two things are done: (1) some example of what apparently is too narrow an object is noted (here it appears to be that a particular case of "the removal of organs from a living donor to save another's life" is too narrowly or summarily called "killing"), and (2) the "totality" point is made — as when Fuchs is cited as insisting that all elements of the act constitute the object of choice. The problem with (1) is that it seems

---

23. McCormick, "Some Early Reactions," p. 27.

arbitrary. Knauer has decided that whatever went on with the organs is better referred to as "saving a life" than "killing." But why? No reason is given. The problem with (2) is, quite simply, that it has no limits. How could one possibly expand the object to include the "totality" of the elements in the act?

For example, let us imagine that it is true that Joe's hand grasped a knife, his hand moved, the knife penetrated Jim's body, and Jim died. Some questions: When did this occur? Where? What was Joe thinking? What happened next? What color shirt was Jim wearing? Were Joe's shoes tied? How much taller was Joe than Jim, or was he shorter? (And so on.) Perhaps, beginning with the question about shirt color, someone will object to this series of questions, saying it has become irrelevant to the act. The clever response (once again) would be to ask which act, since (following the proportionalists' recommendations) we are to look for the object of the act among the totality of elements involved in it. But, beyond cleverness, since the proportionalists have told us to expand the object of the act but have offered no guidance but that we should include all its elements, who are we to decide that details about shirt color or shoes are irrelevant?

In this regard, and to relate this discussion about the object to the larger debate about *VS*, McCormick's offer to the pope regarding how agreement could be reached about intrinsically evil acts is hardly as generous as it sounds. "Let me return, then, to John Paul II's language. He cites as an objection to proportionalist tendencies the notion that some acts are intrinsically evil from their object. I believe all proportionalists would admit this *if the object is broadly understood as including all the morally relevant circumstances.*"[24] Here we have, once again, almost infinite expansion of the object.

As we shall see in greater detail in the next section of this book, there is a way to relate "circumstances" to "object." "Circumstances," says Aquinas in one section where he follows Aristotle explicitly, can be broken into seven categories: *who, what, where, by what aids, why, how, and when.*[25] But he also says that as circumstances, while they are morally relevant to an act, i.e., they mitigate or exacerbate the praise or blame rightly assigned to an act, they are not to be included in the ob-

---

24. McCormick, "Killing the Patient," p. 19.
25. Aquinas, *Summa Theologiae* I-II.7.3.

ject of the action itself. Aquinas's discussions of these matters, while frequently cited in little bits, are not typically investigated at length. This is unfortunate, since these discussions remain unequaled in subtlety, clarity, and comprehensiveness. Any discussion of the "object" of an action, I believe, must begin with what Aquinas has to say about it.

For his part, McCormick turns in a different direction for help about the object. It may indicate where the proportionalists' further study of the object will lead. In addition, I believe it fittingly characterizes the differences that lie at the base of the debate we have been considering in this chapter.

> *Veritatis Splendor* insists that the morality of an act depends primarily upon the object rationally chosen. I think there is very little controversy on that general statement. What is an object? The letter responds: "a freely chosen kind of behavior." When one looks at the past literature and that reviewed above, it becomes clear that the disagreements begin to occur when authors discuss what goes into the object, what counts as a "kind of behavior." . . .
>
> I know of no way to solve this except by appeal to experience. Most people would not view the removal of a kidney from a living donor as an act separate from its transfer to the ill recipient. They would view the whole process as an act of organ transplantation. Contrarily . . . they would judge aborting fetuses for population control, killing for world peace, etc., as fully constituted acts (therefore, with their own intentional objects) aimed by ulterior intent to a further end. I await further comment from others on this matter.
>
> The fact that people disagree about what the notion of object should include, plus the fact that in the textbook tradition the notion of object included or excluded elements depending on what one wanted to condemn as wrong *ex objecto,* lead to a further reflection. It is the question of how determinative of rightness or wrongness the object is. Could it be that this determination is made on other grounds, and then the conclusion is presented by use of the term "object"? If this is indeed the case, then the encyclical's repeated appeals to actions wrong *ex objecto* does not aid analysis; rather it hides it.[26]

26. McCormick, "Some Early Reactions," pp. 27-28.

Rather than to Aquinas, or for that matter to anything peculiarly Christian, in these suggestions McCormick turns toward what seems to be the social sciences, or perhaps the pollsters: What do most people think?

Yet further, McCormick hints at another point that has repercussions not just for how the object, and so also the action, is understood, but also for how theological argument is to be approached. McCormick muses that it may be the case that talk about "object" is merely a means some people use to push their predetermined and (we can surmise) arbitrarily held "morality" on other people. In short, McCormick seems to be suggesting that the arguments of the pope or others are a facade for power, a means employed by some to push others around.

As I have been arguing, the physicalism about action discoverable in the writings of the proportionalists conceives of human acts mainly as instruments by which human beings attempt to mold the physical world a bit more to their liking. As such, acts are essentially a means of having and using power over something other than ourselves, or if over ourselves, it is as if over another self than the one using the power. The power is always used to cause an effect.

In such a schema our gaze will invariably turn to outcomes; human acting, we will presume, is something entirely strategic — what we do to bring about those outcomes we deem desirable. "Manipulation" is the correct term to use in describing what is going on in an act. Since, as J. L. Austin and others have taught us, words spoken or written are themselves kinds of acts, speech acts, then words also become means of power to effect some outcome. In this way the suspicion McCormick voices of the pope's (or others') strategic use of talk of "object" fits perfectly with the presumptions of the physicalist view.

Of course, sometimes people use words and acts with nothing else but outcomes in mind, so having the suspicion that some such thing is going on is not by itself enough to make one a physicalist. However, we should expect that in a physicalist world such suspicions will increase since, after all, in such a world power informs all human words and actions. Such a world will also be a fearful world, for who would not be afraid if she thought of her acts and words, and therefore of others' actions and words, primarily as a kind of arsenal? This kind of world, one riddled with fear, is of course precisely the world

John Paul II believes we have been living in for some time.[27] His warnings against it in *Veritatis Splendor* are timely and apropos, a point that is perhaps all the better illustrated by the reactions of his proportionalist critics.

27. The phrase "Be not afraid," his first public words as pope, is for John Paul II the key exhortation of his papacy. For a brief but poignant synopsis of how and why, see *Crossing the Threshold of Hope* (New York: Knopf, 1994), pp. 218-24.

# 4. Human Acts Are Moral Acts

## 1. Introduction

One of the difficulties with contemporary discussions of action is that they are generally offered in the midst of a project already begun. A philosopher sets out to argue for a certain theory of morality, consequentialism perhaps, and then discovers himself making judgments about the rightness or wrongness, goodness or malice, of this or that human action. Whereupon he asks, what, after all, are these "actions" about which I find my theory compelling me to make judgments? And perhaps he opens an inquiry. But the inquiry will always appear to him as a sort of detour, one he needs to get round in order to get back to the main road.

If one returns to the work of Aristotle and Aquinas, it is apparent that understanding the nature and place of human acts is hardly a detour in their discussions of ethics. Actions are not something they discover as a sort of difficulty as they theorize about morality. To the contrary, if there is theorizing to be done, it is done first and quite self-consciously about actions, and anything said further about morality or virtue will presume this initial analysis.

In this chapter and the next we will attempt to follow along with Aquinas's understanding of action. There are a number of reasons why this will be of help, including that in the current disagreement among Catholics discussed in the previous chapter we found terms inherited from that discussion — "object," "circumstance," and so on. We cannot render Aquinas's highly nuanced account transparent on all points. But if we attend to selected points with some care, we may discover that we have come further along in our understanding of actions than any contemporary treatment is able to bring us.

## 2. Human Acts Are Moral Acts

Aquinas introduces the second major part of the *Summa Theologiae* in the following way: "Since, as Damascene states, man is said to be made to God's image, in so far as the image implies an intelligent being endowed with free-will and self-movement: now that we have treated of the exemplar, i.e., God, and of those things which come forth from the power of God in accordance with His will; it remains for us to treat of His image, i.e., man, inasmuch as he too is the principle of his actions, as having free-will and control of his actions."[1]

As creation comes forth from God, so actions come forth from human beings. They are our works; as God is known by his works, we are known by ours. Moreover, it is by acts that we move toward our last end, which is God. This is written into the very pattern of the *Summa*, which begins and ends with God, with human acts treated in between. Moreover, action itself, its necessity for human beings, is the key to an important theological truth. As Aquinas notes, God might have made us happy by nature, not needing to be moved to happiness by any previous operation. As such, however, our happiness could only have been natural. True happiness, however, surpasses our nature, for it is to be found above us in God.[2] "[N]o pure creature can becomingly gain happiness without the movement of operation, whereby it tends thereto" (I-II.5.7), and human movement is by act.

1. Aquinas, *Summa Theologiae* I-II, Prologue; hereafter cited as *ST.* Unless otherwise noted, subsequent quotations from the *Summa* will be drawn from the translation of the Fathers of the English Dominican Province (New York: Benziger Brothers, 1947). Citations will be included in the body of the text.

2. It is therefore only a half-truth to say that we are creatures who by nature act, for this neglects the fact that our true good is found beyond our nature, and that the attainment of this good requires that we act toward it.

Already it should be apparent that, while it is true that "human actions" are discussed in specific parts of the *Summa*, particularly in the so-called treatise on acts (I-II.1-21), it is hardly the case that Aquinas's "views about action" can be understood apart from his theology. Indeed, this is not just generally true but particularly, for actions are the glue of the whole of the *Summa*'s second part. Since it is proper to human beings to act, our happiness is itself a kind of act, and the passions and virtues have their function in relation to how they move or direct us to this end. This is another reason why it is difficult to speak of "Aquinas on human acts," as if one could capture his view without also treating happiness, the passions, virtue and vice, and law.

Nonetheless, there is much to be found in the first twenty-one questions of I-II, wherein Aquinas explicitly sets about to explore the nature of human action. As the opening quotation to this section indicates, human actions proceed explicitly from the fact that humans are given free will; we are the principle of our actions. Quickly Aquinas turns this point into a distinction: "those actions are properly called *human* actions which proceed from a deliberate will. And if other actions are found in man, they can be called actions *of a man*, but not properly human actions, since they are not proper to man as man" (I-II.1.1).

It turns out to be easy to imagine what might be an "act of man" that is not a human act. Aquinas gives us some examples: "when one moves one's foot or hand, or scratches one's beard, while intent on something else" (I-II.1.1, obj. 3). Human beings do these sorts of things all the time, but they are not human acts. They are movements shared with the animals — which is not to say they are beneath us. It is rather to say that, in the pattern set out by Aristotle, our inquiry is about what sets human beings apart, what is distinctive to them. This is tied up in our being creatures with reason and will, who are therefore capable of deliberating about what we should do, and of doing it.

Aquinas believes this distinctiveness of a human being is part and parcel of her being a moral being. "And since, as Ambrose says, *morality is said properly of man*, moral acts properly speaking receive their species from the end, for moral acts are the same as human acts" (I-II.1.3). For the ongoing purposes of this book, this is an important point. As we indicated in the previous chapters, it is highly typical of modern thought to suppose that morality is something added to human life, or a separable component of it. What we need, it is therefore supposed, is a way to mark out the territory of acts that are moral, or to which moral judgments are rightly applied, from the rest of what we do from day to day. This attempt at a distinction creates a dual need that has much to do with the errors detailed earlier. On the one hand, we need a "theory of morality" to tell us which acts demand moral attention. On the other hand, we need a "theory of action" to tell us, quite apart from any consideration of morality, what makes an action an action.

Aquinas needs neither; or better put, from the start he assumes that as we consider human acts we consider morality, and vice versa. The description of all acts is related to the fact that they proceed from a human being who is, distinctively, capable of deliberation and choice; this makes all human acts moral acts.[3] As the distinction between human acts and acts of a man shows, to label an act "human" (as opposed to being "of a man") is to place it within the realm of what is human, involving deliberation, choice, and the like; this is precisely the same as the realm of morality. The distinctive features that apply in this realm are not merely some among a variety of things about human beings; rather, choice, deliberation, and action all have their place in relation to the final end of human beings, happiness, and so ultimately to God. Human acts, then, have their meaning in terms of this final end to which all other ends are subordinate. "Morality," or the moral life, is a way of speaking about our journey to this end; it encompasses our life in all of its human aspects.

It is important to see that by placing all acts in relation to this final end, Aquinas does not strip them of their relation to that variety of

---

3. David Burrell's important *Aquinas: God and Action* (London: Routledge & Kegan Paul, 1979) makes a number of points that relate to our argument here. As he suggests, "understanding lies at the heart of all activity that is properly called human" (p. 122). This means that we do not have to *bring* understanding to human action, as if from outside it. It also means that the intellect is *active* — we do not just think about acts, rather thinking is necessarily involved in our acting. This profoundly distinguishes Aquinas's task as he treats human action from the modern treatments discussed in the preceding chapters. As Burrell notes, "at no time does Aquinas tell us what an act is. Nor do we need to be told, since we perform acts all the time. The aim of his analysis is not to offer a theoretical explanation of performance, so much as to assemble sufficient reminders allowing us to articulate as best we can that in which we are engaged" (p. 129).

90

proximate ends to which they might also be ordered. Aquinas does not mean to redescribe all acts in terms of the final end, as if, with Joseph Fletcher's "acts of loving kindness," the names of particular acts should be replaced by either "happiness-enhancing acts" or "happiness-detracting acts." Aquinas has a variety of ways of staving off such reductivism, including his extended treatment, in succeeding questions of the *Summa,* of the great complexity of human passions and capacities. Yet the first and most obvious way Aquinas's view avoids the action reductivism we have witnessed at work in modern moral theories, such as Fletcher's situationism, is simply that he does not set about to bring something called morality to bear on something called human action. As we have noted, the thick and complex descriptions that apply in the realm of human action are the *same descriptions* as those of the realm of morality. Indeed, the realms are not two but one and the same.

Since it is so central to this chapter as well as to understanding Aquinas, it is important to deflect a possible interpretation of Aquinas's view that human acts and moral acts are the same. Since human acts are moral acts, it follows that the descriptions of human acts, their names together with any descriptive elaboration, have moral import from the beginning. They signal that moral judgment applies and, in many cases, carry that judgment in their very name. However, this does not imply that the work of moral judgment is completed by an initial description of a given human act. Rather, that is where it begins. In fact, the work of making moral judgments about human acts is work we never leave off, precisely because we are beings who act. The faculty of judgment is involved in everything we do, as well as everything we see and understand others to do.

One might think of this work of moral judgment, as the proportionalists do, primarily in terms of *applying* "moral descriptions" to particular cases, e.g., this particular act of killing is a case of murder, that one of justified homicide, etc. But while it includes this, the work is far more involved. Indeed, as we saw with even the relatively more astute account of James Gaffney, proportionalism's difficulty remains that it separates acts out there in the world from the moral descriptions we (occasionally)[4] bring to these acts with moral

---

4. The term "occasionally" is important for understanding the proportionalists,

terms like "murder." Consequently, our interest in applying these terms in this or that description seems arbitrary, as though we might make an agreement to call a certain other set of actions, perhaps killings done in the month of January, morally bad in a new way, marking our agreement with a commemorating language flag such as "January killing."

The work of moral judgment applies in action descriptions, yes, but it also involves the assessment of the morality of individual human acts, many of which are not prelabeled. There is no need to separate these tasks, although, as we shall later see, there is good reason to distinguish the names of acts, a distinction made possible by Aquinas's assertion that acts can be morally indifferent in their species but never morally indifferent as individual human acts. The distinction according to species draws our attention not to the fact that we apply moral judgments only now and then, but rather that all action descriptions have a moral arrangement. The consideration of "act species" in Aquinas is based on this, for it assumes that each act has a place in what is essentially a moral world.[5] And this is nothing more nor less than to place it within human life, which is, once again, essentially the moral life.

Comments earlier from Elizabeth Anscombe help to clarify the system of act classification Aquinas will go on to display. Recall that she rejected queries from action theorists who pressed for *the* action, wryly remarking that they landed us again in "bare particular country." In response she suggested that her interlocutors pick a description, any description, so long as it was true about what was done. This may appear to support a wild pluralism about actions, as if acts can be named however we like so long as the name fits. And indeed, both Anscombe and Aquinas begin with a pluralism about actions since they hold that a variety of descriptions will undoubtedly be true of a particular act. Yet this sort of pluralism does not rule out further, more discriminating judgments about the act. Indeed, since moral judgment is involved in action and action description from the start, it also can (and must) continue to guide us as we determine which of a

---

for, as we have argued, they display a bedrock physicalism by supposing there is a premoral world to which we (sometimes) apply our moral judgments.

5. See, for example, *ST* 13.1.

number of true descriptions is most important. Aquinas does sustain an interest in naming acts, but it is not that of the "bare particularist" who wants a discrete entity that is itself and nothing else. Like Anscombe, Aquinas will hold that a particular act can be, for example, both a cutting and a murdering (e.g., let us suppose someone cut another's throat as he killed him), but he will go on to say that the two descriptions do not vie equally for how the person's act finally must be understood (and named), precisely because murdering is far more morally serious than cutting. To make this judgment Aquinas neither has to deny that the act was (as well) a cutting, nor does he have to argue for any special moral theory or criterion by which we can tell that murdering is more important than cutting. This is so because, again, human acts are moral acts, and so judgment of an act as moral is already begun when it is determined to be a human act. Hence, in Aquinas, we have a plurality of ways of describing actions coupled with the presumption that a unified thread of judgment must run through our descriptions. This thread does not tie Aquinas to any particular theory of what is moral; rather it relates simply to his key affirmation that all human acts are moral acts.

A brief excursus at the end of the treatise on acts concerning bad art illustrates well how this goes. Aquinas notes in passing that if an artist departs from the particular end related to his art, producing bad art, we might blame him "as an artist." This departure may or may not be a departure from the general end of all human action, which relates to who the artist is as a human being, and for which we hold him accountable morally. So if an artist produces a bad piece of art so that another is taken in, this is a sin, but "not proper to the artist as such but as a man. . . . [For] in moral matters, where we take into consideration the order of reason to the general end of human life, sin and evil are always due to a departure from the order of reason to the general end of human life. Wherefore man is blamed for such a sin, both as a man and as a moral being" (I-II.21.2, reply 2). It follows that in a case where different descriptions of an action might apply, e.g., when an artist's defacing of an icon might be called either "making an innovative artistic statement" or "sacrilege," Aquinas can say that, while both may be true of what was done, the act must principally be considered as an action of sacrilege. This is so because "sacrilege" relates the act to the general end of human life in a way that "innovative artistic statement" does not. An explicitly moral description of an action does nothing more nor less than place that action in explicit relation to that end. And since human acts evidently relate to "the human," and "the human" is ultimately understood in terms of the final end for humans, explicitly moral descriptions of human acts will always take a certain precedence over other descriptions. Hence, while other descriptions may truthfully apply, i.e., the artist *both* makes an innovative artistic statement *and* commits a sacrilege, the latter description, as explicitly moral, takes a certain precedence over the former.

## 3. Escaping Physicalism and Human/Moral Acts

It is important to be clear about the implications of the discovery that in Aquinas there is no distinction between human acts and moral acts. For the lack of a distinction challenges a quite standard set of modern presumptions. Once the force of the challenge is grasped, we can expect objections. For Aquinas's view seems to imply that everything we do that is rightly called a human act is either good or bad for us to do. But for many this will seem absurd. Just now I sipped water. This I did by choice and with purpose — not like stroking my chin, not merely an "act of a man." Yet surely my sipping water was not either morally good or bad for me to do. Aquinas, however, is unequivocal; every human act we do is either (morally) good or bad: "Gregory says in a homily: An idle word is one that lacks either the usefulness of rectitude or the motive of just necessity or pious utility. But an idle word is an evil, because men . . . shall render an account of it in the day of judgment (Mt. 12:36): — while if it does not lack the motive of just necessity or pious utility, it is good. Therefore every word is either good or bad. For the same reason every other action is either good or bad. Therefore no individual action is indifferent" (I-II.18.9).

The assertion that there is no morally indifferent individual human act makes sense in Aquinas precisely because, as we have seen, he begins his treatise on human acts with the distinction between human acts and acts of a man, a distinction that resurfaces in the question just quoted.

Consequently, every human action that proceeds from deliberate reason and considered in the individual must be good or bad.

If, however, it does not proceed from deliberate reason, but from some act of the imagination, as when a man strokes his beard, or moves his hand or foot; such an action, properly speaking, is not moral or human; since this depends on the reason. Hence it will be indifferent, as standing apart from the genus of moral actions. (I-II.18.9)

In contrast to the "acts of a man," for Aquinas human acts will always take their name from their human end. "Now it has been stated above that acts are called human inasmuch as they proceed from a deliberate will. Now the object of the will is the good and the end. And hence it is clear that the principle of human acts, in so far as they are human, is the end" (I-II.1.3). This means that while human acts will always have physical features, they will not be principally named and classified by these features. In contrast, Aquinas intimates that there might be another classification of acts, according to their "natural species."[6] While these acts might be human acts, they are differently described or classified, in terms other than their human end.

6. The following comments help us gain a sense of what Thomas means by "natural species" as that classification relates to the various species of human actions. "It is possible, however, that an act which is one with respect to its natural species, be ordained to several ends of the will: thus the act to kill a man, which is but one in respect to its natural species, can be ordained, as to an end, to the safeguarding of justice, and to the satisfying of anger: the result being that there would be several acts in different species of morality: since in one there will be an act of virtue, in another, an act of vice. For a movement does not receive its species from that which is its terminus accidentally, but only from that which is its *per se* terminus. Now moral ends are accidental to a natural thing, and conversely the relation to a natural end is accidental to morality. Consequently there is no reason why acts which are the same considered in their natural species, should not be diverse, considered in their moral species" (I-II.1.3, reply to obj. 3). My subsequent development in the text of "fularming" is meant to display more clearly the contrast between human acts, which draw their names from their human ends, and other sorts of descriptions. I believe we can be clearer about the significance of the contrast Aquinas here draws between the "natural" and moral species classifications of acts when we attend to a human movement entirely in relation to a physical movement done by a human body (fularming), rather than a physically characterizable result of some such movement, i.e., that there came to be from it that someone was rendered dead — which is what Aquinas seems to mean when speaking of "to kill a man" considered in its natural species.

Aquinas does not develop such a classificatory system, for his concern in the *Summa* is human acts. Imagining an alternative system is helpful, however, since it throws a contrasting light on how, as Aquinas rightly notes, we name human acts according to their human end. Consider the following example of a possible species set out according to a different classificatory system based on the physical positioning of the human body. Suppose we gather all the things people typically do with their arms extended: casting with a fishing pole, offering a salute, serving in tennis, etc. These acts might be renamed "fularmings."[7] (For physical therapists concerned with the movements of the "upper extremities," such a cataloguing makes sense.) Now any one human activity so classified might turn out to fit in a whole variety of alternative physicalist species. Playing tennis would involve fularming, leg extending, waist bending, etc. Or, conversely, any act classified as one in its (imagined) physicalist species might turn out to be multiple human acts, as we are imagining fularming to be involved in casting a fishing line, saluting, and so on.

Explicitly, Aquinas speaks of the act "to kill a man" considered in its natural species. This "to kill a man" (not, mind you, "to choose to kill a man," as spoken of earlier by Rhonheimer) is not yet a human act. Indeed, we use it of others than human beings: "the moose killed him" or "the earthquake killed him." To become humanly classified or named, the natural or material elements of the act must be linked with a specific human end, and they can be linked in varying ways. This is why one act considered naturally, "to kill a man," can be different human acts, since (to use Aquinas's wording) it "can be ordained, as an end, to the safeguarding of justice, and the satisfying of anger"

7. The failure of this sort of classification for the purpose of the essentially human concerns by which we live can be seen in the sort of conversation that might ensue between someone casting with a fishing pole and someone who knows next to nothing about fishing and happens upon him as he fishes. "What are you doing?" asks the newcomer. "I'm fularming, of course. Haven't you ever been to a tennis match?" "Well, I know you're fularming; that's evident. But what's the point of this fularming right here?"

The description "fularming" tells the newcomer nothing that he cannot already observe; moreover, the connection to tennis helps him not at all. For he doesn't want merely to observe and catalogue physical events, he wants to understand the human action. This can only be done by finding out how the action fits into the essentially human purposes, or "ends," of the one who is acting.

(I-II.1.3, reply obj. 3). This is not to say that one instance of killing a man understood as an intentional human act is more than one human act. For in that act the man was either killed in anger or for justice, and is accordingly named. Rather, it is to say that an act named according to what Thomas calls its "natural species" can be rightly named as a human act in more than one way, depending on the human particulars of the doing of that act (i.e., the intention of the one doing it) on a particular occasion to a particular end.

The reverberating charges of "physicalism" considered in chapter 3 relate directly to this. Fularming attends to physical features only. It matters not to the physical therapist if patient P's fularming was done playing tennis, fishing, saluting, or for that matter, by no human action at all but by some external force such as tornadic winds that caused the human arm to be pulled to full extension. As such, if someone described and lived in the world as if "fularmings" or "leg extendings" were the right and complete sort of descriptions of the things human beings do, he would be rightly accused of physicalism. This extreme physicalism is hard to imagine; importantly, "fularming" is a created description that cannot hold a place in our language, unless perhaps in the context of medical treatment. Even such apparently physicalist action descriptions as "kicking" cannot be said to take their principle merely from the physical motion. Indeed, "kicking" as a human action has an intended end, namely, that something be struck with the foot. Plainly kicking specifies certain bodily motions — I cannot kick with my hand. But further, "kicking" draws our attention not just to an extended leg (like fularming) but to whatever the leg is extended to strike. And insofar as it is located in a phrase such as "I kicked *x*" — and not in an odder (although understandable) phrase like "the foot kicked out" — as a matter of course we assume that I intended to strike *x* with my foot. Kicking, then, unlike fularming, is not rightly understood in purely physicalist terms. To be sure, different instances of kicking will be tied to further human intentions, such as "scoring a goal" or "opening a door." We cannot stop in our understanding of what was done in a particular case of kicking with the intention that something be struck with the foot. Nevertheless, kicking as a human action is essentially related not just to a physical movement of the human body, the extension of the foot, but to a human intention that something be struck with the foot.

**97**

## 4. The Voluntary and Moral Acts

As we have said, a key part of coming to understand human/moral acts as Aquinas understands them (and also for understanding why all human acts are moral acts) is in coming to see that all human acts are voluntary acts. Questions regarding the voluntary have already arisen with reference to human intentions. So far in our discussion "intention" can be understood in the broadest sense: P intended $x$ if P meant to do $x$. On this broad definition, all human acts (as Aquinas understands them) are by definition intentional. So kicking is an intentional (human) action if the person who kicked meant for something to be struck with his foot. This is sufficient, as Aquinas understands it, to set human acts apart from the "acts of a man."

What is involved in this broad sense of intentionality can be further analyzed. As we learn from both Aquinas and Aristotle, the analysis is best begun by considering the "voluntary," and the voluntary is best considered by beginning with the concept of the involuntary. Importantly, involuntariness (and so voluntariness) comes in degrees. There is a set of "acts" that are in every way involuntary, what Aquinas calls "acts of the vegetal soul" (I-II.17.8), such as digestion and physical growth. They are things we speak of ourselves as doing (certainly we say "I grow" or "I digest") that are, by their very nature, not subject to "the command of reason." Vegetal acts are pure cases; by definition they are involuntary. Other cases of involuntary action, however, are more variable. Something intrudes in a particular instance to make a particular act less than fully voluntary. For instance, Aquinas holds that the presence of fear can make an act less voluntary, although not completely involuntary (I-II.6.6). Fear is related to violence or force (I-II.6.5), which, when present, renders the act involuntary simply. If some act is forced by another, it falls short of being a human act. Like a vegetal act, it could not have been not done, and so it is not a moral act. Consequently, there is no sense in asking whether it was good or bad for the person to have done it.

Constraint in an act can be partial rather than total. Particular cases of partial constraint or interference can be complicated, and for philosophers, quite interesting. Aquinas gives one type considerable attention: those involving ignorance in some way. Different categories distinguish different applications (I-II.6.8). Ignorance is related to the will *concomitantly* when I do something in ignorance that I otherwise meant to do. I did not know what I was doing, but had I known I would have nonetheless done it. This happens rarely, of course, but it is imaginable. Aquinas gives the example of a man who means to kill his enemy, sees him, but mistakenly thinks he is a deer. He shoots what he thinks is the deer but serendipitously (for him) kills his enemy. This ignorance does not rightly cause involuntariness, but nonvoluntariness, as Aristotle says.

Aquinas uses the term *consequent* to describe those cases in which, while it could be genuinely said that the agent did not know what he was doing as he acted, he nonetheless chose in some way to be ignorant. Two kinds of ignorance fall within this category: *affected ignorance*, where I desire not to know so that I may have an excuse; and *ignorance of evil choice*, when, because of some defect in my character — say I am lazy or impulsive — I do not take the time to learn what I could, and so act in ignorance. In these cases ignorance does not cause involuntariness simply, since the ignorance itself is in some sense voluntary.

The involvement of the will in concomitant and consequent ignorance means the acts done in these kinds of ignorance are human acts (which is to say that they are moral acts). We can be held accountable for them since the ignorance involved does not cause involuntariness simply. A third sort of ignorance, however, does cause it. This is when I am ignorant of some crucial aspect of the situation in which I act and I do something I wouldn't have done had I known it. For this application of ignorance Aquinas uses the term *antecedent*.

It is significant for the ongoing purposes of this book that there is no clear difference between antecedent ignorance and ignorance of evil choice, except that the latter arises from some vice. That is to say, considered in itself there is no discernible difference in the "knowing situation" of a person who acts from antecedent ignorance and another who acts from the ignorance of evil choice. Both act without knowledge of some relevant bit of information, and were it known, each would have refrained from the act. In the first case, however, Aquinas views the connected act as involuntary, while in the second he does not. The difference between these two types of ignorance rests not in the specific state of mind of the agent nor in his personal description of what he was about. It concerns instead the more public matter of what we reasonably expect people to know. For example, we think a father should have known that the paint chips on the wall by the baby's crib might cause her harm; if he is ignorant of the danger, we suppose he is lazy and never bothered to inquire or attend to things as he ought to have. So, if the baby eats the paint chips and gets lead poisoning, our inclination is to blame the father (we call him negligent), for he should have known about lead paint and its possible ill effect on his child. Yet this judgment does not apply to the mother who took her child to day care in a government office building in Oklahoma City lacking the knowledge that the building was that day targeted by terrorists. Like the father with the paint, had she known about the terrorists she would never have taken her child to the building on that fateful day. But — and here's the difference — she could not have reasonably been expected to know about the terrorists, so we have no thought of blaming her when her child is killed by the terrorists' bomb. We have only sorrow in our hearts for her.

This discussion of ignorance connects to earlier points made in the first chapter of this book regarding actions and their homes. The meaning of a specific act of mine is not rightly located only by my state of mind when I acted — i.e., that I meant to do this or that, or that I, for instance, simply felt like clasping my hands three times in an hour — but also how that state relates to who I am expected to be in a community. As we progress further in Aquinas to consider the will's involvement in an act, it is important to keep in mind that this is not strictly an internal matter, as if only the one who acted can say what he willed. Further, we should not suppose that the moral (human) expectations we place on one another come to apply only after a human act is performed and described. As we have just seen, with the distinction between the ignorance of evil choice and antecedent ignorance, moral expectations and notions will figure strongly, not only in how a particular human act is rightly described, but also in our determination of whether a human act was done at all.[8]

The significance of this point will become clearer as we move

8. As we shall see in chapters 7 and 8, the notion that someone *neglected* to do something is entirely dependent on these sorts of expectations. The determination that someone "neglected" often is entirely unaffected by the self-description of the activity of the person to whom we are attributing the neglect. For, of course, the notion of neglect already implies that person's inattentiveness, his failure to be properly aware of justified and commonly shared human expectations for action.

along. At present we can conclude our concern with Aquinas's account of the voluntary by noting that our principal interest in discussing involuntariness is to locate those human activities that, either partially or completely, fall outside of the realm of human action. This makes plain, once again, how important the distinction between human acts and the "acts of a man" is for Aquinas.

As a final note, the distinction between "acts of a man" and human acts will often require testing in a particular circumstance. From simple observation we sometimes cannot tell if what someone does is a human act or an act of a man. For instance, a particular case of my scratching my nose could be either an unthinking response to an itch or a signal to an assassin to do his work.

To help us think through these sorts of cases, Elizabeth Anscombe has helpfully adopted the convention of imagining different kinds of responses to an observer querying an actor about why he did what he did. The actor might refuse the application by saying, "I was not aware I was doing that."[9] Such a refusal amounts to a claim that what he did was not a human action (a claim an interlocutor may or may not go on to dispute). The application of the question "Should you have done *x*?" follows the same pattern. The rejection of the question might come in the same form: "I didn't know I was doing *x*," or perhaps, "I had no choice" — although this latter response will have a broad range of meanings. In any case, the point is that if what a person did was a human action, the question "Should you have done *x*?" always reasonably applies. While there is a gray middle where questions of why or should will be debated, there are clear cases, and these clear cases help us see the sense of the distinction and how it can rightly be disputed in the middle. For example, if I say, "I digested my food" or "I grew four inches" or "I slept poorly," and you say, "Should you have?" I will take your question to amount to a misunderstanding, rejecting it with such a reply as: "Well, it happened. I really had nothing to do with it." In effect, I am saying: your question does not apply precisely because what I did was not my human action.

(As Anscombe also notes,[10] it is worth adding that the response "I don't know" or "I'm not sure" does not amount to a rejection of her

9. Anscombe, *Intention* (Ithaca, N.Y.: Cornell University Press, 1963), p. 11.
10. Anscombe, pp. 24-25.

**101**

"why?" or our "should you have?" question. Indeed, it accepts its terms, even if its speaker might resist the summary application of praise or blame to the action. We do things all the time that we are uncertain are right to do, although we hope they are. Quite unlike cases of "murder" or "stealing," the moral judgment of these actions is hard to make, and this holds praise or blame at abeyance. But this does not make them any less moral or human actions.)

## 5. Minutiae

As we have said, Aquinas's discussion of voluntariness is one key way he marks out the subtle boundaries of human action. Vegetal acts plainly fall outside this territory, and present a solid place to begin as Aquinas approaches the territory of human acts. Considerations of voluntariness also remind us of the moral assessment that human acts necessarily require, since, as Aquinas holds, a judgment about good or evil applies to every human act. If a particular thing done can be shown not to have been done voluntarily, then assessment in relation to the good does not apply. Conversely, if the act was voluntary, then the terms "good" or "ill" necessarily apply.

I am well aware that the idea that every human act is good or evil will ring strangely in modern ears. Could Aquinas actually mean that every human act done — including such acts as sipping water, pouring coffee, mailing a letter, etc. — is either good or bad? To return, however, to the crucial claim in the *Summa*, this point is entirely clear.

> For since it belongs to the reason to direct; if an action that proceeds from deliberate reason be not directed to the due end, it is, by that fact alone, repugnant to reason, and has the character of evil. But if it be directed to a due end, it is in accord with reason; wherefore it has the character of good. Now it must needs be either directed or not directed to a due end. Consequently every human action that proceeds from deliberate reason, if it be considered in the individual, must be good or bad. (I-II.18.9)

As we shall later consider in greater detail, Aquinas's designation of the act "considered in the individual" marks it off from the act "considered in its species." Thomas holds that an act can be morally indifferent according to its species,[11] even if no individual act (note: all acts actually done by someone are "individual acts") can be morally indifferent. This is an important clarification, for it makes plain that Aquinas is not alleging that "sipping water" or "mailing a letter" is, in virtue of its very description, either good or bad. Rather, the point is that a particular instance of sipping water or of mailing a letter is (indeed, must be) either good or evil.

Contemporary judgments may not stray so far from Aquinas's view as at first it seems. Suppose John mails a letter to Jerry in which he makes a death threat. We would say that in this instance it is bad for John to mail his letter to Jerry. Indeed, modern resistance focuses not on whether a particular instance of mailing a letter might be good or evil; rather it focuses on whether *every* instance can be described and elucidated in these terms. This is because, for moderns, the realms of human action and moral action are not coextensive, as they are for Aquinas. Put another way, for moderns some (many) particular human actions are morally neutral or indifferent, whereas for Aquinas there are no morally indifferent particular human acts.

Because of this difference modern moralists feel obliged to mark out a territory called "moral" separate from Thomas's territory of human/moral acts. As we observed in chapter 2, modern moral theorists frequently circumscribe the territory of the moral with a foundational moral principle. If, for instance, what is moral is defined by treating persons never only as means but also as ends (e.g., as Kant holds), then morality will come to bear on human action when some person is treated as ends or as means. However, if no one is treated in any way at all by some human act — e.g., I sip water, pour myself coffee, etc. — then morality is thought simply not to apply.

We have discovered in previous chapters that when morality is independently defined in this way, invariably the definition turns back to wreak havoc with human action. This fact should open us to the possibility that the ancients were closer to the truth. Perhaps, in other

---

11. "It may happen that the object of an action does not include something pertaining to the order of reason; for instance to pick up a straw from the ground, to walk in the fields, and the like: and such acts are indifferent according to their species" (*ST* I-II.18.9).

words, the modern penchant for marking out a special territory of human activity called "the moral" as distinct from "the nonmoral" is based upon a mistake. To be fair, however, not all objections to the idea that all individual human actions are either moral or immoral are theory linked. Practically we behave as if many actions we do, or observe others doing, simply don't matter morally. What of this fact? Is there a way it can be accounted for in Aquinas's view of human action?

In fact, he has a quite clear response. In effect, he agrees. Some actions matter very little morally — which is not to say they don't matter at all, something Aquinas could not say and remain consistent. According to Aquinas, there are human acts that are morally *insignificant,* even if not morally indifferent, which can be given the label "moral minutiae." Aquinas discusses them when speaking of "counsel," which is what we take as we deliberate about what action to choose. Counsel is necessary if a course of action admits of doubt. Yet not all actions do. This occurs in two types of cases.

> Now, that something in relation to human acts admits of no doubt arises from a twofold source. First, because determinate ends are gained by determinate means; as happens in the arts which are governed by fixed rules of action; thus a writer does not take counsel how to form his letters, for this is determined by art. Secondly, from the fact that it little matters whether it is done this or that way, which occurs in minute matters, which help or hinder little with regard to the end aimed at; and reason looks on small things as mere nothings. Consequently there are two things of which we do not take counsel, although they conduce to the end, as the Philosopher says: namely, minute things, and those which have a fixed way of being done. (I-II.14.4)

There are some human actions, perhaps the great majority that we do (if one were counting), about which it makes little sense to deliberate — which is to say something important for Aquinas, since the good of an action depends on its relation to right reason. In fact, with some individual actions we have a moral reason not to deliberate. Some examples of senseless deliberation might be: Should I write with this pen or that one? Should I make my letter *A* this way or that way? Should I mail this letter? On the face of it, these are minutiae — it does not matter much morally exactly how they are done.

That deliberation is rightly bypassed about these human acts (we need not take counsel about them) does not mean they are not human acts. We do them by choice, and with purpose. As such they are human acts, and so moral acts, and so acts for which we are responsible, including our delegation of their status as minutiae. We must therefore be open to challenge regarding whether or not we are right not to deliberate about them.[12] In this sense the category of human acts we are calling minutiae has an important fluidity. That someone regards something as minute does not make it so; hence, what acts the category contains is rightfully always a matter for moral debate. For Thomas the category must exist since we do not (and should not) take counsel about everything we do. However, once the category has been identified, like the minutiae themselves, there is little reason to investigate it further. Aquinas expends no further effort analyzing minutiae, nor does he develop additional act species by which to classify them. The description or classification of acts according to their "species" has a practical end: to locate them in relation to the true end of human life. Since the identification of a broad class of acts as "minutiae" does this, little else needs to be said about the classification in general.

12. There is subtlety in this point. For while Aquinas holds that it is necessary for us to relegate certain actions to the category of minutiae, since otherwise we would be deliberating endlessly, he continues to hold that the category of actions marked (by a particular person or society) as minutiae remain moral actions, and hence worthy of praise or blame. This opens up the interesting case where people disagree about what is a trifling matter. While we all must operate with a (very large) category of human acts we treat as minutiae, it is also true that we must be ready to investigate this classification if it is reasonably brought forward by another as not trifling at all but actually quite morally important. As a key example, what some men regard as routine behavior in relation to women arises from ingrained vice or institutional evil. A particular man who, by institutionalized or cultural habit, proceeds in his actions as if such matters are routine or trifling is nonetheless responsible for what he does when he treats a woman badly.

## 6. Moral Actions and the Virtues

We have made much in this chapter of the fact that in Aquinas's treatise on acts in the *Summa,* the realms of morality and of human acts are exactly coextensive — that for Aquinas all human acts are moral acts. This point is not a discovery about Aquinas.[13] However, by placing it in the context we have placed it, side by side with contemporary debates about action, we can more clearly mark its significance for any account either of action or of "morality." In the *Summa* Thomas carries his discussion of morality far beyond the treatise on human acts, the section we are specifically investigating. But the equivalence of human acts and moral acts is crucial for all subsequent sections, both the more remote section on passions and virtues as well as those questions that complete the section specifically dedicated to human acts.

Questions 1-21 begin by discussing the last end of man and proceed to an account of human action. Question 22 initiates a discussion of passions, of habits, and finally of virtues and vices. We need good habits, which are the virtues, to form the passions. So formed, the passions move us or dispose us to act well. Indeed, moral virtues are nothing more nor less than the perfection of a power to act, or, in another definition, they are operative habits (I-II.55.2). The journey that is the moral life requires that we have power to do the right thing well. As habits, as powers of the soul, the moral virtues stand in potentiality with respect to act. They equip us to do the key work of the moral life, to move toward our final end. And we move in this way by our actions.

A distinction between human acts and moral acts would do nothing less than abort Aquinas's project. Had he, somewhere late in the treatise on acts, drawn such a distinction, the subsequent sections on passions and virtues would be superfluous. For the passions, the need for habits, the relation between appetite, intellect, and will — are all

13. Ralph McInerny makes the point clearly throughout his *Aquinas on Human Action: A Theory of Practice* (Washington, D.C.: Catholic University Press, 1992). For example, early on he says, "Now that we have some idea of what counts as a human act and what does not, it is clear that all human acts are moral acts and all moral acts are human acts" (p. 9). As well, Karol Wojtyla's work *The Acting Person* proceeds on the basis of this view. (See, for instance, the introductory discussion on pp. 8-14 where the future pope lays out the groundwork of his study.)

essentially *human* characteristics. It is human beings who perform human acts, and in their acts they proceed toward (or away from) their final end. So which acts are good, which conduce toward this end, must be determined in relation to the many-splendored thing that is human nature. When this is given full display in the *Summa* in the sections beyond question 21, those on passions, virtues, sins, etc., we can return all the more clearly to see which are good and which are bad acts.

In a similar vein, it is important to see that the subsequent discussion of the virtues cannot imply that they are instrumental skills we might use to act well after having determined, by another mechanism, such as a monistic moral principle, what makes moral acts moral and so distinguishes them in kind from other, "nonmoral" human acts. That is, as if the virtues were merely the tools we need to do a certain prespecified task well, or which might motivate us to do what we know from some other source to be what we ought to do. Virtues are comparable to skills, at least in a certain sense. For example, they are like baseball skills in that we need them to play baseball and cannot acquire or keep them without practice. However, there is an important difference, for the virtues are related directly to the passions, which are, as Aquinas says, "in our soul" (I-II.22.1).[14] Unlike baseball, the moral life is not something human beings might *decide* to become good at, as if they might just as well have decided to become good at soccer or gardening. Rather, that the virtues are necessary follows from the fact that one is a human being. To be born a human being is to be born into the game of morality — which of course makes it not a game at all, but life, pure and simple. So it is that moral actions take their shape in relation to the passions and the moral virtues that form them. Moreover, as we come to have the virtues, so we can see what are good or bad actions, and why they are good or bad.

Another way of putting this is to say that we cannot know what human acts in particular are until we know something about what sorts of beings humans are. To discover this we must consider the passions, and so also the virtues (and vices). We are, for instance, the sorts

14. For a full account of the place of the passions in relation to the moral life, see Simon Harak's *Virtuous Passions: The Formation of Christian Character* (New York: Paulist, 1993).

of beings in whom fear arises, and who are prone to act from fear. Our understanding, even our identification and description, of a whole range of acts is related to this essentially human feature — acts such as "flight," "cowardice," "resistance," "bravery," "retreat," "attack," "perseverance," etc. As these descriptions show, we do not carry out our actions just in relation to the fear we have, as if one feels fear (passion) and so runs (act). Rather, as human beings, we are capable of knowing our fear, of asking whether we should do what it is telling us to do, and of acting even as we fear in a way that is not controlled by it.[15]

The four cardinal virtues can be placed within this context. They are cardinal because related to each is a set of passions or operations that move us to or direct our action. So temperance curbs the excitable passions; fortitude strengthens those passions that might cause us to withdraw; justice guides the operations of the will so we can determine what is due to others; and prudence directs us to pick out and do what is right to do. (See I-II.61.2.)[16]

---

15. I do not mean here to rule out that nonhuman animals might not also act in a certain way, responding in different ways to their fears. Clearly animals have fears, and do things in response or relation to them. Moreover, I suspect we are ready, most of us, to say that many different species of animals are capable of acting courageously. This, in fact, points to another virtue in Aquinas's (and Aristotle's) account since it begins with animal passions or appetites. The human virtues are what temper or strengthen or direct these passions in a distinctively human way — toward our end, or toward happiness.

Recently Alasdair MacIntyre has worked to reconnect the discussion of human life with nonhuman animals. Far from denigrating human beings, this connection reminds us that the human virtues arise in relation to the sort of creature God made us to be, including that we are rational and dependent, as well as that we are bodily, that we live together, and that we are subject to death, to sickness, to being overrun by certain passions, etc. See MacIntyre, *Dependent Rational Animals: Why Human Beings Need the Virtues* (Chicago: Open Court, 1999).

16. Mention of the role of prudence returns us once again to the discussion of act. For the choice that is so key to determining whether a genuinely human action has been performed (that it was voluntary), if it is the right one, "is made by prudence, that counsels, judges and commands in those things that are directed to the end" (I-II.65.1). Indeed, the discussion of prudence that comes fifty questions after Thomas discusses choice in direct relation to act, evidently revisits it. These functions — counsel, judgment, and command — are the explicit subject of questions 12 through 17 in the treatise on acts. As necessarily being about matters that could be other, human acts are uniquely the subject of choice and reason. We could do either $x$ or $y$; but rightly to determine that $x$ is better than $y$, and to choose it, we need prudence.

Human actions, then, have their meaning, and sometimes even their names, in relation to the sorts of creatures we know human beings to be. However — and this is a point to which we will return when discussing the crucial relation in the treatise on acts between the act of the will and the external action — it does not follow from this that actions are rightly placed only in relation to the human person. We cannot, along the lines of Joseph Fletcher's "acts of loving kindness," redescribe all human acts entirely in relation to the virtues: this was a just act, that was an intemperate act, this other a courageous one, and so on.

To be sure, we do sometimes name acts in relation to virtues and vices. So I might say to my son after catching him taking more than his share of birthday cake, "You were being greedy, that's what you were doing." I use this description because it places my son's act in an explicitly intentional and moral context in a way that "taking two pieces of cake, the others only having one" does not. In like manner, Aquinas follows roughly this pattern when he works to classify sins according to their species. For instance, murder is principally a sin of injustice, adultery of lust, and therefore of intemperance, and so on.

Yet virtue/vice action descriptions cannot displace or subordinate all others. For while they might tell us of the actor, they tell us nothing specific about the *world*, and it is in the world that human actions have their home. Like Fletcher's "acts of loving kindness," taken by themselves, virtue/vice descriptions of actions are overly abstract and therefore untrustworthy, for they can be easily turned to the describer's purposes. We cannot act well without the virtues, certainly; but also we have the virtues *in order to act*. As embodied creatures, we act in the real, physical world. Acts, we must remember, are where the virtues and vices meet the world. Without act, the virtues are merely pleasant names. To be sure, we need the virtues to see the world well. But — and this is a key point particularly for Pope John Paul II — in human actions, freedom, which is implied by human action, must be allied with truth. Virtue/vice–based action descriptions therefore cannot entirely take over for those action descriptions that specify what we do in and to the world as we act. In a similar way, morality is not merely attitudinal. Kant was incorrect; mere good will is not enough. To be one who in all respects acts well, who proceeds to her final end, the good person must see and act in the world truthfully, which is to

109

see and act in the world as it is in all its particularities. Particular action descriptions ("she kicked," "I sipped water," "he murdered") ensure that this close touch with the world will not be let go.

# 5. Naming Human Actions

## 1. Introduction

In chapter 1 we considered briefly some of the questions regarding human action that have occupied action theorists in contemporary analytic philosophy. How are actions individuated? What is the relation between one description of an action, such as pulling the trigger, and another, such as shooting in a bull's-eye, when both seem to apply to the same action? Or, when descriptions of actions compete, which one do we choose as a description of *the* action, if there is such a thing?

These questions have been given a distinctively modern form and flavor by the action theorists. Yet they are genuine questions that have been addressed in other times as well. It should not surprise us that Aquinas has something to say about them — in fact, a great deal. Of course, his answers will take their place in the framework of thought we have identified, one much informed by the central affirmation we have identified, namely, that human acts are moral acts. As we shall see in this chapter, within this framework questions of action identification, individuation, or classification of human acts can be answered in ways that are inaccessible if one begins with other assumptions such as those dominant in our present time.

## 2. Species Classification of Human Acts

Near the end of his treatment of human acts, Aquinas turns to a discussion of how acts should be classified. At first this may seem odd. There are some things, like flowers or birds, whose classification makes immediate good sense. Others things, however, seem resistant to a classificatory scheme. Suppose someone sets out to classify moments in the day, or different thoughts I had this morning. Would there be a point to this? Moreover, wouldn't any classification of these kinds of things turn out arbitrary?

Actions at first appear similarly resistant to classification. As Anscombe observed, there is an oddity even in counting many human actions — so we rightly wonder if the further classification of things that cannot even be counted is simply out of the question. What may appear as yet a further difficulty, as we have heard from Aquinas, is that actions derive their species from their end, so we cannot classify them in any complete way merely by marking the observable physical movements they involve as we might do with, for example, different instances of "fularming." Perhaps an observer could mark out as separate events, even count, the number of times someone's arms were fully extended in the manner that athletes in training count their push-ups. Yet the point in our discussion of fularming was to show how the "acts of a man" differ from human actions, since we do not name — indeed, do not see — casting a fishing line and serving a tennis ball as instances of the same thing, even if they might involve almost precisely the same bodily movements.[1]

I do not believe, however, that these points show that the classification of human acts is impossible; rather, it is evidently difficult and complex — and as it is done, if it is to be done, the reasons why it is useful must stay before us. One point in particular settles the question of whether act classification is possible: we already do classify acts, for we name them, and naming cannot but be an inchoate form of classification.

---

1. Interestingly, it takes reflection, even experimentation, to confirm that casting a fishing line and serving a tennis ball are related movements, even for those very familiar with each motion. On the other hand, the close relation between, say, the action of baiting a fishing hook and casting a fishing line is automatic; we do not have to think about them or try them out to see their connection. And of course, the physical motions involved in each are very different.

I do not intend, in this chapter, to build a system of act classification. However, if someone were to set out in such a direction, two things would need to stay before her, both detectable in Aquinas: First, any classification would need to begin by carefully attending to the names we use for human actions — we should not make up new ones for the purpose of classification. Second, and relatedly, she would need to keep before her at all times that classification of human acts had a practical end. The latter point illumines why, while he works to put one or the other particular act into different species, Aquinas never feels compelled to develop a fully exhaustive system of act classification.[2] In a particular case we will have a reason to classify a particular act; and that will lead us, with respect to that particular act, to think about where it rightly fits within what Aquinas thinks of as the genus[3] of human acts. For this we don't need an exhaustive taxonomy of human acts so much as some general guidelines that will allow us rightly to name and classify a particular act as we have need.

Let us suppose someone asked how we should classify a particular thing done: "P's washing his hands." Our initial response might be bewilderment. How do you mean, classify? Yet, interpreting the query charitably, we would begin looking for a category into which the action washing one's hands might fit. And here, undoubtedly, we would seize on something like hygiene. Washing one's hands is more like

2. By leaving the category of insignificant acts undesignated, Aquinas in effect suggests this. He is not interested in cataloguing all the species of acts he can find, as one might butterflies.

3. In Aquinas's classificatory system the genus is "human acts," as opposed to, say, "acts of a man." The earlier delineation of the human and the voluntary, therefore, could be read back as a marking out of the genus. The genus classification also relates human acts to a good, since it is by acts that humans attain their end. Moreover, as we shall discuss further in the text, further classifications within the genus will similarly concern the good, in progressively finer terms:

> Hence a fourfold goodness can be considered in human action. The first is the goodness an action has in terms of its genus, namely, as an action, for it has as much goodness as it has of action and being, as we have said. Second, an action has its goodness according to its species, which it has from its appropriate object. Third, it has goodness from its circumstances — its accidents, as it were. Fourth, it has goodness from its end, which is related to the cause of its goodness. (I-II.18.4 — Oesterle translation).

taking a shower or brushing one's teeth than it is like, say, waving goodbye or dealing out cards. But this is interesting. For, consider that the movements associated with washing one's hands are far more similar to dealing out cards than those involved in taking a shower. But we would not think to associate the act of washing one's hands with the act of dealing out cards. Why is this? It is because taking a shower and washing one's hands share an end, what we have called hygiene, and actions take their names from their end.

The fact that we far more readily associate washing one's hands with taking a shower rather than with dealing out cards reveals something else that is important in understanding human acts. This is that classification by end relates not just to what was done, but to why it was done. And to ask why something was done by someone is, in effect, to ask whether it was good that it was done, just as we assume that the one who acted had some good in mind, real or apparent.

Were we concerned to teach someone, perhaps a young child, about how to keep herself clean, we would want to instruct her about both washing her hands as well as taking a shower. The answer to her query about why she needed to learn either action would be roughly the same. Taking a shower and washing one's hands both relate to the human good of personal hygiene — and this provides both their "what" and their "why." Put more generally, with respect to human actions, the question "Why should I do *x?*" or "What is the good in doing *x?*" is intrinsically related to the question "What (sort of) action is *x?*"; and this is so because, in Aquinas's language, human actions take their species from their end.

This brings us back to points made in the previous chapter. Since human acts are moral acts, our concern about a particular human act — how it should be named and classified, etc. — will not need to *become* moral, for it is already from the start. Or, put now in relation to the example just used, "washing one's hands," the doing and the naming, brings a particular set of human behaviors into relation with some good, actual or apparent,[4] that human beings pursue.

---

4. The distinction between actual and apparent goods is key to the whole of the second part of the *Summa*. For, as Aquinas holds, all human beings pursue their last end, which is happiness. What occurs, of course, is that this end is misidentified, and so an apparent good is pursued as if it were a true good.

This gives us insight into the practical end of Aquinas's classification of human acts. For his treatment of act classification proceeds on the assumption that the reasons we will have for classifying this or that particular act will always be moral reasons. That is, we will want to know what this or that particular act is precisely because we will want to make some judgment about whether, why, and in what ways it is good or bad to do it.

This point finds expression in the *Summa* in I-II, question 7, where Aquinas offers a brief excursus on whether the theologian should consider the circumstances of human acts. That he pauses indicates something of the practicality of his inquiry. The implication in the asking seems to be that if circumstances need not be considered by the theologian, the inquiry can be left off at this point, the numbing complexities and tiny distinctions that follow in later questions left unmade or unnoticed. But of course, Aquinas answers that the theologian *must* consider these complexities, for at least three reasons.

> Circumstances come under the consideration of the theologian, for a threefold reason. First, because the theologian considers human acts, inasmuch as a man is thereby directed to Happiness. Now, everything that is directed to an end should be proportionate to that end. But acts are made proportionate to an end by means of a certain commensurateness, which results from the due circumstances. . . . Secondly, because the theologian considers human acts as they are found to be good or evil, better or worse: and this diversity depends on the circumstances, as we shall see further on. Thirdly, because the theologian considers human acts under the aspect of merit and demerit, which is proper to human acts. (I-II.7.2)

Each of these reasons places our classificatory interest — as theologians, but surely also as human beings who cannot but be concerned with our happiness or with good or evil — in relation to moral judgment relating to particular acts. Hence, any further inquiry will have this as its goal: it will wish to investigate human acts in relation to the comprehensive human concern of which acts should be done and which should not be done.

As Aquinas's reference to "circumstances" implies, while properly begun with the names of human actions, the inquiry is not completed in the naming. In fact, while a name for a given human action provides a place to *begin* an inquiry into its true moral status, we may actually discover in the inquiry that the name itself should be revised. Consider again the action (taken in general, or as a species) "washing one's hands." Since we suppose that hygiene is a good, we will generally suppose that a particular case of washing one's hands is good. However, the description by itself does not imply this with any sort of necessity. A child's saying "I just washed my hands" is more likely to bring forth praise from her or his mother than "I just kicked the cat" or "I just made a noise," but this does not mean that every particular act of washing one's hands is rightly thought to be good. For instance, "[Pilate] took water and washed his hands before the crowd, saying, 'I am innocent of this man's blood; see to it yourselves'" (Matt. 27:24). Plainly, Pilate shouldn't have washed his hands, as the story behind this text implies. And for this judgment to hold we do not need a new term supplied as if the description "washing one's hands" had already settled the matter that to do so in a particular case was ipso facto good. In Pilate's case, the good associated with washing hands has been trumped by the circumstances of this particular hand washing.

In another case, or even category of cases, the good of washing one's hands (the good of hygiene) can be heightened. This heightened good may appear in a new action name. For instance, suppose I live and work among the sick. If these circumstances are stabilized or perhaps institutionalized, a new description can arise. Take, for example, the action description "scrubbing in" before an operation. Note that if someone says "Dr. A didn't scrub in," this carries a much heavier moral weight than "A didn't wash his hands"; indeed, it implies he didn't do something he should have.[5] This is because the institutionalized context of the act has heightened the good of hygiene.

A way to understand what is going on here is to return to the relation between Aquinas's claim that every *individual* human action is either good or evil (I-II.18.9) and the claim that immediately precedes it in the *Summa*, namely, that human actions are not necessarily good or

5. It is not the case, however, that the description "washing my hands" must be replaced by another description like "scrubbing in" for it to carry moral weight. This is so because, unlike "digesting my food," "washing my hands" is a human action. As we have said, *x* is a human action if the question "Should you have done *x*?" can be rightfully asked of it.

evil according to their species (I II.18.8). Human acts cannot be morally indifferent in their individuality, but they *can* be indifferent *according to their species*. That is to say, it is possible to describe a human act in general terms, e.g., "walking through the fields," with nothing being implied in the description about whether it was good or bad for it to have been done.[6] So, the knowledge conveyed by the species description "walking through the fields" gives us no guidance at all about whether it was good or bad for a particular man to have done it. "Walking through the fields" is an instance of an act species that is indifferent, as opposed to certain other acts whose species classification already implies or suggests a moral judgment (like "stealing" or perhaps even "washing hands"). Aquinas describes these indifferent act species:

> Every action takes its species from its object; while human action, which is called moral, takes its species from the object, in relation to the principle of human actions, which is the reason. Wherefore, if the object of an action includes something in accord with the order of the reason, it will be a good action according to its species; for instance to give alms to a person in want. On the other hand, if it includes something repugnant to the order of the reason, it will be an evil act according to its species; for instance, to steal, which is to appropriate what belongs to another. But it may happen that the object does not include something pertaining to the order of reason; for instance, to pick up a straw from the ground, to walk in the fields, and the like: and such actions are indifferent according to their species. (I-II.18.8)

If an individual act is marked in its description to be morally indifferent by species, and if we have a reason to inquire into it morally,

---

6. Earlier we noticed that the description of a human act could easily be confused with the description of a movement. Now, insofar as individual human acts are never morally indifferent, one might suppose that a shortcut to determining whether a particular description is either of a human movement or a human act would be to ask if the description specified morality in some way. In cases like "almsgiving," "littering," or "stealing" this occurs. (All cases of littering and stealing are human acts, and they are all wrong.) But we have now discovered that there exist species descriptions that are in fact of human acts (and not just movements) that do not carry this force. They are indifferent as to the morality of the act that was done.

then we will need to investigate its circumstances further. As we shall see, sometimes this investigation actually leads to a reconsideration of what name we should apply to the act; i.e., placing it in another species. As well, the circumstances of a particular act have significant power to make it good or evil even if they do not change its name. "It sometimes happens that an action is indifferent in its species, but considered in the individual it is good or evil. And the reason of this is because a moral action, as stated above, derives its goodness not only from its object, whence it takes its species; but also from the circumstances, which are its accidents, as it were" (I-II.18.9).

Here the reader is perhaps tempted to throw up her hands in dismay. What is the point in persisting in the view that acts are rightly divided into species if (to recall a point from the previous chapter) so many of our individual acts are morally insignificant (minutiae) and therefore need no species classification and, as we now discover, many of our "species" descriptions are morally indifferent, and so bring us no further in determining whether a particular act is either good or bad — is supposedly the practical point of species classifications?

Yet there is, I believe, good reason to persist with Aquinas. It should be noted that only *some* species descriptions are morally indifferent. And since the moral identification of an act is what we most require — i.e., what the theologian, as well as the rest of us on our journey to our final end, should care most to know about an act — we know that if an act is indifferent according to its species, then we can look to its circumstances to reach a judgment regarding it. Moreover, although Aquinas states repeatedly that determining species in the natural world is a different sort of enterprise than in the world of human acts, which is governed by reason, there is an important commonality. Species classifications of whatever kind *fix* a thing in a category from which it cannot be easily moved. While I might tame a fox and rename him "my pet," he is yet a fox. His foxness is fixed; who he is is not up to me, nor, for that matter, to the community of language users who happened to use the term "fox" in specifying the species name. In a similar way, I might redescribe an act of adultery as an "act of loving kindness," but it is still an act of adultery, whatever the circumstances.

When we begin to consider the fixedness of human acts and the reasons why fixedness might be important, we must recall that Aquinas believes there is a truth about every act, an essentially moral truth. This truth can be known, always by God and sometimes by us. He holds that not only individual acts are wrong, but whole species, such as the species of act called "adultery." A particular act of adultery is wrong because, and just insofar as, it falls within the species "adultery." The classification of an act under "adultery," therefore, conveys to us something very important, namely, the truth that this act ought not to be done.

One might object that we do not need species classifications to tell us that an act is wrong or right since we have a rich fund of virtue and vice descriptions that can carry our judgments to particular acts. Yet as we noted at the close of the previous chapter, virtue descriptions, while important in the extended moral evaluation of a particular action, are insufficient in themselves to differentiate actions. If I say, for instance, that S did something courageous, you will want to know just what it was that S did. And to get this description we will need to turn to the world in which the action was done. But — and this is something Aquinas has shown us plainly in his emphasis on the humanness of human actions — this cannot be found in a "physicalist" or natural description. So if I say "S's legs propelled S's body and it subsequently covered a small oval object," this does not help in displaying the thing S did that I supposed courageous. What I need to say is that S smothered a live hand grenade. When I do this, I set the act plainly in the human world where it belongs, the world of human ends and purposes.

The use of the plural "ends" in this last sentence is quite important. For although Aquinas holds that all of what we do can be related to our final end, as drawing us nearer or directing us further away, the ends of particular acts can relate to this one end in a great variety of ways. Or, as he puts it, while each act relates to our final end (this is the same as to say that it is either bad or good for us to do), it also relates to a "proximate end" from which it generally takes its name. "One and the same act, in so far as it proceeds once from the agent, is ordained to but one proximate end, from which it has its species: but it can be ordained to several remote ends, of which one is the end of the other" (I-II.1.3, reply obj. 3). Harking back now to the debates in chapter 3, we can reintroduce the term "object" as rightly referring to this one proximate end for a particular action.

The use of the term "proximate" suggests nearness. One way to think of it, then, is as what is closest to the agent's intention in the particular case in which he acts. And not infrequently this holds, as when I insert the key to unlock the door, of which I will say, if asked, that what I am doing now as I insert the key is unlocking the door. However, in the naming of an action, there is no formula that can be used with precision to determine what is the proximate end of something done that can be tied always in a prescribed way to my intention. This is true for a number of reasons, including that we often perform actions with more than one intention, often with no intrinsic relation one to another. For example, if I write to my mother to say we will be unable to visit, I write both to stay in touch and to inform her that we won't be coming. I don't do one of these for the sake of the other, and neither end is more proximate to what I am doing when I write the letter.

All this implies that further complexities regarding ends and objects have yet to be considered. What we have established thus far, however, is that the fixing of an action in a description is important to Aquinas, and to all of us, since we need a way to say what the action is. Moreover, we need such descriptions if we are to proceed further toward a correct and full-bodied moral judgment about what was done, if one is called for.[7]

In a species description, particularly as it informs us of the object of an act, we receive a description of the action not just in relation to a particular agent's purposes, but also in relation to the world — and by "the world" we mean here not merely the "natural" or physical world, but the intentional, human world in which it takes place. In order to see how Aquinas works toward this end, it is necessary to attend to his distinction between the internal act of the will and the external action.

## 3. Internal Acts of the Will and External Actions

While Aquinas uses the language of "species" of human acts as early as the first question of the *Prima Segunda*, he does not fully specify

---

7. Importantly, the moral judgment of the act and the truth about it are not separate concerns. Indeed, for Aquinas the concern for the right moral judgment about an act is the same concern as for the truth about it, as a human action. For human acts are moral acts.

what he has in mind until question 18. In the intervening sections he introduces additional notions that, if we attend to them carefully, will provide further clarity about how species designations might be rightly applied. One of the most important of these terms is what Aquinas calls the "circumstances" of an action. The literal meaning of the term is helpful: circumstances are those things that surround an act. As such, they make sense in relation to the idea that an act has a primary substance or identity, a center that can be surrounded. As Aquinas says, circumstances are "whatever conditions are outside the substance of an act, and yet in some way touch the human act" (I-II.7.1). While Aquinas thinks circumstances can be extremely close to an act — they touch it and, as such, often are key in determining its relative goodness or malice — they remain essentially distinct from the object of an act, what might helpfully be thought of, in this context, as the act's center. And it is by object and not by circumstance that an action has its species. In a word, "circumstances" and the "object" of an act are codependent notions. Both can determine the morality of an act, but one surrounds the act while the other identifies its center or core.

Identification of the center of an act is complicated in Aquinas's schema by his further division of the act into two parts: the *interior act of the will* and the *external action*. When any act is considered, it must be with regard to both, but always formally with regard to the interior act of the will and materially with regard to external action (I-II.18.6).

While the division is drawn partly to correspond to certain scholastic categories Thomas was working with, there is a practical resonance in it that applies today. In a given act I perform there is, on the one hand, this thing I am doing and, on the other, my deciding to do it now. If I am walking through the field right now, there is "my walking through the field" and there is my walking through the field just now in order to do something, perhaps to get to Grandmother's or to find clues to a murder. (Please note that "walking through the field" is understood as an intentional action in contrast to, say, "my legs transporting my torso through a field.")

According to Aquinas, *both* the act of the will *and* the external action have an end or object. In the case considered, the end of the will, the reason or purpose I have in walking through the field just now, is to get to Grandmother's. The thing I am doing, the external act, also has an end: it is, simply, to walk through the field. (This may sound redundant, but we must remember that the specification of the end must occur in some form in the action description, for without such a specification we have no human action.)

The complication here becomes apparent. We have discovered that both the external act and the act of the will have an object; however, as Aquinas informs us repeatedly, they are not different acts but two parts of the same act. So how are we to know which object, that of the will or that of the external act, is the object of this one act (whatever it is)? Or, further, how are the two different objects (if they are different) related to one another in the act?

As we have seen already, the external act of, say, "walking through the field" can be related in different acts to a diversity of objects of the will: "getting to Grandmother's," "searching for clues to a murder," and so on. One thing that follows from this, which Anscombe encourages as well as Aquinas, is that actions can be considered under a variety of descriptions, whichever ones are true of them. It is true in the situation we are considering both that I am going to Grandmother's and that I am walking through the fields, so what I am doing can be rightly placed under either description.

In the end Aquinas will suggest a way this plurality can be honored in our language and also cut through, should we need to come to some clear moral assessment of what exactly was done or come to one primary (i.e., species) description of the thing being done. Before moving to this, however, he introduces yet another layer of complexity regarding the fact that not only are there (at least) two descriptions that apply to every act — one involving the object of the will, the other the object of the external action — but also that two different objects can be related in a variety of ways.

More often than not, this relation is one of independence, namely, that the end of the act of the will is not intrinsically related to the end (object) of the external act. Consider, for instance, the case in which a man is "walking through the fields" in order to "find clues to a murder." In the particular case of this man's doing it, the two are related, yet taken by themselves there is nothing about the (species) description "walking through the fields" that ties it to the (species) description "looking for clues to a murder," as is shown simply enough by the fact that if we come upon a man walking through the fields we do not assume he is looking for clues to a murder.[8] The independence of the two descriptions in this case is placed in clearer focus when contrasted to another sort of relation, what Thomas marks as a case in which the object of the external act is "ordained" to the object of the will. For instance, "to fight well is ordained to victory" (I-II.18.7). The idea is simply that "fighting," the external act, has its sense in relation to the end of the act of the will, namely, to win. In other cases, however, the relation between the terms of the twofold action is accidental, as in our case of the man "walking through the fields" and "looking for evidence of a murder."

To review what Aquinas's analysis has so far revealed: Human acts can be described in a number of ways. There are many possible true descriptions of what someone is intentionally doing. However, this does not mean that the descriptions are arbitrary or that, if we have need, we cannot find our way through the labyrinth of true descriptions to find one that principally identifies what was done in a particular case. When we set about to do this, to find the right name for what was done, we need to search out the object of the action, not merely its circumstances. Yet, with regard to the object, we must be aware of the complication that virtually all human acts can be divided in two, into the external act and the act of the will, and that each of these has itself an object or end. While sometimes the ends are related, more frequently they are logically independent, being brought together in a particular act by the one who acts.

With these things in mind, we can proceed with Aquinas's analy-

---

8. It is important that, as observers simply coming upon this man, while we don't know he is looking for clues to a murder, we know with certainty that he was walking through the field. This means that we know when a person is acting, and generally we know at least one true description of what he is doing. When I say "know" here, I am not using it in the restricted, technical, and essentially Cartesian sense that is even yet being debated in analytic philosophy. There is, of course, always the possibility that the man I see walking through the fields has a radio transmitter in his head controlled by an evil scientist who has taken over the man's brain. In this case, the man would not be acting since he is doing nothing under his own control. Yet when Wittgenstein's critique of "certainty" is in the background, where he shows us that the strict philosophical sense of certainty is a chimera, I am as certain that the man is engaged in the human action of walking through the fields as I am that he is a man and not a ghost. This is sufficient for me to say with meaning that I am certain that that man is walking through the fields.

sis. In discussing what exactly was done in a particular case of a person's acting, at least two further questions are involved: First, how is an action individuated — what are we focusing on, and how is it drawn out from the stream of activities we pass through so as to be called one act? And second, what is the proper name of the act once individuated? In brief, I believe Aquinas's analysis equips us to respond to these questions in the following way: the act of the will individuates, whereas the name of the act (its object) is determined either by the will or the external act, whichever is more morally salient.

That it is the act of the will that individuates is suggested by the fact that the will controls "my doing the action just now." The will, in this respect, is said by Aquinas to be the initiator: "the end [of the will] is the last in execution; but first in the intention of the reason, in regard to which moral actions receive their species" (I-II.18, reply obj. 2). In this sense the end of the will is what I set out to do, even if it is the last thing accomplished. It is the movement of the will that demarcates the act in time: it sets a course and, unless interrupted, pursues it until it is through, at which time it turns to something new. This brings the interesting outcome that I can do one act in the midst of another act. If I am walking through the fields to visit Grandmother, and as I walk I spot a rare species of finch at the edge of the field in a tree close to where the path leads, then I commence to do another act as I walk onward. I have changed from "walking through the field/to get to Grandmother's" to "walking through the field/to get a closer look at a rare type of finch." And when the finch flies away, I can go back to walking to Grandmother's. They can be considered as two acts (not one or three), as marked by the end of the will.[9]

9. This analysis is suggested by the following comment from Aquinas: "For continuous walking is one action, considered in the natural order: but it may resolve itself into many actions, considered in the moral order, if a change take place in the walker's will, for the will is the principle of moral actions" (I-II.20.6).

In our example, it is true that I am still walking to Grandmother's as I walk to look at the finch. (If I had to change my course to see the finch, the demarcation would be clearer.) In this way it seems to me possible to do two things at once: I am *both* walking to Grandmother's and walking to get a better look at that finch. I mean this in a different way from the "action trees" philosophers have set up where it is imagined that I am doing one thing for many different reasons. So before I walk to Grandmother's, I think it will be good to get some exercise, and so as I walk to Grandmother's I do so also to

There is a sort of power, then, in the interior act of the will to mark out the action to which a description needs to be applied. However, this power does not extend so far as to always determine the principal name (description) of the action. Instead, for Thomas this is determined by the "order of reason" as it regards (judges) what is done. And since we are discussing human (moral) acts, reason attends to the species of good or malice the act involves, in both its objects. Now the object of the will, the end, is more determinate, and in a sense more private, since it is directly related to what the agent sets out to do. But the object of the external act is more public; it cannot be described apart from its place in the physical world we all share. As such, it is more resistant to a privately inspired redescription (such as an "act of loving kindness").

We have now moved to the second question asked above. Once an act is individuated, how is it to be named? Naming, as we have seen, is related for Aquinas to species classification. Thus far we have seen that this classification is tied to the proper object of the act, since the object determines what the act is, while the circumstances surround it, making it better or worse. The will initiates and moves toward an object, yes, but we must remain aware that the external act also has an object. And we cannot assume that the object of the will is always the

---

get some exercise. Were I merely walking to get some exercise, I wouldn't go to Grandmother's, or if I did, it would not be right to say that I was walking to Grandmother's but rather that I was walking *as far as* Grandmother's — and if she's in, perhaps I'll stop by. The difference can be seen by whether I judge what I did to have been accomplished. (In the former case, if Grandmother weren't in, I'd need to come back later.)

It seems, however, that while it is possible, doing two things at once is not as easy as we might suppose. For there is a certain capturing of the attention that occurs when, in one external action, my focus changes. This is what gives sense to the notion of "being interrupted." In this case of seeing the finch on the way to Grandmother's, it seems to me better to say that "I was on my way to Grandmother's but was interrupted, pleasantly so, by that finch, at which I am just now trying to get a better look." I am implying, then, that at any one time it is generally right to say that I am doing one thing, not two or more. It does not follow from this, however, that an action cannot be resumed — and as such is still the same act. So there are not two acts, "walking to Grandmother's before I saw the finch" and "walking there afterward." Writing this book is something that takes some time, and it has been interrupted frequently, but it seems to me counterintuitive to suppose that I am doing different things each time I sit to write the book. This is surely how we talk: today I'm going to do just what I did yesterday, I'm going to write my book.

identifying object of the act, what it is named for. Sometimes it is, but not always.

On what ground does Aquinas think the object of the will can be overridden in the naming of the act? In broad terms the ground is simply that all human acts are moral acts. Since this is true, the moral value of an act will always play the determinative role in its naming. Or, put in another way, the type of good or evil in the thing done determines how we should regard it as a human act.

This is not to say that every human act must have a moral name. As Aquinas has painstakingly pointed out, naming has to do with species designations, and species designations are in general. While it remains true that all individual human acts are either good or bad, it is not required (indeed, it would be impossible) that we always carry a moral appraisal about in the act's name. Naming has, in this sense, other functions than evaluating an action morally, a point that allows us to draw the process of naming an act and morally evaluating it apart without separating them entirely. But — and this is the way naming and moral evaluation are always yet connected — if a moral species name applies to what was done, it cannot but figure in the naming of what was done. So, for example, in a case in which no moral determinative species name applies, then the act can be named in terms of one of the morally indifferent species names that are true of it, and moral evaluation can be added in other words. If, however, a moral species name applies, then it can only be trumped by another moral species name, never by a morally indifferent species name.

Put another way, when an act is indifferent with respect to its species, it is in effect free to become good (or bad) in a particular case. Principally this is accomplished by the specific act of the will by which, as we have seen, a person decides to do a thing now, and to a certain end. Yet when the thing done — understood now as the external act — is not indifferent according to its species, as in stealing or almsgiving, the internal act of the will, even if it seizes on its own end first and later wills the external act as a means, cannot entirely overcome the good or the bad already set in the object of the external act. So while an act within a morally indifferent species of act can be made good or bad as an individual act by a good or bad will, a good or bad species of external act, when taken up in a particular case, has a certain independence from the goodness or malice of the will that takes it up. The following quote from Aquinas helps display how these complex relations can come together as someone wills to do an external act that carries a morally charged species name.

> External actions may be said to be good or bad in two ways. First, in regard to their genus, and the circumstances connected with them: thus the giving of alms, if the required conditions be observed, is said to be good. Secondly, a thing is said to be good or evil from relation to the end: thus the giving of alms for vainglory is said to be evil. Now, since the end is the will's proper object, it is evident that this aspect of good or evil, which the external action derives from its relation to the end, is to be found first of all in the act of the will, whence it passes to the external action. On the other hand, the goodness or malice which the external action has of itself, on account of its being about due matter and its being attended by due circumstances, is not derived from the will but rather from the reason. Consequently, if we consider the goodness of the external action, in so far as it comes from reason's ordination and apprehension, it is prior to the goodness of the act of the will: but if we consider it in so far as it is in the execution of the action done, it is subsequent to the goodness of the will, which is its principle. (I-II.20.1)

In the example Aquinas uses, the object of the will and the object of the external action are accidental to one another: the end of the will, vainglory, has no intrinsic connection to the giving of alms, which is to say that the goodness of almsgiving is not derived in any way from the goodness or evil of vainglory. Indeed, in this case there is a conflict between an evil end of the will (vainglory) and a good object of the external action (almsgiving). This makes the case more complex than those cases where an act involves an external act that is indifferent by species, such as walking through the fields. An action whose external act is walking through the fields is made good or bad simply by a good or evil act of the will (for example, to visit with Grandmother or to aggravate Mr. MacGregor, the field's crotchety owner).

In further analysis, it is important to remember that in dividing the act of the will and the external action, Aquinas does not mean to divide

127

the action itself. It remains one. However, the division of the action into the two parts means that the determination of its goodness or malice can now relate to two different sources in the act: the will of the one who takes up the act, or the act done. Either source can supply good or evil. When one supplies good and the other evil, as in giving alms for vainglory, Aquinas is plain that while the evil can be mitigated by the good, it cannot be entirely overcome. Moreover, the evil must figure centrally in the naming of what was done. So, for instance, if an evil external act, such as stealing, is taken up for a good (moral) reason or concern on the will of the actor, it is nonetheless an evil done. Robin Hood steals, even if his stealing is not as bad as the stealing the duke of Nottingham does when he takes what is due the poor. Robin's stealing is mitigated by his goodwill while the duke's is not.

The following quotation both summarizes the analysis to this point and takes the further direction it suggests:

> The interior act of the will and the external action considered morally, are one act. Now it happens sometimes that one and the same individual act has several aspects of goodness or malice, and sometimes that it is but one. Hence we must say that sometimes the goodness or malice of the interior act is the same as that of the external action, and sometimes not. . . . We must therefore say that when the external action derives goodness or malice from its relation to the end only, then there is but one and the same goodness of the act of the will which of itself regards the end, and of the external action which regards the end through the medium of the act of the will. But when the external action has goodness or malice of itself, i.e., in regard to its matter and circumstance, then the goodness of the external action is distinct from the goodness of the will in regarding the end; yet so that the goodness of the end passes into the external action, and the goodness of the matter and circumstances passes into the act of the will. (I-II.20.3)

Aquinas here reviews the types of relations that can stand between the two ends in each act, i.e., the end of the will and the end of the external act. Indeed, following his analysis we can delineate six different combinations as produced by the two different parts of the act. These are: good will/derived good external act; good will/different good external act; good will/evil external act; evil will/derived evil external act; evil will/different evil external act; evil will/good external act. Yet since the act is a unity, these different and in some cases disparate elements must be brought together under a description. But which description? And why that one?

In two combinations where the good or evil of the external act is derived from that of the will, the conclusion is easy. The external act, considered by itself, does not put up any resistance to the end to which the will puts it. Like walking through the fields, it is indifferent in its species and so merely follows the good or evil of the will, deriving its good or evil from it. However, in the other combinations there is an independence between the interior act of the will, its end, and the external act considered with respect to its end (object) that marks its species. In some cases the independence involves a conflict between a good and an evil. To deal with these, Aquinas notes that "for a thing to be evil, one defect suffices, whereas, for it to be good simply, it is not enough for it to be good in one point only, it must be good in every respect" (I-II.20.2).[10] It follows that in the two combinations listed where evil and good together are involved, the act must be marked according to the species of evil done or willed, in either the external act or the interior act of the will. In the remaining cases where there are two goods or two evils, then the unified act is best named under the good that is the highest with respect to the order of reason or the evil that deviates the most from it.

## 3. Reason, Language, and the Stability of the External Act

We have returned, circuitously, to a key concern of chapter 3. Aquinas's position on "intrinsically evil acts" is that there are some. For him, while it can mitigate it, a good will cannot overcome an evil external act. If the thing I am doing is evil, I cannot make it good by doing it now for the best of reasons. It cannot be good to steal to help

10. To be truly and fully good, Thomas states that it must have a fourfold goodness: with respect to its genus, its species, its circumstance, and its end. An action can be easily good in one of these ways while missing goodness in another (I-II.18.4).

the poor; it cannot be good to torture someone for the good of the country; it cannot be good to kill an infant to curtail population growth; etc. Whatever the circumstances surrounding the external act, and whatever the good intentions of the actor, these acts are sins according to their species.

Now this will not really be news about Aquinas's view. The above analysis had as its point not so much to discover this basic position in Aquinas, for it is well known, but rather to undertake an investigation of Aquinas's general understanding of action. The conclusion that there are intrinsically evil acts is one of a number of results. While it may be an important conclusion to establish in certain circles, it does not take us that much further in understanding Aquinas's view about action in its full subtlety. Rather, if the analysis so far is useful, it will be in opening up the details. If the debate among Catholics is to progress, it may need to be in relation to these details and others that lie buried beneath the surface of Aquinas's view of the moral/human life, which we have only touched. Yet precisely because of the intricacy of these details, one might wonder how far Aquinas's view has taken us *practically*. Indeed, part of the intricacy relates to the fact that Aquinas believes careful attention must be paid to the details of the acting situation with respect to every individual human act. Hence, one wonders how much can be said in advance about how a given particular action is to be understood. Put another way, perhaps the distinctions between circumstance and object, between act of will and external action, etc., are so supple that they can be worked through only as we go to a particular case.

Jean Porter has recently emphasized this point. She is concerned that Aquinas's notion of the "object" of an act not be used as if it were an abstraction, something that could be known before considering a particular circumstance in which some particular act is done. Taken as such, emphasis on the object might excuse us from the careful work required in determining what is to be done in a particular circumstance, or, as well, the judgment about what in fact was done in a particular case — how what someone did is rightly named and therefore evaluated. I concur with Porter on this general point: the notion of the "object" can easily become objectified and overplayed. However, we must stop short of attributing to Aquinas's analysis such a fluidity that almost anything can be the object of an act, and therefore the source of its identifying species. As an illustration of the complexity about object, Porter uses an interesting example Aquinas gives where the object of an act (and so its species name) passes through a series of changes, demonstrating, at least to Porter, that "object" is hardly something one can use to settle a debate about how actions work.[11] Aquinas describes the case as follows.

> [Unlike] nature [which] is determinate to one thing . . . the process of reason is not fixed to one particular term, for at any point it can proceed further. And consequently that which, in one action, is taken as a circumstance added to the object that specifies the action, can again be taken by the directing reason, as the principle condition of the object that determines the action's species. Thus to appropriate another's property is specified by reason of the property being another's, and in this respect it is placed in the species of theft; and if we consider that action also in its bearing on place and time, then there will be an additional circumstance. But since the reason can direct as to place, time, and the like, it may happen that the condition as to place, in relation to the object, is considered as being in discord with reason: for instance, reason forbids damage to be done to a holy place. Consequently to steal from a holy place has an additional repugnance to the order of reason. And thus place, which was first of

11. Porter is right to say that the object of an action cannot be determined prior to that action being done in the world. So if someone uses the concept of "object" as if it has the power to settle what was done before the details of the relevant situation are investigated, he or she misuses it. On the other hand, by choosing the example she does, Porter's treatment appears to suggest the opposite view, that the "object" of an act can be almost anything at all, and so we can't use it as we argue with someone about whether or not a particular action is rightly named. Were that her point, I believe she would be mistaken. As I think careful analysis shows, what Aquinas designates as the object in this case is entirely consistent with the patterns he has otherwise laid down throughout his discussion. See Jean Porter, "The Moral Act in *Veritatis Splendor* and in Aquinas's *Summa Theologiae*: A Comparative Analysis," in *"Veritatis Splendor": American Responses*, ed. Michael Allsopp and John O'Keefe (Kansas City: Sheed & Ward, 1995), pp. 278-95.

Problems about the "object" arise for modern thinkers when they conceive it abstractly, as if part of a theory of action. But this is not Aquinas's idea at all. The doing and describing of an act already involves the object; it is not something brought to it to reach some theoretical understanding of what was done. As David Burrell rightly characterizes Aquinas's discussion of act and object, "an act cannot be described without characterizing its object." *Aquinas, God & Action*, p. 122.

all considered as a circumstance, is considered here as the principal condition of the object, and as itself repugnant to reason, either for or against, it must needs specify the moral action whether good or bad. And in this way, whenever a circumstance has a special relation to reason, either for or against it, it must needs specify the moral action, whether good or bad. (I-II.18.10)

This example might be taken as a challenge to the analysis that has been given about objects and species, as if Aquinas has fallen into a contradiction. To begin, there is the matter the example is specifically designed to address: whether circumstances can determine species. As Aquinas earlier states, in one logical sense circumstances cannot determine species insofar as they are *defined* as those things that surround the substance of an act, and as such are accidents. (This is how Aquinas initially defines them in I-II.7.1.) When a thing is the principal condition of something, it cannot be its accident. In this example Aquinas speaks of something that in most cases is accidental to the substance of the act done, namely, place, but which becomes in this case essential.

Yet Aquinas defines "circumstance" in another way in I-II.7.3, where he follows Tully's list of seven "circumstances": *who* acted, *what* he did, and *by what aids, where, why, how,* and *when* he did it. According to the list, "where" is a circumstance. In this particular act, place turns out to be essential, the thing according to which it has its species. In this second definition, the list of seven, Aquinas need not be thought to contradict himself. The list specifies seven features of acts that are generally circumstantial; it does not define circumstances logically as what is nonessential.

Yet if the example does not involve a contradiction, it continues to puzzle. Why should sacrilege displace theft as the principal species? Are we to imagine that this is what the actor had in mind? Much more likely he meant to steal, and the fact that what he stole was in a holy place hardly crossed his mind. To name the act in terms of place might suggest (to the proportionalists or others) that Aquinas here is given over to the ill effects of physicalism. For what seems to have occurred is that the "external act" has its object in the physical features of the world, i.e., that the theft was from a holy place — features having little to do with the intention of the human being who acts in them.

How might we respond to this objection? We know that for Aquinas to say of someone, call him Joe, that he committed the sin of sacrilege implies that what Joe did was *voluntary*. If it can be shown that it was not voluntary, then no sacrilege was committed, since sacrilege is a human act, and all human acts are voluntarily done. For instance, suppose, fantastically, that Joe is the captive of a group of antireligionists on a campaign to destroy holy sites. They have wired his brain to a transmitter and are controlling his body from behind the church parking lot. This would be an instance of what Aquinas calls "violence" that renders the act involuntary, so Joe, at least, is not guilty of sacrilege, nor for that matter of stealing. Indeed, he does nothing — nothing human, that is.

If we assume, as we must to proceed with this case as a discussion of a human action, that Joe steals freely, it might be true that he is unaware that he is stealing from a holy place. Here we encounter ignorance, which is, as we recall from the previous chapter, at the edge of voluntariness. But in rendering a judgment about voluntariness with respect to ignorance, the type makes all the difference. And of course, ignorance comes in a variety of types. Perhaps Joe's is *antecedent* ignorance. He is fresh off the boat from a foreign land and enters the first building he can find to steal something. It's a church, but he doesn't know this; in fact, he doesn't even know what a church is — there aren't any in his land. Furthermore, it is dark in the church and he can't even recognize any signs that this is a place of worship — he merely grabs the first weighty object he touches and runs. Yet this determination of "antecedent ignorance" holds, excusing Joe of sacrilege (he didn't do it), only so long as his ignorance was not "concomitant." Perhaps the knowledge that Joe lacked, that he was stealing from a holy place, would have made no difference had he possessed it: he would have taken the holy object anyway. If this turns out not to be so — i.e., had Joe known he was stealing a holy object, he would have immediately put it down and gone somewhere else to steal — it follows that Joe's act is *not* one of sacrilege, but rather one of simple theft.

Under these conditions, then, Aquinas would hold that the act was not a sacrilege. Yet plainly in the example he means us to suppose they don't apply, that the thief steals from the holy place knowingly and freely, and so committed sacrilege in his theft. What the thief thinks, or how much he thinks, about the thing he steals may be relevant circumstantially, but it is not species determinative. All we need for sacrilege is that the thief know, or rightfully could be expected to know, that he is taking a holy object.

It is important to note that Aquinas's view is not physicalist. It is not merely a set of movements that Joe's body goes through that we point to by the term "sacrilege." To say that something was "taken," that it was "someone else's property," that the place from which it was taken was a "holy place," etc., etc., is already to enter the intentional, human world in which actions have their home. So when we speak of the object of the external act as taking something from a holy place, we are already speaking of something that can be known for what it is as an object only within the human world, which is where human actions necessarily take place.

There may be one more objection about the species classifications themselves. If, as we now discover, an act can move so easily from one species to another, from theft to sacrilege, how do the species categories actually function to define the act for what it is? Why are there two species categories, and how are they related? And why is one, sacrilege, Aquinas's choice over the other, theft, as the primary species of the act?

We should recall that Aquinas has said that a specific act may be considered under more than one species. It is true, after all, that what Joe did was *both* an act of theft *and* an act of sacrilege. Depending on its particulars, it may be in other species as well. Yet it is nonetheless true that Aquinas believes sacrilege trumps theft as the act's primary species designation. Why is this?

The answer to this question takes us to the heart of Aquinas's project. Recall that for him all human acts are moral acts — and so each individual act is either good or bad, it cannot be indifferent. The goodness or malice of an act, then, is always the rightful focus of an inquiry concerning what a given act is. Unlike classifying butterflies, our concern in classifying acts is practical, not taxonomic. We want to know how close a particular act came to hitting the mark, to being a truly good act.[12]

---

12. Among the concerns about how close an act is to hitting the mark will be our interest in praising or blaming someone for doing it. However, this is hardly the sole concern. For example, we should want to know how we have sinned so we can rightly confess what we have done to God and to others we have harmed, and to turn from our evil

There are a great variety of ways in which human beings will and do good or evil. Moreover, in any particular act the actor is capable of subtly directing or nuancing what he does by what he pursues in the act, how he fits it to the situation, and so on. Hence, many human acts are open to an intricate investigation concerning the goodness or malice of what was done, even if certain minutiae do not merit this full investigation. When an investigation is undertaken, the first step is to identify the act. This is where species classifications come to bear. Yet the investigation does not cease with the classification of the act, for there are very many factors surrounding the act that affect its relative goodness or malice — what Aquinas calls circumstances. These must be examined, for they can change how the act is judged morally.

Given that an act's relation to good or evil is its principal (and most real) characteristic, then it must be named in relation to the type of evil or good that is the most serious. If an act falls in more than one species of good or of evil, as does the theft/sacrilege under consideration, the place to begin in naming it is with sacrilege. This is so because, for Aquinas, sacrilege is a more serious sin than theft, at least in its species. (From this it does not follow that all cases of sacrilege are worse than all cases of theft, for sufficient mitigating or aggravating circumstances may apply that cause a particular theft to be a worse sin than a particular sacrilege.) Sacrilege is a direct injury to God, and is opposed to the virtue of religion (II-II.99.1-2). So, to proceed in understanding what was done in terms of our essentially human/moral interest, the act must be marked as sacrilege, and the variety of its circumstances further considered in relation to that principal classification.

Aquinas's view that sacrilege is a more serious sin than theft will likely be greeted with material opposition in our contemporary context, but this tells us as much about the anomalies of our own moral understandings as about his moral understandings. In fact, reflection about common contemporary presumptions reveals the opposite of what one might expect. Far from dispensing with a hierarchy of moral

---

ways. We should want to exhort others, which is not the same as blaming them. We should want to understand the varieties of ways human beings sin so we can pass on wisdom about how these can be avoided, or the variety of ways people can be good so we can rightly enjoy them now and teach our children to enjoy them in the future.

descriptions, in our times we depend on them all the more, partly because we are inarticulate about them and, relatedly, have less sense about how our descriptions might be arranged on some rational pattern. Consider the following imagined conversation as an example of how such descriptions function.

> "I'm feeling kind of guilty."
> "Why?"
> "I broke a promise."
> "Oh? What did you do?"
> "Well, I promised Jim I wouldn't kill him, but I broke my promise."
> "What?! You killed Jim?!"

Or, as we might say to this interlocutor (with Aquinas's assistance), the act you committed was both the breaking of a promise and a killing. But it must be principally classified under the species of killing, for this is the more serious evil. That this is true about your action is made no less so by your private choice to describe it as a promise breaking.

In brief, the classification of actions according to species and in relation to our moral understandings persists, and Aquinas's analysis both of how these classifications work formally as well as of the material concerns any pattern of classification will display remains directly relevant to the naming and doing of human action, in any time and culture.

# 6. Moral Notions and Moral Acts

## 1. Reprise on the Failure of Moral Theories

Emergence from a discussion of Aquinas on human acts into the contemporary scene requires some adjustment of the eyes. His understanding plainly differs from much contemporary thinking. As we have emphasized, prominent among the differences is Aquinas's supposition that human actions are the same as moral actions — with the significant consequence that no theory of morality is necessary to distinguish the moral from the nonmoral within human action. For him, rather, moral considerations already apply to all human acts just insofar as they are human acts. Consequently, Aquinas expects moral considerations will have a great deal to do with how acts are named; and when there is some question about which name of an individual act should be counted most important, a moral name will always trump a morally indifferent one, and a more weighty moral one a less weighty.

This set of implications — the lack of a need for a moral theory, the presumption of the involvement of moral considerations, and a charted course for deciding on the principal name of an individual action — could be thought to simplify how action and "morality" are addressed. Another set of implications, however, makes the process more complex. Recall that for Aquinas the "why" of any human action will already be at least partly included in the "what." So if someone says he just washed his hands, we will assume that he did so to get them clean. Moreover, his doing so will make sense precisely because we assume that he shares with us the idea that that hygiene is a good. The action "washing one's hands" in this way has a home; it fits within a set of practices in the human life that does not need to be justified precisely because its very existence already implies that it is. In MacIntyre's terms, it is intelligible.[1]

Put in other terms, there is a good buried within the intelligible human action of washing one's hands. And it is this that gives rise to the complexity. For there are any number of such buried goods. Our actions, as intelligible actions, presume a whole world of what modern thinkers like to call "values," but these are not something we might buy or exchange on an open market, nor are they enormous and free-floating ideals like "freedom" or "utility," but are rather things like warm porridge, lively conversation, or clean hands. The world of human action, like a great forest, is dense with such goods.[2]

There are, I have been implying throughout this book, quite serious repercussions when the great complexity of this forest of goods that supports human action is ignored, as it has been by so many thinkers since Aquinas, whom we might call the premier forester of all time. What occurs as a result of such ignorance is illustrated by a poignant exchange near the end of the first act of Robert Bolt's play *A Man for All Seasons*. The play's central hero, Sir Thomas More, cuts a similar figure to Aquinas, although his expertise in the play is in the complexity and subtleties of the laws of England. The exchange is between More and the young iconoclast, Roper, More's future son-in-

1. It does not follow from this that every time anyone washes his hands he does this only to get them clean — he may have other reasons as well, such as that he happens very much to enjoy the gentle splashing sounds produced by the action. Nor is it unimaginable that someone might not share with most of the human community that hygiene is a good. If this occurs, however — and we should want to confirm it in the man's life and practice, i.e., that he no longer takes showers, really doesn't wash his hands, etc. — then not just his action (or refraining) will become somewhat unintelligible to us, but he will as well.

2. The unintelligible actions considered in chapter 1 of the hand-clasping man or the questioner at the bus stop serve as reminders of how we assume specific goods in action. When we ask, "Whatever could this man be doing?" we are signaling that we recognize no goods (or "values") that could lie within the behavior we have witnessed.

law. The dark end to which the play proceeds, More's imprisonment and subsequent execution, is both preceded and precipitated by the developing corruption of Richard Rich. Midway through the play an opportunity presents itself for More, then Lord Chancellor and able to do as he pleases, to arrest the increasingly corrupt Rich, who almost certainly will harm More and his family if he is not stopped. In the exchange Roper urges More to arrest Rich, not because he has broken any law but because he is a bad man who is likely planning some serious evil. As More allows Rich to leave, the exasperated Roper protests that he has thrown away the chance to stop Rich from doing great harm. More responds to Roper with force:

> MORE: And go he should, if he was the Devil himself, until he broke the law!
> ROPER: So now you give the Devil benefit of law!
> MORE: Yes. What would you do? Cut a great road through the law to get after the Devil?
> ROPER: I'd cut down every law in England to do that!
> MORE: Oh? And when the last law was down, and the Devil turned round on you — where would you hide, Roper, the laws all being flat? This country's planted thick with laws from coast to coast — man's laws, not God's — and if you cut them down — and you're just the man to do it — d'you really think you could stand upright in the winds that would blow then? Yes, I'd give the Devil benefit of law, for my own safety's sake.[3]

I believe what Bolt's More says here about laws applies as well to the great variety of action descriptions available to us in language and life. They are a great forest covering the land. Certain modern moral reformers, iconoclasts like Roper, are like lumberjacks equipped with great buzz-sawing theories. As Roper might have it, the theories shift all moral authority to themselves, thereby cutting off the authority residing in the existing moral notions. Equipped with their theories, buzz-sawing moralists set about the daunting task of checking every one of the trees in the forest for moral validity according to their theory. The trees need to justify themselves in terms of the saw — in ef-

3. Robert Bolt, *A Man for All Seasons* (New York: Vintage Books, 1990), p. 66.

fect dictating a clear-cut of the old forest, to be resown subsequently with the seedling progeny of the saw.[4]

Of course, the great tree-cutting project being carried out in various phases since the Enlightenment has not been completely successful, to its own benefit, precisely because, as MacIntyre points out, for the Enlightenment to apply moral judgments to life, it needs a life. That is, it needs a history that is carried by the practices, languages, and actions of a people to theorize about; it cannot of its own accord produce such a life. So, as MacIntyre notes, while Kant's "doctrine of the categorical imperative provides me with a test for rejecting proposed maxims, it does not tell me whence I am to derive the maxims which first provide the need for the test. Thus that Kantian doctrine is parasitic upon some already existing morality, within which it would allow us to sift if the test it provided were a reliable test."[5] Like Roper, were the lumberjack theorists to cut down all the trees to get to the devil, there would be nothing left of the moral/human life for the theorists to theorize about.

## 2. Jean Porter and the "Meaning of Morality"

Since the middle of the twentieth century, beginning with Anscombe's watershed article "Modern Moral Philosophy"[6] (1958) and culminating with the publication of MacIntyre's *After Virtue* (1981), the theory-based approach to morality we associate with the Enlightenment has become increasingly problematic. Many have tried to imagine what might be involved in its abandonment. Simultaneously, and relatedly, new attempts to revive older thinkers and modes of thinking about ethics have been made. Yet it has not been so easy for even a new generation of thinkers to shake the theorizing habit. Game attempts to understand morality and moral action outside of the Enlightenment's

4. Our own time is one in which moral theories are bringing forth new notions. What we have all come to know as "politically correct" terminology is a blatant example of this.

5. MacIntyre, *A Short History of Ethics* (1966), p. 197.

6. Anscombe, "Modern Moral Philosophy," in *Collected Philosophical Papers*, vol. 3, *Ethics, Religion, and Politics* (Minneapolis: University of Minnesota Press, 1981), pp. 26-42.

theoretical paradigm have been short-circuited as modern thinkers re vert to terms and questions they profess to leave behind. Jean Porter's *Moral Action and Christian Ethics* is one such attempt to get beyond certain modern moral theories, to return to an older vision rooted in Aquinas; it nonetheless falls prey to bygone Enlightenment problematics. Porter is not without insight into Aquinas's views of human action. However, she cannot appropriate his view fully because she continues to carry modern presumptions about "morality" that are incompatible with it. For our purposes, it is instructive to pass through Porter's views, noting her mistakes, to see more plainly which modern presumptions about morality and human action must be relinquished if the view of human action found in Aquinas is to be fully appropriable in our present age.

As Porter notes, "contemporary work in the philosophy of language and moral philosophy has established that a moral theory in the modern mode is not possible."[7] Practically, the Enlightenment theories have turned out to be thoroughly reductive of our actual moral lives, as, for example, Edmund Pincoffs has argued in his *Quandaries and Virtues*, revealingly subtitled "Against Reductivism in Ethics."[8]

Porter appears convinced by these critiques. However, she is troubled by certain features of the "nonreductive"-virtue approach offered as an alternative to the Enlightenment pattern of moral thinking. As she says, for Pincoffs "there is finally no way to get beyond the surface of moral language, to an underlying rationale or purpose in terms of which to systemize that language."[9] This creates a practical problem for Pincoffs when he moves on to make substantive moral judgments about, for instance, the superiority of education to indoctrination. It is difficult to see how such normative claims can be sustained in the moral world of the consistent nonreductivist. Or, according to Porter, for Pincoffs the problem becomes that he simply cannot appeal in moral argument "to any standard other than the practices of his own community to give content to the ideals of the virtues and vices."[10]

7. Jean Porter, *Moral Action and Christian Ethics* (New York: Cambridge University Press, 1995), p. 200.

8. Edmund Pincoffs, *Quandaries and Virtues: Against Reductivism in Ethics* (Lawrence: University of Kansas Press, 1986).

9. Porter, p. 129.

10. Porter, p. 132.

I concur with much of Porter's criticism of Pincoffs. I am suspicious, however, that the assessment has a negative effect on Porter's own work. For an account can now be given according to which the contemporary nonreductivist reaction to Enlightenment philosophers' views of morality loses something they had, namely, rational grounding. Hence, to defend against new approaches like Pincoffs's that stay only on the surface of our morality, Porter supposes we will need to recover the firmer rational ground thinkers like Kant sought, even if that grounding cannot be had in the form of a theory.

In a word, Porter's appropriate dissatisfaction with the lightness of contemporary accounts that remain on the surface of moral language unfortunately draws her back to the Enlightenment concern about the rationality of morality. And so she goes hunting for what she calls the "meaning of morality." This is revealed in the following programmatic statement with which she opens the hunt: "If moral thinking does not function in accordance with the model of modern moral theories, can it be said to be rational at all? As we shall see, it is the case that good moral thinking is rational in its character."[11] From this point Porter sets about to work empirically, gathering some of our "basic moral concepts" together and asking about their relation. Do we follow rules as we use moral concepts? And can these rules, if they exist and we can identify them, be characterized in such a way that we can have confidence in the "rationality" of their various patterns?

Porter warns us not to expect too much from this work. Moral concepts are, after all, "empirical concepts." That is to say, they are not a priori concepts but rather function to gather together certain entities or objects in the world under a classification (Porter gives "man" or "gold" as an example).[12] As the point is made by Friedrich Weismann, from whom Porter borrows terminology, empirical concepts are necessarily "open textured." As Weismann holds, while we use the concept of "man" (in the sense of "person") readily and commonly in our discourse, its scope is always open in the sense that we cannot specify exactly and empirically the range of creatures to which it applies. This is revealed by the fact that were we to come upon a creature who "looks like a man, speaks like a man, behaves like a man, and

11. Porter, p. 44.
12. Porter, p. 22.

is only one span tall,"[13] we would have to think hard about whether to call him a man. The question of whether this creature is a man cannot be settled beforehand; moreover, as he appears before us, we should not be surprised to find disagreement among language users. The disagreement and uncertainty do not, however, imply that the concept "man" is useless or indistinct; in fact, we use it all the time, applying it with ease in most instances.

By pointing out the complexity of the application of empirical concepts to particular cases and by suggesting that moral concepts are empirical ones, Porter means to break with any simplistic understanding of how rules are followed in moral rationality.

> [T]he understanding of a moral rule (or any rule) is not logically prior to some comprehension of the cases to which it does, or does not, apply. We do not begin with a general rule, which is grasped in some mysterious analytic way, and then applied to particular cases. To the contrary, if one is to follow a rule at all, it is necessary to begin with a set of cases that are recognized as unproblematic instances of that rule, together with a set of cases in which it is generally recognized that the rule does not apply. In order to follow a rule, one applies it to relevantly similar cases, unless there is some reason to call its application to a given case into question. If there is some reason, then the case is a borderline or ambiguous case, and (if it is important enough) it may well become the focus for moral dispute. But in the majority of cases, there will be sufficient warrant, based on analogies with non-problematic cases, to either apply the rule in question or to decide that it does not apply in this situation.[14]

Impressed by Weismann's work on empirical concepts and (quite rightly) concerned to appreciate the complexities of moral concepts and rules, Porter is led to give something of a freestanding empirical analysis of moral concepts as they are employed by contemporary language users. Once again, Porter means to overcome the Enlightenment presumption that we need a comprehensive theory to access rightly the morality in our lives; in fact, morality runs throughout our

13. Porter, p. 23.
14. Porter, p. 35.

language in the various moral concepts we use repeatedly, and with understanding — meaning at minimum that we are quite capable of following rules with respect to their usage, so long as these rules are understood in a way that is appropriate to the application of "empirical concepts." Like Pincoffs, then, and unlike Kant or Bentham, she means to consider how these terms actually function in our lives and language. But unlike Pincoffs and more like Kant, she believes that good empirical work on these concepts will yield sufficient commonality so that it will be possible to gather them together under one roof. Thus "morality" becomes legitimately characterizable and properly unified. Listen to how she characterizes the problem she sees, and how she hopes it will be solved.

> The heterogeneity of our basic moral concepts may suggest that they have nothing in common, beyond counting for us as moral concepts. If this were the case, then we would have to give up any hope of making sense of the concept of morality, at least on the basis of the moral concepts we share. There would be, so to speak, no sense to make, and nothing to be learned from moral concepts beyond the sheer fact that we do count these and those particular kinds of notions as moral concepts.
>
> However, this conclusion would be too quick. There are some unifying threads which run through most of what we would count as the basic moral concepts. While these strands of unity do not comprise a moral theory in the Kantian sense, they do offer a basis for the more limited claim that we do have a coherent concept of morality.[15]

In sum, then, this is Porter's project. She hopes to look carefully at some basic moral concepts to see if there is sufficient connection and unity among them in order to venture a well-founded and coherent characterization of the concept of morality.

What can be said about the project in the light of our treatment so far of human action?

To begin with a general objection, we might ask what precisely is meant by the term "basic"? How do we know which concepts count as basic in morality? This is a question that is especially important to

15. Porter, p. 47.

Porter's empirical method. Since she cannot begin, like Kant, with a moral theory, she must sort through our language to find moral terms to investigate. But clearly their number is astoundingly great. Pincoffs and Robert Audi have compiled a list of well over two hundred English terms that imply moral judgment. The list is principally about judgments of character,[16] and as such does really touch on the terms we have for actions such as murder or theft or adultery, which turn out to be Porter's pick as "basic" notions.[17] Yet why are these properly basic? Why not investigate instead terms like "fornication" or even "littering"? We need an argument that these notions are "properly basic."[18] Yet on Porter's empirical procedure, i.e., that her analysis is undertaken in the manner I have called "freestanding," such an argument is very difficult to give.

Yet I do not mean to dwell on this objection. For our interest is not just in the procedure Porter adopts as she responds to the tugs and tussles of the contemporary debate about how, or how not, to overcome the difficulties of modern moral theories without losing moral rationality altogether, but rather in how this relates to the view of action we have discovered in Aquinas. When we turn our attention in that direction, it seems to me that Porter, despite the fact that she uses some particular texts from Aquinas well, ignores the shape of his general account in which, as we have emphasized, it is crucially true that all human actions are moral actions.

To see the relevance of this basic affirmation, we need to return to Porter's appropriation of Weismann's discussion of "empirical concepts." As she supposes, moral concepts are a subset of empirical concepts. Depending on how one wants to cut things up, there might be some good sense in drawing out this comparison. For instance, if someone thought moral concepts were a priori concepts, like the number two, then it might be helpful to point out that they plainly refer to things in the world — and in this sense are more like the concept "man" or "gold" (favorites of Weismann that Porter also em-

16. See Pincoffs, pp. 76-77.
17. Pincoffs, pp. 76-77.
18. The term is a favorite of Alvin Plantinga's, although used in a different context. See, for instance, his "Reason and Belief in God," in *Faith and Rationality*, ed. Alvin Plantinga and Nicholas Wolterstorff (Notre Dame, Ind.: University of Notre Dame Press, 1983).

ploys) than like concepts such as the number two. But since this is as far as Porter's analysis goes before she turns to specific moral concepts like "murder" (i.e., she tells us simply that moral concepts are empirical, nothing more), we are left with the impression that there is one very large set of concepts called "empirical," which is unlike at least one other set (i.e., a priori concepts), and within this large set is to be found a subset of concepts named "moral."

The lack of analysis at this level forces Porter's question about the "meaning of morality" to arise either too early or too late. Having told us only about the huge set of empirical concepts and the subset of moral concepts but of nothing in between, she speaks about the possibility of the irrationality of moral concepts as if it were a crisis. As presented by Porter, that a concept is "moral" seems to amount to little more than a declaration in the language that here is an empirical concept we praise or blame. Conversely, this seems to imply that we might be settling, or our language is settling, on things to praise or blame in helter-skelter fashion. This is the possibility Porter wants to address with her empirical investigation of basic moral terms. She hopes to show that there is a rational pattern discoverable in our moral concepts or attributions. This pattern, if we find it, will lead us to the meaning of morality.

Here it is helpful to recall the structure of Aquinas's thought about morality in the *Summa*. His analysis of human action is importantly positioned *before* he speaks of the details of moral terms. As we put the point earlier, Aquinas does not begin a discussion of morality and then turn in the midst of it to a discussion of human action. Instead, he begins discussing morality with a discussion of human acts. And this is essential, since what it means to be a human/moral person is to be the "principle of one's own actions," as "having free will and control of one's actions." But Porter does not follow Aquinas on this, for she offers no general discussion of the human person, no account of the relation between human action and human personhood, and makes no mention of Aquinas's key view that the realm of human action and the realm of morality are the same. Without any of these points made, Porter seems to forget that a "moral concept" like "murder" is plainly distinguishable from an "empirical concept" like gold insofar as it, as Aquinas would note, is a human action and as such derives its species from its end. Missing the middle step of action, Porter believes she must go looking for the meaning of morality among the great array of moral terms in our language — and that if she doesn't find it, morality will be in danger of slipping into irrationality. This is doubly unhelpful. On the one hand it creates a crisis of rationality that isn't there, and on the other it teaches the unwary reader that "moral concepts" are to be understood as a sort of grab bag of notions that are distinguished from other empirical notions only insofar as they carry something like praise or blame along with them, a praise and blame that might be based on nothing more than a whim.

What I mean to say is that Porter gives herself work that is not only unnecessary but is also based on an important mistake, one traceable to the Enlightenment. Given Porter's critique of Enlightenment theories of morality, we can anticipate that she will not answer her question about the meaning of morality in terms of an Enlightenment theory. Instead of proposing a theory, Porter, after investigating such "basic moral concepts" as "murder," "lying," "theft," "adultery," concludes that all moral concepts to some degree express a commitment to non-maleficence. As she concludes in her investigation, "non-maleficence provides the focal meaning for our concept of morality"[19] — and this common thread is sufficient to save our moral concepts from irrationality. But it is not the answer to the question Porter poses that is the problem, it is rather the very posing of the question itself. To reiterate, the posing of the question implies that unless morality is characterizable in some unified way, unless, that is, the concepts of morality can be linked either by theory or by common threads of the sort Porter proposes, then we shall have to conclude that it is irrational. And to imagine that our moral concepts might all turn out to be irrational in this way implies that our moral concepts are rightly grouped separately from the rest of our operative concepts from day to day, and as such must be given a footing outside this life. Morality is split from human life in Porter. By contrast, in Aquinas human life and morality are held carefully and consistently together by human acts that are, once again, the same thing as moral acts.

But what is the alternative to Porter's pattern of analysis? Is it to deny that morality has meaning, or that it follows a rational pattern? Plainly not. Rather, with Aquinas, it is to see that morality has mean-

19. Porter, p. 54.

ing in the same way that human life has meaning — and this of course will involve us in describing and categorizing human action in ordered ways. To do this we rightly turn our attention, as Porter does, to moral terms. What we should not imagine as we investigate, however, is that all these terms need to turn out some core meaning of morality. With this objective removed, we can proceed to notice great variation in our moral descriptions, at the same time as we see patterns.

## 3. How to Do Things with Moral Notions

We began our discussion of Jean Porter's book on action by noting her dissatisfaction with Edmund Pincoffs's approach since, for him, "there is finally no way to get beyond the surface of moral language, to an underlying rationale or purpose in terms of which to systemize that language."[20] The difficulty for Pincoffs, then, will be in finding a platform from which to offer genuine criticism of moral language. This criticism is not incorrect about Pincoffs, although not so much because of what he does with moral terms as because he defines virtue as "dispositional properties that provide grounds for preference of persons"[21] rather than tying the virtues to the end of the human person, as Aquinas does.

To tighten her own proposals so as to avoid Pincoffs's looseness, Porter, I believe, misperceives the threat of the irrationality of morality largely because she leaves aside the central affirmation in Aquinas that human actions are moral actions. Instead, she sets about to find, in moral terms, a core meaning of morality and so falls back into Enlightenment problematics. When Porter worries as she does about the rationality of morality, she seems to have slipped back into the view that "morality" or moral judgment, and therefore moral terms that carry such a judgment, comes to our human lives or human actions from *outside* them. If we imagine this, that moral judgment arises in or is brought to bear on our lives from outside, we cannot ask whether our morality makes sense without asking at the same time if our lives make sense. But, as we have attempted to show in a variety of ways,

20. Porter, p. 129.
21. Pincoffs, p. 82.

the picture that separates moral judgment from life is false. Moral judgments and the moral terms that imply them do not come to human life in this manner. As we have been emphasizing throughout this book, they are in human life, or more strongly, they are the very stuff of human life. This means that they have already an essentially rational structure since they are necessarily linked to how a group of human beings, one large enough to have a language, actually lives (or once lived) in the world. Moreover, they are rational within that group insofar as they require that the person who rightly uses them has a practical grasp of the way of life of the group and has made it her own. This requires that she be able to follow a rule with respect to a set of moral notions. And since the rules are about human actions (and not mere movements), rational understanding is required if they are to be rightly followed.

Julius Kovesi's *Moral Notions* attends with wisdom and precision to the complicated ways in which competent language users follow rules with respect to moral notions. While Jean Porter gives Kovesi's treatment some attention and J. M. Brennan makes note of it briefly in the introduction to his book *The Open Texture of Moral Concepts*,[22] by and large the book has been neglected in discussions of morality and action. Kovesi wrote his book originally to address the fact/value distinction much discussed at the time of its issuance. Kovesi wished to show that many values *do* follow from facts, that "is" can imply "ought." He was concerned not only with what we typically think of when speaking of moral notions, terms like "stealing" and "murder," but also with more mundane concepts such as "table" or "dirt" that display what Aquinas would call "goods," the sort we noted in our earlier discussion of washing one's hands.

In considering the relevance of some of Kovesi's insights, it is helpful to return to the moral notion of murder. Someone can murder someone else in many ways: by stabbing with a knife, pouring a bit of poison into a drink, flipping a switch, etc. So following a rule with respect to the application of the term "murder" demands some considerable rational capacity. For instance, we expect young children to be able to point out the set of objects that are yellow long before they can

---

22. J. M. Brennan, *The Open Texture of Moral Concepts* (New York: Barnes & Noble, 1977).

point out the set of human actions that are murders. These expectations demonstrate the relative complexity of the latter application. As Kovesi puts it, moral notions like murder "are not the objects of our senses. They are the object of our reason."[23] As our attention to both Anscombe's and Aquinas's work has already suggested, we make a mistake if, in following a rule with respect to "murder," we fix on what is available to our senses by themselves (if this can be imagined), such as the quick movement of a sharp, glinting object (a knife) or a white powdery substance (some poison) dropping lazily into a teacup.

This is not to say that murder is something *supplied* by our reason to the physical world. The outcome, after all, of murder is a dead body. Indeed, murder is about *both* human intentions *and* physical changes in the world. What we need, then, is a distinction without a division. Not unlike Aquinas's distinction between the internal act of the will and the external act,[24] Kovesi adopts the terms "material element" and "formal element" to point out two different sides to a notion like murder. As he sees it, any murder involves a series of bodily movements. But by themselves these movements cannot prepare for the application of "murder" to the series. In order to follow a rule with respect to these different series of movements, that is, to identify them each as "murders," we need to attend to the formal element in the notion "murder."

Moral notions are not by any means the only notions that, according to Kovesi's scheme, possess both a formal and material element.

23. Julius Kovesi, *Moral Notions* (London: Routledge and Kegan Paul, 1967), p. 18.

24. There is also some considerable difference, for Kovesi tends to treat the "material element" as if it is mere bodily movement while Aquinas, as we have seen, thinks the "external act," as well as the "internal act of the will," derives its name from its end. This actually leads to certain mistakes on Kovesi's part, since his teleology is underdeveloped, and so is less able to draw us to see how action and morality are both teleological at their center — and thus to see their essential relation. (Lamentably, Kovesi gives no indication of having read the least bit of Aquinas.) However, the Wittgensteinian interest in following a rule with respect to the application of a term propels Kovesi's investigations, while Aquinas is concerned to bring us to think in terms of species, and to be able to determine into which species a particular act falls. Kovesi will therefore be more attentive to what we do as we name, rather than what are the rightful names in a particular case. His attention to this process is a helpful addition to Aquinas's reflection about how the act of the will or the external act rightly plays a role in a particular naming.

Kovesi observes that how we follow rules with respect to notions like murder is not really different from how we follow rules about many other notions, although, as he points out, there are some notions such as "yellow" that do not call for much of a formal element in their application.[25] This is why they are among the first young children learn. The complexity of the application typically expands as the formal element is more prominent. But we should see that this complexity comes quite quickly as we move beyond terms like "yellow," which is actually more unlike most other notions than like them. So, for instance, even a notion like "dirt" features a fairly prominent formal element about which one must know a good deal before rightly (i.e., with reason) using it. "Not only does the notion of dirt imply standards, but unless we understand why we list as examples of dirt custard on a waistcoat and sand on a lens but not custard on a plate or sand on the beach we would not know how to continue the list."[26]

What is going on in a notion as it is meaningfully applied in relation to its formal element is best seen as the notion is learned. So Kovesi invents a notion and imagines its being taught by a philosophy instructor to his class.

> First he [the instructor] coins a silly word — 'tak' for instance. Then he draws various figures on the blackboard. The figures are of various shapes but some of them have a little pointed projection. He points to the figures with the projections and says "These are 'taks.'" Then pointing to the others he says: "These are not 'taks.'" . . . Soon the students would be able to say themselves whether a newly drawn figure is to be called a tak or not. The impression we get from this example is that we can follow a rule by observing empirical similarities only.
>
> There is, however, something strange in assuming that the pupils can leave the classroom and say: "Now we know the meaning of 'tak.'" This is so not only because they may never see any taks outside the classroom; after all they might, on occasion, see figures that exhibit the characteristics of taks. If however they see one,

---

25. With respect to "yellow," Kovesi comments that we "do not even need to introduce a formal element here, and we can follow a rule in using the word 'yellow' by observing an empirical similarity" (Kovesi, p. 35).

26. Kovesi, p. 38.

what are they to do then? . . . What is the point of the word 'tak'? The instructor gave no suggestion about this, and consequently did not teach the pupils the meaning of the word. . . . Without the need for 'tak' in a way of life we will not start forming the notion or using the word, and the word will not acquire meaning.[27]

Kovesi's point is that notions, moral notions but all sorts of other notions as well, arise within the context of human interaction with the world and with one another. The interaction is not just any sort, but it is purposeful. If they are to mean something to us, there needs to be a point in selecting out the pointy objects from the others. If we don't know the point, while we might after one lesson be able to select taks from among a collection of various shapes, we have no idea what we are doing as we select or why taks are to be distinguished from non-taks. Since this is so, Kovesi holds that, while we might be able to identify one, we do not really know what "tak" means.[28]

If we say nothing more about taks than that they are pointy objects, it is very difficult to imagine them really being a notion at all. If we persisted and nonetheless called "tak" a notion, then it could be thought irrational, that is, absolutely arbitrarily chosen, and having no discernible sense whatsoever. Like the man who clasps his hands three times in an hour, if someone dedicated his life to the investigation of taks, identifying and cataloguing any tak he sees, we would have no idea what to make of him. Barring the existence of such a man, it is hard to imagine that "tak" could have any life beyond the one philosophy class in which it was "taught," since students would have no reason to remember it. To retain the notion as a notion, we need a point in having it — or, in Kovesi's terminology, we need some sort of operative formal element. For this to be supplied the notion must become rational, i.e., it must be tied by reason to something that matters to human beings.

Suppose, for instance, it is discovered that clouds regularly take on a tak-like shape just before some notable meteorological event occurs, perhaps a hailstorm. Something, we assume, is going on in these clouds that makes them take this shape. If we are to go further in in-

27. Kovesi, pp. 39-40.
28. This point is related to the one made earlier with the help of Aquinas, namely, that with respect to human actions, "what" typically implies at least some "why."

vestigating it, we'll need a name for the pointed clouds — and why not "tak"? So "tak" takes root in our lives, and henceforth can be used with meaning and sense.

Note that while taks are in the natural world, their naming as taks relates clearly to human purposes. Hailstorms are something we are interested in for a variety of reasons, and want to investigate. Like the great majority of our notions of the natural world, there is a sense in which the notion "tak" construed in this new weather-related way is about us, or at least about the world in relation to us.[29] In distinction from this, and to begin to make our way from taks toward moral notions, Kovesi notices that there is another set of notions that relates to us in a dual way: they are not only *for us* to use as we interact with the world, but also *about us* as we do so. "A scientist needs his fellow scientists because the nature of his activity is such that it must be governed by publicly accessible criteria, but he does not need his fellows to provide the very features and aspects that he selects for his notions. In the case of our moral and social life on the other hand, it is our wants and needs, aspirations and ideals, interests, likes and dislikes that provide the very material for the formations of our notions."[30]

Kovesi's contrast between what a scientist does as she describes and what we do in "our moral and social life" is enlivened by the distinction noted earlier, drawn by Aquinas, between acts according to their "natural species" and acts understood as "human acts." Kovesi is not drawing his contrast between notions formed, on the one hand, about nonhuman objects in nature and those formed, on the other hand, about human objects. After all, science is quite capable of inspecting human life in the same manner it inspects things like geological formations or meteorological events like "taks." Rather, the difference lies in that human wants, needs, and aspirations figure at least twice in the notion, not only in the purpose we have in forming the notion but also as intricately related to the things about which the notion

29. One human purpose, simply wanting to know what is, serves as the basis for some of our more technical terms about the natural world. But even this desire "wanting to know" is something about which we make judgments, in the sense that some cases of "wanting to know" seem to us to be irrational. What do we make of the person, for instance, who wants to know (count) the precise number of trees that now stand upon the earth?

30. Kovesi, p. 53.

is formed. Here are some examples that begin an almost endless list: "writing," "arguing," "theft," "courage," "love," "soap," "gun," etc.

This sampling of notions begins with three actions as a way of demonstrating that the sorts of notions Kovesi has been discussing are strongly tied to what we have to this point been calling the human world, or the world of human action. Yet the list also includes other notions that are not descriptions of human actions per se, but nonetheless depend for their sense upon the character and existence of human action.[31] That is to say, "courage," "love," "soap," "gun," and innumerable other notions have no meaning unless there are such things as human actions in the sense that Aquinas has displayed; and unless we presume this world, we cannot use or follow rules about them. For instance, someone cannot know the meaning of "handgun" unless he or she knows that humans sometimes set about to quickly and without warning bring about the death of certain people or animals. Lacking such knowledge, as in the initial lesson about "taks," were this person shown a variety of objects including a number of guns, he or she might by shape be able to pick out another handgun, but plainly could not go on to connect these with a rifle or a bazooka.

In effect, actions spread their meaning into the surrounding territory. In Aquinas's terms, this meaning is rooted in some good, real or apparent.[32] The complex understanding of and knowledge about these various goods, real or apparent, is what allows us to follow a rule with respect to the application of the notions of this type: to know that and why this dropping of a bit of powder in a glass and that stabbing with a knife are both rightly called murder, or (moving between related notions) why "washing one's hands" is rightly connected with "taking a

---

31. Kovesi's treatment of "table" is particularly enlightening. He notes that the use of the term "table" is governed by its formal element in a way quite similar to the notion murder. Table is not merely a flat surface having four legs, but it is understood by us more in terms of how we write or eat. In this way the Romans, who did not eat on tables, did not really share our notion. See Kovesi, pp. 3ff.

32. The addition of "real or apparent," of course, makes all the difference. To understand moral notions one must understand both that human beings pursue what they see as good and also something about the particular things they typically see as goods. Plainly, however, there is room for disagreement about what are the real goods of human life. It is in this disagreement that various moral notions will compete.

shower" rather than with "dealing out cards," and why "soap," even though an object and not an action, is far better grasped (as a notion) by relating it to washing one's hands or taking a shower than by attending to its usual color, shape, or consistency.

While the very large set of notions we have been discussing makes sense only as these notions relate to the human (and therefore moral) world, it does not follow that they are all rightly called moral. Soap is intrinsically related to the human good of hygiene, yet it is in an important way unlike the term "murder." Unlike soap, murder immediately calls forward a specifically moral interest related to the praise or blame of some person, act, statement, or policy. It calls forward our faculty of judgment, requiring that we consider the goodness or evil of the thing done. To be sure, this press to make or confirm a judgment about good or evil is aroused in different company and by different things, as one can learn easily enough by spending time in certain religious groups or among feminists. Moreover, there are different degrees of the arousal itself, from mild to extremely serious, as in the case of the term "murder." For this reason, the category of notions we call "moral notions" must remain indistinct. We will need to be content with a graduated scale on which "murder" is clearly a moral notion, "soap" is not, and "abandonment" lies somewhere in between.

It is important to keep in mind that we are speaking here about notions and not about particular acts or persons. It is possible to reach a moral judgment about almost any particular act done or attribute possessed by a given human person. Yet all our notions, even those Kovesi describes as being about us twice, do not carry this judgment with them. Aquinas, of course, has made essentially this same point about species of human actions, namely, that acts can be morally indifferent with respect to their species. Aquinas's discussion, however, is improved on by further distinctions in Kovesi's treatment. In Aquinas's scheme some species terms (notions) are morally indifferent but others are morally weighty, suggesting a fairly strong either/or. What Kovesi points out is that moral notions vary in their degree of openness or completeness. "Murder," for instance, is a complete or closed moral notion in the sense that its use settles our moral judgment of a particular act. "Wrong murder" is in this sense redundant. "[I]f someone understands the notion of murder or stealing, to say that they are wrong does not give him any more information."[33] There is a story behind every murder, but when the term is applied to the story, a moral judgment is carried in the application itself. The story may continue, and the judgment may be mitigated, but it cannot be overcome.

It is important to pause briefly to remind ourselves that "murder" does not simply carry an independent moral judgment to some already established location in the world, as though someone did it (the murder) and we come along later with a moral term to mark it as wrong. Rather, "this is murder" is a truth claim about the world, about what someone did. To be sure, when a criminal investigator discovers a dead human body, he does not know if murder occurred, and so does not employ the term in his initial description. Yet, if in his investigation certain conditions are satisfied, he will conclude that a murder occurred. In this conclusion he decidedly does not apply the term "murder" simply to mark his belief that this particular killing was a wrong one. "Wrong" or "right" is not added in after the description. The investigator is saying, simply, that it is true that P was murdered. The truth claim includes within it a moral judgment, which can never be separated from the claim. This is so because the whole investigation proceeds within the context of human actions in which moral judgment is essential; apart from this context there would be no sense in the investigation.

If we are conscientious, we will do similar investigations all the time, although they will typically be of matters of less moral weight than murder: I have an exchange with a colleague in my department and wonder afterward if he has insulted me. I think about it, and conclude he was simply in a hurry. These investigations do not start from scratch every time; indeed, if they did we could not have a moral life. For it is the very pattern of this life that it contains known objects like "insults" and "murders" which are the means of judgment as well as the reason for investigation. The pattern is carried along in many ways, but nowhere more clearly than in our moral terms, such as "murder" and "insult."

What Kovesi helps us see is that "murder" and "insult" are relatively "complete" moral notions in the sense that they imply moral judgment in virtually every description. Other notions are more "open"

33. Kovesi, p. 26.

in that the judgment they carry is less definitive. As a (quasi-)moral notion that is more open than murder, consider "abandonment." Abandoning something (or someone) is not the same as leaving it, although one can't abandon something if he doesn't leave it. The difference between abandoning and leaving is tied up in our moral judgment about what was done. But by itself saying that "P abandoned X" does not settle our moral evaluation of what P did in the same way or to the same degree that "P murdered X" plainly does.

Combined with certain things, the abandonment that P did might tighten. For example, generally we believe that some things ought never to be abandoned, like our mothers. So if I say, "You abandoned your mother," I don't need to add "and you shouldn't have." This point is brought home by the fact that if you believe what you did was not wrong you will reject my characterization and say, "I didn't abandon her, I only left her for a time," rather than saying, for instance, "I know I did; sometimes it's good to abandon one's mother." "Abandoning mother" is a relatively complete moral notion, to use Kovesi's language, whereas "abandonment" by itself is more open. Abandoning a building, while not generally thought to be something good, in some circumstances might be unquestionably the right thing to do. And when we hear that someone abandoned a cave, we think even less about whether he should have. Here, clearly, part of the complexity in the notion "abandonment" comes from the fact that it does not by itself specify what is abandoned; we can abandon both mothers and houses. Murder, on the other hand, is more specific about its object: murders are done to people, not inanimate things or even animals.

It would be a mistake to conclude from this contrast between abandonment and murder that the relative completeness of a moral notion corresponds to the moral seriousness of the action the term describes. The notion "litter" is a relatively complete moral notion in the sense that "littering is wrong" is redundant.[34] To be sure, we

---

34. The way littering is complete is also different from the way murder is complete. The terms limit their scope in different ways. Unlike murder, which can only be done to human beings, almost anything thrown out of my car on the highway can't count as litter — although, to be sure, throwing a human being out does not count. What littering spotlights, however, is not so much what is thrown out but the manner in which it is thrown, namely, carelessly. So if I have a good reason to throw something out of my car on the highway — suppose, for instance, there is a very angry man in the car and he is reaching

sometimes put up signs saying Do Not Litter along the highway. Yet the "Do Not" functions quite differently in such a sign than in the sign Do Not Pass. For Do Not Litter we could substitute without loss in meaning something like Remember about Littering, something that would clearly not work with passing.

The logic of "littering" includes the idea that it is always wrong to litter — it is a complete moral notion. But plainly we do not think it is worse to litter than to abandon one's mother. As we have said, the relative completeness of a moral notion and its moral seriousness do not correlate. This demonstrates that we must expect and attend to a great variety in our moral descriptions. On Robert Bolt's metaphor, our moral lives are planted thick with moral notions, and like the great variety of trees that cover the land, we cannot assume that each will equal the other in height or span, nor in how it puts out its leaves. What we can know, as Bolt's More tries in vain to teach the young and overeager Roper, is that without the trees there is no defense against the devil. Without moral notions there simply is no moral life — and, as we have been saying, without a moral life there is no human life.

Herein lies the future of moral inquiry: namely, the careful and critical attention to the great variety of our descriptions. We have returned, in Joseph Dunne's phrase, "back to the rough ground."[35] Covering this rough ground will require particular judgments about how an action or person can be morally described. But it will also require attention to the range of general moral notions that is available for use in particular descriptions. And here we cannot suppose that the same language of description will always and everywhere be available. Since, as Kovesi rightly noted, moral descriptions are tied by at least two cords to the human life — they are for us to use, but also about us the users — then what we can say is inextricably tied up with who we

---

for a stout stick lying on the seat between us — then I can say, with sense, that my throwing the stick out the window in this instance was not littering.

35. This is the title of Dunne's impressive book: *Back to the Rough Ground: "Phronesis" and "Techne" in Modern Philosophy and Aristotle* (Notre Dame, Ind.: University of Notre Dame Press, 1993). It is an illustration of how interesting as well as intricate an analysis of the moral life can be — perhaps the surest way to illustrate just how impoverished discourse about morality has become in an age so dominated by Enlightenment theorizing.

are. Moral notions, those notions human beings apply to human life, will in this way be less stable than human descriptions of the nonhuman. After Adam names the animals, the human community will have an easy time keeping a species designation like "fox" in place, so long as foxes keep up their fox lives and now and then wander into our backyards. Indeed, while we might change the name for fox, as we do from language to language, what the name refers to will continue to present itself to us, and in its presence remind us of its name. With moral designations like "adultery," however, we have greater power, since we can to some degree make the thing disappear in the renaming. Or, perhaps better put, in our moral renamings we do not just change the name but we change the thing, and so change ourselves, and not necessarily always for the better.

## 4. On the Significance of Moral Memory

It follows from the previous analysis that morality cannot be divorced from community in the simple sense that moral descriptions must be sustained by a group of language users who not only speak in certain patterns but also act on them. While we who live in these communities cannot abstract ourselves from the patterns and descriptions, we can notice them and argue about them. This will give form to a moral discourse.

This discourse can be about certain nuances in moral life and language. For example, the nuance of difference between "not staying with" and "abandoning" is important since it allows us to make fine moral distinctions as well as to express them to one another. Moreover, this is a matter not just of settling on one description that is best but of having the language to tell a story into which particular human actions can be fit.

That there is a vocabulary and story behind our actions has been a subtext of many of the points made so far in this book. As we saw in the first chapter, action theorists have generally proceeded with the assumption that we should begin discussing human actions in abstraction from any story or "home." As we argued, this actually renders actions unintelligible, like the hand-clasping man. In the end we simply do not know how to speak about what he is doing. If, like the action theorists, we abstract human actions from the common moral vocabulary we use to speak of them, we in effect render all actions no longer human actions, treating them instead like homeless bits of behavior. The burden of this book is to reverse this movement, and to return human action to its various human homes — which is, as we suggested in relation to MacIntyre's example, to recall that human actions must be at least minimally intelligible.

Of course, when the activities of the hand-clasping man are first placed before us, they seem unintelligible because *he* is unintelligible. Yet over the course of our discussion of moral notions and the language we use to describe human actions, it should have become clear that the description of human action *x* involves not just what is presented us by someone doing *x*, but how *we* (the describers) are able to root the *x* that is done in a description. And different kinds of descriptions of human action will be more or less available to us as we have a vocabulary of human action, which is in effect a moral vocabulary. As a further point, we should now more clearly be able to imagine that moral vocabularies might become impoverished: we simply might lose a way to describe well what a particular person is doing.[36] And this is not merely a point about language but also about action. That is, we may lose the capacity even to *do* certain things, to engage in the actions for which we have lost descriptions.

Were we interested here in apologetics, the point could be made that the richness of a community's moral vocabulary could be a strong reason to consider the claims that community makes, and that its philosophers or theologians articulate and refine, about ultimate matters such as the nature of God, the world, and human life within it. In this context, I have not meant to hide my own view that the moral vocabulary of Aquinas, for instance, is far richer than the dominant moral talk of our own time, and that this is a reason to suppose that on many points he is much closer to the truth about human life than we are.

36. That the dominant discourse of medical ethics has been increasingly represented by theological critics is a case in point of this impoverishment. It by and large lacks the capacity to speak truthfully and in any nuanced way about what actually is done in medicine. See, for instance, Courtney S. Campbell, "Religion and Moral Meaning in Bioethics," in *On Moral Medicine: Theological Perspectives in Medical Ethics*, ed. Stephen Lammers and Allen Verhey (Grand Rapids: Eerdmans, 1998), pp. 22-30.

Apologetics is not the focus of our inquiry. However, reference to it in this context reminds us that, lying behind apologetics, communities represent themselves to one another in terms both of what claims to truth they each make, as well as of what path of life they believe is the best to pursue. This alerts us to the inevitability of theology in the sense that any community displays in its moral vocabulary what it supposes is most true, best, and most worthy of human pursuit. Theological reflection both limits and enlivens our moral lives. It limits them in the sense that it circumscribes what sorts of moral terms and therefore what form of life might be possible. For example, the presentation of and emphasis upon the moral term or notion "adultery" within Judaism and Christianity, tied as it is to the covenant at Sinai and to the teachings of Jesus, limits how sexual relations outside the sacrament or institution of marriage can be understood and described. It enlivens the moral life just to the extent that accent on "adultery" sets a context in which further nuances of the moral life relating to marriage are discoverable. This is true not only of human life within marriage but also in other parts of human life in which close relations between two persons are involved. The connection in such cases may be analogical rather than direct, but no less revealing and filled with normative force, as is illustrated by the powerful analogical use made by the Hebrew prophets of marriage and adultery to portray the relation between God and Israel. The nuances of notions will in this way and others spread out horizontally, affecting other terms and descriptions as well. The notion of "fidelity," for instance, while likely understandable apart from a social context in which "adultery" is meaningful, would almost certainly not be understood or displayed in the same manner, with the same set of possible nuances, in a context where adultery holds its meaning.

The richness of moral discourse is provided, then, not just by the existence of certain words in our moral or action vocabulary, but by the analogies and stories by which they can be elaborated, related, nuanced, or even slightly changed in application. Since the judgments of morality are always particular, any application of a general term to a particular case will involve careful investigation and also the right sort of telling of the story in which a particular action was done.[37] This may

---

37. This is the casuistical tradition of ethics at its best. For an elaboration and fuller

require many citations of cases that a particular action is both unlike and like. Plainly all of these cannot be covered with one or another moral term or notion. Indeed, since, as we noted earlier, the "what" of any human action is tied inextricably to the "why," we will need to know the details of the situation that might have made a person choose to act as he or she did. As Kovesi notes, sometimes "we have not got a single term to sum up the whole situation in which one ought to do one thing rather than another. We need a whole novel to state all the relevant facts."[38] Indeed, it is important to hear these full stories not only in cases when no single term can sum up what is true of them, but also in order to determine what particular term is rightly to be applied. In an imagined case of someone leaving his mother to "join the Resistance, we would have to discern whether it is a case of leaving, forsaking, abandoning or deserting a mother. Which of these descriptions is the correct one depends on the relevant facts of the situation."[39]

The power of novels and stories, which is essentially a moral power, extends yet one step more. For stories not only illustrate our judgment, and give us time to display that judgment in its details, they often become the means for further and ever more subtle judgments. Stories involve not just situations but also persons who live in them; and it is often in the stories of these persons that we come to see what is possible for a human being to do and be, extending both to the depths and heights of human character.[40] Consequently, stories themselves can serve as the foundation of genuinely new moral notions.

This can happen in the most mundane ways. For instance, my son once had a soccer coach who, while a fine coach in many respects, was prone to fits of shouting from the sidelines at the players. Many parents disapproved, and during the fits we would grumble and commiserate. This became a shared memory, a story or set of stories that we

---

display of this point, see Stanley Hauerwas, "Casuistry as a Narrative Art," in *The Peaceable Kingdom* (Notre Dame, Ind.: University of Notre Dame Press, 1983), pp. 116-34.

38. Kovesi, p. 112.

39. Kovesi, p. 117.

40. Notably the display here is not just of one or the other act, but of the virtues and vices out of which the acts proceed, particularly if the story or novel extends over time. As MacIntyre suggests, if you wish to find out something about what the virtue of constancy involves, you should read Jane Austen's novels. See Alasdair MacIntyre, *After Virtue* (Notre Dame, Ind.: University of Notre Dame Press, 1981), pp. 222-26.

later found we could evoke quickly by the use of the coach's name, or by a brief imitation of his peculiar style. The behavior Mr. Mansfield (not his real name) displayed was distinctive enough for us on occasion to be able to refer to it simply by conjugating his name: "mansfielding." Now and again we saw this same sort of behavior displayed by other coaches — and we as a group were particularly adept at recognizing it. Because of the judgment we had shared in the prolonged experience of Mansfield, we were able to extend it to other cases. Armed with the specific wrongness of "mansfielding" — and this was quite specific, combining not just his shouting but also the misplaced intensity, the inordinate desire to win, etc. — we found that we were able to go on to make other judgments about other coaches. "Mansfielding" came to have meaning and also to carry judgment; indeed, its meaning and judgment were tied to one another.

Located within a very small community, "mansfielding" lacks the scope and power to become a widely shared notion. Whether or not such stories become terms, however, they can guide and direct judgment on a quite large scale. Consider, for instance, the notorious occasions when someone in the role of coach did something no one in that role had done before — at least no one so publicly — that commanded our moral attention: Billy Martin of the New York Yankees kicking dirt on the umpire's shoes or Bobby Knight of Indiana University throwing a chair onto the basketball court. To my knowledge neither of these cases has given rise to a specific notion, but when coaches or managers misbehave, these episodes are readily at hand for comparison and contrast. They help us form new specific judgments about what is or isn't right for a coach to do.

Kovesi's work on these matters, and ours in elaboration, makes clearer a point that Jean Porter also emphasizes — and which she traces back to Aquinas. This is that "moral reasoning is not deductive but analogical."[41] As Kovesi puts it, when we go about making our moral judgments we are looking for what amounts to the "same thing." And in rejecting that something is the same thing as something else, we must provide additional analogical support. When, for example, one brother maintains to another that his leaving Mother was simply a case of leaving while his brother's was a case of aban-

41. Kovesi, p. 114.

doning her, he must be able to draw out factors within his situation that mark it as more like some other situation than like that of his brother. Existing moral notions constrict what this brother can say by their undeniable relevance; for instance, the very notions of "brother" or "mother," understood not merely biologically but morally, imply that brothers share certain responsibilities to their mother, but it does not follow that they are always the determinative notions in a final description of what is really going on in their situation.[42] But this can be shown only if one brother can successfully describe his situation by story or analogy so we can see why it is, in important ways, unlike his brother's.

As is illustrated on a very small scale with our group of soccer parents, for us to go on making and discussing particular moral judgments about actions or persons, we must carry a shared moral memory. We do this partly in our moral notions, but also, in more complicated fashion, these notions are stitched together in various ways by stories we continue to tell about our shared pasts. Indeed, the terms are often rooted in the stories — when they stand free, they actually have a tendency to develop clay feet. To be revived they may need again to be related to some key piece of the shared stories, so long, of course, as these continue to play some vital role for those who tell them. Conversely, sometimes that a particular notion is vital to us will prompt a return to the story or set of stories that once informed it, giving it full life and sense. The moral notions and the storytelling, the remembering, vitally interact, as the telling of the story of slavery in the United States interacts with Americans' ongoing description of certain acts as instances of "racism." Importantly, these stories and notions become active in setting meaning patterns for the actions we

---

42. See Kovesi's discussion of this case on page 140 of *Moral Notions*. This example is particularly intriguing since operative family notions such as "brother" will vary from one to another culture, not on whether (moral) responsibilities apply to them, but exactly how. So, for example, the operative existence of the notion "elder brother" might settle and locate this moral difference in a particular culture such that it is quickly clear that one brother did indeed abandon while the other merely left. The example illustrates the need for an account or a detailed story to divide the judgments about what each brother did precisely because the notion "elder brother" does not function in this way for most of us — i.e., we assume each son's responsibility to his mother is the same, irrespective of birth order.

perform. This is why what I do as a white American male with or to one of my black colleagues will (sometimes) rightly be interpreted, even described, differently from what I do or don't do with another white male colleague. Put in the context of points made earlier, the context of my human action, its home, is not set solely by my intentions or even my individual story, but by the human world I inhabit, which is necessarily a communal world, with a communal history. A human "I" is necessary in any human act, but what I did when I acted (or, as we shall see in the next chapter, failed to act) is not entirely up to me to determine. It must instead be located within the ongoing language, life, and story of those with whom I live. It is we together who must sustain my action in those words and stories that constitute our shared moral memory.

The necessity of a moral memory brings us once again face-to-face with the reality that moral notions and the stories that sustain them can come and go in communities of language users, or be significantly changed in their meaning. In the context of a complaint about the lack of moral memory in the contemporary West, this could be taken as a lament. Yet it is important to see that the process by which a people acquires, abandons, or reorients moral descriptions is not by itself lamentable. Christians, in fact, have been great ones for abandoning or radically reorienting moral terms. As Nietzsche saw, what Christians did with the term "pride," turning it from pagan virtue to Christian vice, is a particularly good example of this. For his part, Nietzsche's own push for the "revaluation of all values,"[43] which included, importantly, a radically revised account of the moral virtues,[44] is a coherent attempt to reorient our moral memory once again. As this exchange between Nietzsche and the Christians makes plain, while the idea of a change in the vocabulary or stories upon which our morality rests is offensive to neither, particular changes will be a matter of the greatest

43. Nietzsche, *The Anti-Christ* (New York: Penguin Books, 1968), #62.

44. E.g., part 7 of *Beyond Good and Evil* (New York: Vintage Books, 1966) is entitled "Our Virtues." While MacIntyre's contrast in *After Virtue* between Nietzsche and Aristotle as the two genuine moral alternatives for our time has been criticized and alternatives suggested (e.g., see Scott Bader-Saye's chapter "Abraham or Nietzsche" in his *Church and Israel after Christendom: The Politics of Election* [Boulder, Colo.: Westview, 1998]), Nietzsche remains the clearest moral alternative to the Christian or Jewish moral traditions of memory in the West.

**165**

concern to both. For Christians, for instance, the loss of power of a notion such as "sacrilege" (as used in the previous discussion of Aquinas) may not only mean that certain human actions will be redescribed (with no remainder) in other, more commonly used terms like "theft," it may also mean that certain other actions such as "consecration" will empty of meaning and actually be difficult if not impossible to perform. Indeed, for Christians, it is hard to imagine a more important task than the maintenance of what we have been calling a shared moral memory. Without it, very many of our human actions will be difficult to distinguish from a random clasping of the hands.

# 7. The Importance of Not Doing Something

## 1. Obstacles in the Way

Imagine a man walking down a twisting mountain path. The path is well-worn but apparently not much used recently, for a variety of obstacles block it. The first is a large, fallen tree. When he reaches it, this man leaps over nimbly and continues along his way. Rounding a corner, he encounters a second obstacle, this time an old tire. Hardly breaking stride, he clears the tire easily, although by no means hurriedly — he is apparently in no rush. Some more twists and turns, and a third obstacle presents itself, this time a human corpse. Knowing something, now, of this man's agility, we are not surprised to see him, with only the slightest effort, spring neatly over the dead human body in the path and continue down the mountain.

Or are we surprised? In fact, we are very surprised, even outraged. This man has given no sign whatsoever that he recognizes another man's corpse as anything different from a fallen tree or an old tire. Our outrage may extend, even, to whoever is relating this little tale of the nimble man on the mountain path. Who could continue to tell of this man's agility when he has just nonchalantly hopped over a dead man?

If this little vignette of the nimble man has effect, it is due to the abrupt intrusion of the corpse. We begin by imaging a man walking along a path and then, suddenly, a dead human body. The surprise is important and revealing. Stories or examples in moral philosophy are more often used to illustrate some point already made or to elaborate a moral problem already discussed. The discussion might be of some sort of killing, and descriptions are trotted out to try on some point or another. We might play with the description "John killed Jane," changing it to "John sighted down the barrel," or "John's finger squeezed the trigger," or "Jane's body fell to the ground." We began with a philosophical puzzle about action and then came to the descriptions so that the degree of detachment in our speaking of Jane's death or of her body has a context. Taken from it, it seems odd, even eerie. If John really killed Jane, what could it mean for us to play about with this description, parsing it out into "John's finger squeezing the trigger," "Jane's body falling to the ground," and so on?

I suspect that the infinite parsing of actions into little events is made easier if the action is of monumental effect, such as murder. Partly this is a matter of avoiding boredom. Philosophical discussions about what the action "brushing his teeth" involved ("John's rotating his wrist," "John's trying out a new and improved toothpaste," etc.) might be sustainable for some time among diehard action theorists, but hardly among the rest of us. What does it matter precisely how we describe John's teeth brushing? When the protracted discussion is, however, about killing, we are interested, not only because it is a bit titillating (it is that), but because killing (and death) is of the greatest significance to us and so the details surrounding it are already heightened in our normal experience. If someone says, "Tell me, down to every last detail, every precise movement, what you saw as you watched John kill Jane," I understand what he is asking, and why. The same request for my observations of John brushing his teeth seems silly, even a bit irritating.

Back to the nimble man. We can see that something like this level of heightened interest is what he lacks. He fails to see the corpse as monumental; it is merely an object to him, an obstacle in his way. It brings from him no shudder of horror, not even a heightened curiosity.[1] Not

---

1. Of course, context will matter. The example implies that the man is not in some urgent hurry; were he, we would not view his failure to stop and at least inspect the corpse as necessarily a lack. We would presume he has a good reason not to stop. Or if we discover that in the area where this man is walking there is a war on, and dead hu-

only the man's behavior but also the man himself repel us. What sort of man could he be?

It is important to see that the revulsion we feel toward the nimble man is difficult to account for according to the standardized tools of analysis used in modern moral philosophy. After all, he had nothing to do with the death of the man in the path: we surely can't charge him with murder. Moreover, since what we have here is a dead body and not a living person, it is a bit difficult to find a rational being who is harmed by the nimble man's nonchalance.

But to look in this way for a specific harm done, one rational being to another, clearly misses the point. The problem is not so much with the *outcome* of the man's leap over the corpse. It relates instead to what it reveals about his soul. How does he see the world? What, if anything, does he love? It is correct to say that we are chilled by him, and this is not just by his action or lack of action: he, the man and his way of seeing and living in the world, chills us. This is not to say that his manner or person seems merely distant or odd to us. We do not say afterward: "What an odd thing to do, simply hop over the corpse like that." No, something is deeply wrong here. The nimble man sees wrongly. When the corpse appears to him as just another obstacle in his pathway, he misperceives it; he does not see it for what it truthfully is.

We shall return to this point about seeing things truthfully nearer the end of this chapter. For now, however, I should like to explore another interesting feature of the example of the nimble man, namely, that we are concerned not so much about what the man did, but rather with what he *didn't* do. He didn't notice, didn't stop, wasn't horrified, etc.

---

man bodies are a common sight, then, while we may not excuse his nonchalance, we will understand it. As with Kovesi's brothers and the French resistance, a whole novel may lie behind what we just saw the man not do.

For our purposes, however, we need not stretch the story out. For we are interested here in presumptions. And our presumption is that, unlike his leap over the fallen tree, this man's leap over the corpse must be explained before we will hear any more about his trek down the mountain.

## 2. When Something Is Not Done

In medical ethics, especially in conjunction with discussion of euthanasia, thinkers sometimes speak of "refrainings." Although this is not always clear in the literature, a "refraining" involves someone's consciously not doing something he could have done, e.g., the doctor refrained from giving his patient the treatment. "Withholding" is another term used, particularly as in the "withholding of lifesaving treatment."

Within this medical context a discussion has gone on that poses interesting questions about how doing something, acting, is related to *not* doing something. James Rachels, a philosopher and contemporary proponent of euthanasia, has advanced the thesis that no moral significance can be assigned to the "bare fact" that in one case one acted and in the other case one did not,[2] and applied this point to the current debate about euthanasia. In a now famous article in the *New England Journal of Medicine*,[3] Rachels worked a kind of magic by thinking up an inventive and ultimately quite powerful example. Suppose there are two men, one named Smith and the other Jones. Each has evil designs on his young cousin from whose death he stands to benefit. Now, as it turns out, Smith kills his cousin. He waits till he is in the bath, then sneaks in and drowns him. Jones has the same plan, but it so happens that just as he enters the bathroom with the intent to kill, his cousin slips, bangs his head, and lands facedown in the water. Jones merely needs to stand by and gleefully watch his cousin drown. Unlike Smith, he did not drown his cousin, he only refrained from saving him from drowning.

Rachels moves rather quickly in drawing conclusions from this example, concluding that they amount to the same thing morally. And I do not think that he is in this instance wrong. But we must move more slowly to see why.

Aquinas holds in the *Summa* that "omission and commission are found in the same species of sin."[4] "Sin" is not a word Rachels uses,

2. James Rachels, "Reasoning about Killing and Letting Die," *Southern Journal of Philosophy* 19 (1981): 465.

3. James Rachels, "Active and Passive Euthanasia," *New England Journal of Medicine* 292 (January 9, 1975): 78-80.

4. Aquinas, *Summa Theologiae* I-II.72.6; hereafter cited as *ST*.

but it does important work in Aquinas. Indeed, "sin of omission" loses meaning when changed, as it is among some interpreters, to "*act* of omission."[5] This is not only because, as we have implied, there is no discernible act. Rather, the more important difference is that "sin" already implies a moral classification whereas "act" does not.[6] This is one way we can begin to see that Aquinas's claim, while related to Rachels's, is also different from it. Rachels imagines that his example shows there is no moral significance in the "bare fact" that Smith acted while Jones did not since we evaluate both Smith's action and Jones's inaction as equally morally reprehensible. I am not sure Aquinas would make this judgment until he knew more about Smith and Jones, yet since evidently for him what each did was a sin, then according to his claim just noted, it certainly could be that what Smith did and what Jones didn't do are rightly to be found in the same species of sin.[7] For the sake of the argument, let us suppose Aquinas would say that they are: we will suppose that Jones's omission and Smith's commission lie in the same species of sin. In more contemporary parlance, we could say that what Jones did (or didn't do) morally amounts to murder, since plainly that is what Smith did to his cousin.

We can characterize the agreement of Rachels and Aquinas in the following way: neither thinker believes that because a particular refraining or omission is an omission and not a commission, it is therefore, based on that fact alone, morally different from another particular action or commission. However, herein lies a key difference. Because Aquinas has the category "sin" and, moreover, believes sins can and should be classified into different species, his assertion that omissions

---

5. See, for instance, Eric D'Arcy's *Human Acts* (Oxford: Clarendon Press, 1963), pp. 41ff.

6. As we have said, all particular acts imply moral classification, but not the designation "act" itself, since it can be understood by species, and acts can be morally indifferent according to their species. "Sin," on the other hand, plainly implies moral judgment.

7. That they are in the same species of sin would need to be argued out. It is unclear how this would be done unless one had a system of classification something like Aquinas's, which is extremely subtle and elastic. Rachels, as a kind of utilitarian, will have a far less subtle classification system — if he has any at all. (It is arguable that for the utilitarian there really is only one sin, namely, not maximizing pleasure.) It is not necessary for our argument, however, to enter into the simplicities or complexities of some classification of sin. All we need here is the general point — and this seems evident — that Smith's doing and Jones's refraining seem very close to one another morally.

and commissions are found in the same species of sin directs us to a closer inspection of the meaning and context of what was done or not done. In contrast, Rachels universalizes his assertion about the insignificance of the "bare fact" difference in this particular case so as to bring him to the conclusion that we determine the moral worth of actions or "refrainings" all on the same scale. To be more explicit, Rachels seems to suppose that because in one case in which two people, Smith and Jones, had some relation to someone else's death, one actively and the other passively, and this amounts to the same thing morally, then it must follow that all commissions and all omissions wherein someone is related to someone else's death amount to the same thing. This is how Rachels emerges as a proponent of euthanasia. For, he reasons, if we think letting someone die is sometimes morally right to do, then it must be right in these same cases to kill.

It is perhaps easiest to see what has gone wrong with Rachels's argument by noting what he should have concluded instead. As his example shows, the fact that one person participated in evil by doing what he shouldn't have done and another person participated in evil by refraining or neglecting to do something, does not imply that the one who participated by doing rather than by not doing should be judged the greater evildoer. In his refraining, Jones participated as much in (and, we are assuming, the same kind of) evil as Smith did in his action. What we should look to, then, is the type of evil, and the sort of participation.[8] With this factor in mind, and with careful

---

8. Technically, an omission cannot be a good; indeed, omissions cannot be indifferent. Omissions are by definition sins. Or, as the word implies, omissions are rightly assigned when something one should have done is not; it is omitted. This is why the designation "refrainings" must be kept together with the designation "omission," for while omissions can be refrainings and refrainings can be omissions, there are omissions that are not refrainings and refrainings that are not omissions. For instance, there are clearly cases of good refrainings such as, for example, the resistance to some temptation. What marks a refraining as I am using the term is an act of the will not to do something. If this thing that is willed not to be done should have been done, then the refraining is also an omission. Yet, as will become important in our analysis, there are omissions that do not involve this direct act of the will. One doesn't decide not to do what he should do, rather he simply doesn't do it. The thing that he doesn't do in this case is nonetheless rightly called an omission. A failure to do what one ought to do out of culpable ignorance is an example. Other examples could be cited as well, such as when one fails to notice when one should act due to carelessness or laziness.

thought case by case, we cannot help but see that one refraining from giving lifesaving or life-extending treatment can be radically different morally from another case. For instance, Jones's refraining from acting to keep his cousin alive is radically different from Karen Quinlan's parents or doctors refraining from acting to keep Karen alive. Similarly (and obviously), actions done to bring about death, killings, can be radically different, e.g., Smith killing his cousin in the bath and, say, Achilles killing Hector.

Aquinas's discussion of human action and omission is attentive to these sorts of differences; he sets about to distinguish acts, whereas Rachels sets about to lump them.[9] Either account, however, brings a fact before us that cannot but have repercussions for our treatment of human actions. This is that the particular moral judgments we make of our own or others' interaction with the world apply not just to cases where we act, but also to cases where we do not act. Moreover, these judgments are not necessarily of different types; that is, we cannot say that because someone did something we should judge him differently from someone else who didn't do something. This casts the judgments and descriptions we have been discussing as judgments about actions in a different light, since they are also not only about actions but also about cases of not acting. This implies that our concern in these descriptions and judgments is not just about particular cases of someone acting, someone intentionally doing something to bring about a certain end, but also about something broader, which involves human involvement with or participation in good and evil.

Yet the link between our judgments about what someone did and what someone didn't do also introduces a puzzling question. In chapter 1 we discussed some of the difficulties philosophers have had in individuating particular human actions. If particular human acts are

---

9. As we suggested, it is likely that for Rachels, a utilitarian, there is but one type of evil, namely, states of diminished pleasure, and but one type of participation, namely, doing or not doing whatever is in one's power to bring these states about. If this is so, the universal extension of his bare-difference doctrine makes a certain kind of sense. That is to say, if one believed the only principle that one should live by was that one should always act to maximize pleasure, then a not acting to maximize pleasure would always amount to the same thing (morally) as an acting not to maximize pleasure. As we have tried to suggest in this book, however, such a monism obliterates the moral language, the ancient landmarks, that make morality and action intelligible at all.

hard to individuate, won't cases of not acting be doubly so? When someone acts, there is at least some observable movement, even if it is as small and subtle as a wink of the eye or a curl of the lip. Yet this is lacking when someone doesn't do something. So how do we know when to say of someone that he didn't act?

The terminology "refrainings" mentioned earlier implies some determination or decision on the part of the one who refrained or withheld that he would not do what he could do. Indeed, a refraining might be thought a kind of action in itself insofar as it involves a specific act of the will, as Aquinas would call it, or some mental event, as Davidson might prefer. Yet before we go looking for signs of a mental event, we must note that "refraining" does not very clearly cover other cases in which we wish to speak of someone's not doing something. In the account of the nimble man, for instance, we have no indication that he "refrained" from stopping at the corpse. He didn't decide not to stop and so proceeded on; he merely didn't stop.[10] But we want to talk of his not stopping.

Points made earlier from Aquinas bear on this problem, particularly those made about ignorance. As in our illustration of Aquinas's category of the ignorance of evil choice, suppose a father failed to know anything of the danger to children presented by peeling paint and so does nothing to keep his child from it. The child eats the paint and gets lead poisoning. Here the father doesn't do anything — he doesn't act, not even in his mind or will. Rather, he simply fails to see the peeling paint as a threat to his child.

What concerns us about the father is that his ignorance renders him unable to act well with respect to the physical health of his child. In this state, eventually he will either fail to do what he ought or he will do something he ought not to do with respect to his child, or both. If the father repeatedly feeds his child large quantities of sugary liquid and the baby's teeth rot, we relate the consequent rotting teeth, the child's ill health, to the father in the same way we relate the child's lead poisoning.

The point, then, from this example and that of the nimble man is

---

10. Note that it seems absurd to speak of the nimble man's (or anyone else's) "failing" to stop at the fallen tree. The example of the nimble man is meant to imply that he sees the corpse exactly in the same way he sees the fallen tree.

that we want very much to pick out "cases" in which particular people don't do something, and this is often irrespective of whether they have marked themselves as not doing it by some act of the will. But now, how we pick out these cases is, at present, a mystery. Our problem might be turned around in another way. Presently I am doing something: writing a book. As we have seen, this might be described or parsed out in other ways: "composing a sentence," "typing on the computer," "thinking about human action" — all true descriptions of what I am now doing. The variety of descriptions generates some confusion since it makes us unsure about how they relate to one another, or which one should be picked as the species description of the action. However, this confusion is limited by the fact that there are only so many ways what I am doing can be described as a human action. It is plainly false, for instance, that I am right now sailing a sailboat. By contrast, there seems to be no such limit on the number of true descriptions that can be given of what I am *not* doing. I am not playing volleyball, not going sailing, not eating cake, not reading a novel, not exploring Antarctica, and so on, infinitely.

Earlier, when the volleyball-playing young man on the beach claimed to be playing chess, we could hold him to the truth, limiting his descriptions by his activity. Yet how do we do this about a case of someone's not doing something? Suppose, for instance, the ignorant father resists our description of his "not removing the paint." Certainly it is true, he says, that I did not remove the paint, but it is also and equally true that I did not tweak my baby's cheek, sing him the first verse of "New York, New York," or take him on vacation to the Rocky Mountains. His challenge is not that the description "he didn't remove the peeling paint" is untrue; rather it is that its application to him is no different from all the other true descriptions of what he didn't do. He asks, why and how does "he didn't remove the paint" apply to him in any different way than all these other true descriptions of what he does not do? Why shouldn't he be able to choose vacationing in the Rockies as what he was not doing rather than removing the peeling paint?

One way of beginning to craft a response is to note that something happened that was related to his not removing the peeling paint that was not related in any comparable way to his not vacationing in the Rockies: namely, his child became ill with lead poisoning.

Since a baby's taking ill is humanly important to us, we want to know more about it, including whether it might have been easily prevented in some way by some other human being. Yet consider here another example, taken from actual medical history, the well-known case of Infant Doe, who suffered from Down's syndrome and whose death in 1982 in an Indiana hospital was caused by a repairable esophageal obstruction. What brought this case to the attention of the American public was the fact that Infant Doe at first was dying, and later actually died. The fact is, human beings (usually) consider the death of a human infant, or of any human being, of considerable importance. It is a monumental event. Consequently, when a human infant dies and there are other human beings intimately involved with her or him, we go looking for factors that might relate the action or nonaction of these living human beings to the death. Our interest and concern is rooted in the importance of the event and determines our search.

It does not follow that if no morally important event occurred, no one failed to do something.[11] Rather, like Aquinas's point about minutiae, when something of insignificance is involved, our moral attention is rightly lessened; as we would waste time thinking too hard about minutiae with respect to acts, so we would waste time thinking too hard about whether someone was involved in a relatively insignifi-

---

11. Sometimes the fact that attention is drawn to an omission is a good deal a matter of luck. For instance, my children leave their toys lying about on the floor frequently enough, but I only occasionally trip over them. When I do I am much more inclined to launch an inquiry as to which child left this toy right here, even though it was a matter of luck that I tripped over this toy today while yesterday I stepped over another toy lying on the floor without noticing it. With Bernard Williams, I do not believe that luck can be entirely factored out of the moral life. See Williams, *Moral Luck: Philosophical Papers, 1973-1980* (New York: Cambridge University Press, 1981), pp. 20-40. However, as John Bowlin correctly interprets Aquinas, the success or failure of an action, while in many cases a relevant consideration about how the action is to be regarded in all its subtlety, is not itself sufficient to transform the act's species. As Bowlin argues, Aquinas's view is superior to Williams's on this point: it responds to contingency and fortune (Williams's luck), but is not awash in it. See *Contingency and Fortune in Aquinas's Ethics* (New York: Cambridge University Press, 1999), especially pp. 66-76. I became aware of Bowlin's book after much of this book was already written. His is an extraordinary treatment of Aquinas on these points and others, many of which are relevant to my own analysis, and, I believe, generally complementary with it.

cant human event. For example, while it is true that one of the house staff did not straighten the pillow on the bed when he or she cleaned the hotel room, it would be silly to expend much energy inquiring about precisely which person it was. These insignificant cases set aside, we can see that a characteristic of cases of "not acting" is that inquiry about them proceeds in the opposite direction from what we might expect.[12] Rather than beginning with the not acting and looking forward to some result, we begin with an event or circumstance of some importance and then look around for someone's not acting. Infant Doe died, and this is of the greatest human significance, so it makes sense to ask if someone didn't do something he or she should have with respect to it. Did someone fail to save his life?

This last question points out that, like actions, "not actings" must be attributed to particular human beings. That is, we cannot just speak of "neglecting to save Infant Doe's life" without asking to whom this might apply. As he lay dying in his bed, any number of us knew of Infant Doe's plight. It was widely reported. A host of doctors and hospital administrators were involved, the case was considered by the courts, and so on. Who, then, let Infant Doe die?

While this question of *who* connects not acting to acting, it also distinguishes it. When someone acts he makes some bodily movement, even as slight as a wink. The movement is a kind of self-designation that signals involvement of that bodily person who moved with whatever the action brought about. In the case of a death, for us to say that someone killed, a causal chain needs to be traced between the death and that person's bodily movement: Tony winked, which Al knew was a sign that he should tell Johnny to make the call to Randy, who waited with his semiautomatic in the phone booth by the midnight diner. The death of the man at the midnight diner can be traced

---

12. This is not to be taken, however, as an absolute difference between acting and not acting. For inquiry about someone's acting also frequently begins and proceeds on the same basis, i.e., something of considerable human significance is discovered (e.g., a human corpse) and we go looking for a human action that might be related to it. As I try to extend the point in the text, in acting the actor self-designates. As such, he can be more easily seen as initiating a conversation about what he did by doing something. In most cases of someone's not acting, someone else initiates the conversation. In either case, however, the actor does not control this conversation — a point that is better seen in relation to not acting than acting, but is no less true of the latter than of the former.

in this way back to Tony's wink — and we can say that Tony killed. However, in the case of someone "not acting," the linking cannot be done in precisely this same way. Moreover, since there was no human movement, there is no one human agent who, in his action, calls attention to himself. Coupled with the fact, just mentioned, that the language of "not doing something" has broader range — i.e., as we noted, there are many more true statements about what I am not doing right now than about what I am doing — it seems once again that we will have some considerable trouble saying of a particular person that he or she did not do something, as in our considered case of exactly who "did not save Infant Doe's life" or who "allowed Infant Doe to die."

Aquinas, however, helps us here by opening another way besides that chain of actions and movements illustrated above whereby particular human beings are linked to significant human events.

> Now one thing proceeds from another in two ways. First, directly, in which something proceeds from another inasmuch as the other acts; for instance heating from heat. Second, indirectly; in which sense something proceeds from another through this other not acting; thus the sinking of a ship is set down to the helmsman from his having ceased to steer. — But we must take note that the cause of what follows from want of action is not always the agent as not acting; but only then when the agent can and ought to act. For if the helmsman were unable to steer the ship or if the ship's helm be not entrusted to him, the sinking of the ship would not be set down to him.[13]

While it is true that many people did not steer the ship, according to Aquinas only one, the helmsman, "caused" the ship to sink by not steering it. The ship's sinking is "set down" to him. Why is this? It is because, as helmsman, he stands in a special role with respect to the ship's course; as helmsman, he was both capable of and responsible for steering the ship. Applied to the Infant Doe case, of the very many people who did not save him, only a few, we believe, were in a role with respect to his health such that they both could and should have done something to save his life. These are plainly his parents and his

13. Aquinas, *ST* I-II.6.3.

doctors, and likely as well the judge that presided over his case.[14] So, from among all the people of whom we can truthfully say they did not save Infant Doe's life, we single them out; they are the ones who "let Infant Doe die."

It is important to note that, for Aquinas, being in the relevant role is not sufficient by itself; two additional things must be true: the person in the role who didn't act must have had both the power to act and the responsibility to act in this specific case. These conditions are closely related to those offered with respect to when a bodily movement is rightly taken as a human action, although with a subtle difference. The first, the power to act, is the same, for it involves force. With respect to action, if someone was forced to move in a certain way, then the result that came of her forced movement did not in the necessary sense proceed from her; it was not her action. Similarly, if some external force held someone from doing something (suppose the helmsman was bound and gagged in the brig), then we do not say that he refrained from or failed to act.

The second condition, while related to the conditions applicable to human action, contains a subtle difference. Or, perhaps better, it becomes necessary to state it in cases where someone doesn't act, whereas it is entailed in cases where someone acts. The condition requires that we check to see if the person whose role is to fulfill a particular charge, steering the ship or caring for a baby's life or health, was in fact entrusted with it on the occasion of the ship's sinking or the baby's dying. For good reason responsibilities can reasonably be passed off. Suppose, for instance, that the helmsman had been ordered by the first mate to tend to a sick sailor while the first mate took the helm. He remains the helmsman, but the responsibility of steering the ship was temporarily not his. In such a case it is incorrect to "set down to" the helmsman the ship's sinking. In contrast, if we consider a case in which someone acts, his action is itself a kind of self-designation of responsibility. So if some sailor shoves the helmsman aside and spins the ship's wheel, sending it on the rocks, in so doing he has made himself the cause of the ship's sinking. By

14. See Allen Verhey's "The Death of Infant Doe: Jesus and the Neonates," in *On Moral Medicine: Theological Perspectives in Medical Ethics*, ed. Stephen Lammers and Allen Verhey (Grand Rapids: Eerdmans, 1998), pp. 708-15.

willing so to act he has placed himself in a relation of responsibility to what comes about in his action.

When someone acts, he places himself in a relation of responsibility with respect to the act's direct end. In his action he designates himself as the agent of the direct outcome. In a killing, then, someone acts to bring about the death of some human being. By some movement of his body he brings it about. Yet when someone is allowed to die, no such self-designation occurs; only the death occurs. So we need to inquire concerning the persons in those roles that included the responsibility that the death be prevented — if it could have been prevented.[15] We may discover no one was in this role. Or we may discover that the role perhaps does not specify what we might have assumed it would specify. (There are, for instance, some deaths from which we do not suppose the role of physician requires saving, such as, for instance, those of terminal patients for whom lifesaving treatment would be burdensome.) Or we may discover, as in the case of Infant Doe, that preventing death was indeed someone's responsibility: that a particular person or persons could and should have prevented the death and did not. In such a case we are warranted in taking the step, the one Rachels makes into a giant leap that simply forgets about

15. A way to see the difference between omissions and commissions, and how the latter involves someone's self-designation or responsibility by his action while the former must wait for a determination of who is in the responsible role, is to note that for persons arriving in a foreign culture, questions of role are the most pressing and also require the greatest amount of explaining and investigating. In other words, the rules and roles of a culture, assumed and subtle, come most to light when there is a question about who didn't do something. On the ship, a kind of culture in its own right, we will want to know who besides the helmsman might also have been designated to steer and what he was doing when the ship ran up on the rocks. Or in baseball, if the throw comes to the plate and no one is there, we will want to know who was supposed to be there. How a culture understands and handles omissions is in this way particularly revealing of the moral commitments of that culture, more revealing than the acts a particular person might do in that culture. This is because acts express not only the culture but also the individual actor, whereas omissions are related only to the culture as the basis for the expectation. Relatedly, when omissions weaken in their moral force, or when a culture feels the need to specify the details of its roles in contractual terms so that omissions can be turned into commissions (e.g., "since you failed to do so-and-so as it is stated in your contract, you have violated, breached, etc. [action terms] your contract") — plainly the state of things in present Western culture — this reveals that the culture has become a kind of society of strangers with minimal moral agreements.

particulars, of suggesting the moral equivalence of some cases of a "letting die"[16] (a not acting) with some cases of killing (an action).

This equivalence, now more nuanced, must carry us back to our ongoing discussion of human action with some important implications. If we are to better understand human action, we must see that the set of entities covered by that term includes as well specified cases of not doing something. The significance of the movement of the human body is not by this dispatched, for all cases of not doing something in the relevant sense include that something could have been done — that the one who didn't move could have. Rather, the movement is relativized. That is, what is key is not that a particular movement did or did not occur, but rather how the movement or nonmovement related to occurrences or things in the world that matter for human beings. Moreover, the essential connection between certain cases of not doing something and certain cases of doing something makes plain that it is not up to individual human agents to determine either what these things that matter are or how his movement or nonmovement related to them. None of us will allow the nimble man to have his own world of human action.

It is more easily recognized in this context (i.e., where certain cases of acting and cases of not acting are drawn together) how we

---

16. There is an oddness about the description "letting die." As noted above, as sins, what Aquinas calls "omissions" are necessarily failures to act as we ought. Taken as an omission, the "failing to prevent someone's death" implies that it should have been prevented. Yet "he failed to prevent her death" (in this sense) and "he let her die," as we typically use that phrase, are not linguistic equivalents since we sometimes will say that so-and-so did the right thing when he let her die. In many cases the sole reason we use words to call to someone's attention that something was not done is that we believe it should have been done, e.g., when the catcher fails to field the throw to the plate. In the case of "letting die," however, there appear to be other reasons involved. I believe there are two at least. First, as we have said, death is of *monumental* significance. Consequently, we are terribly interested in almost all factors surrounding it, including especially the relation of other human beings to it. The term "letting die" places some human being in a relation to the death (he could have done something to prevent it but didn't) without implying that he should have prevented it. Second, the description "letting die" has a kind of contemporary life that it did not have formerly. This is because modern medical technology has made preventing someone's death more possible than it once was. It is therefore far more frequently the case that people today refrain from acting to extend someone's life than it once was. The new plentitude of these sorts of cases makes a description like "letting die" useful.

may have been misled by the self-designation of responsibility that occurs in a human action to overemphasize individual agency. In a modern environment we are tempted to imagine that what I do is, in effect, what I invent. Conceived as such, the world in which we act is emptied of moral significance, except the significance I choose to bestow on it with my initiated action. Omissions show the falsity of such a picture. For they make sense only in a world that is already imbued with moral significance, one in which, for example, helmsmen are to steer, physicians are to care for the sick, and all people are to be shocked and saddened by the sudden discovery of a dead human body. As we have been suggesting throughout this book, it is also in this morally imbued world that actions make sense, which is why actions and omissions can be found in the same species of sin.

## 3. Vision and Virtue: Art and the Moral Life

The accumulated weight of the foregoing discussions cannot but affect how we go on in discussing and doing ethics. No human action (or omission) can be understood apart from the place it has in the moral/human world. This world is brimming with moral notions and nuances of great variety — trees, as it were, of countless species. Inattention to this world and/or the outright denial that it exists creates in us a lack of sense or insight into it. And without a grasp of this world, how can we act well within it?

As we have just seen, one of the ways the inattention to the details of the moral world has been perpetuated is by the notion that human action is a mode by which a particular actor carries his or her internally located agency outward into a naked world — one that, to extend our analogy, has been clear-cut of any and all standing significances. As the noted theologian Stanley Hauerwas maintains, our modern mode of thinking tends to equate action with self-creation, and as such ignores the significance of what he calls "vision." "Christian ethics has succumbed to modern man's one-sided understanding of himself as actor and self-creator. . . . The metaphor 'vision of the good' provides an important corrective to this dominant image of 'man the maker,' for ethics has more to learn from art than from the more 'willful' aspects of our behavior. Of course I am not trying to deny the importance of ac-

182

tion for our moral behavior, but actions must be based on our vision of what is most real and valuable."[17] From this point, Hauerwas proceeds to argue, with the help of Iris Murdoch, that "the moral life cannot be divorced from the substance of the world. The ethics of vision is therefore the ethics of realism."[18] Hence, unlike the modern moral philosophy which "has ignored the significance of vision because it is still tempted, in a Kantian fashion, to reduce morality to a single formula,"[19] an accent upon art, rather than principle-determined action, gives us a far clearer (and truer) picture of the moral life; this is "better understood on the analogy of the aesthetic mode of seeing and beholding than in terms of action and decision. For the right answer is mainly a matter of really *looking* while avoiding the constant temptation to return to the self with the deceitful consolation of self-pity, resentment, fantasy and despair."[20]

The preceding series of quotations from Hauerwas are all drawn from the essay "The Significance of Vision." In it he covers an extraordinary stretch of ground — one might even say too much ground. I believe, however, that he is on to matters that are absolutely crucial for recognizing the significance of the work so far done in this book. He begins by associating the terms "actor" and "self-creator." This is not a necessary association, as he admits in the next sentence when he notes that he does not mean to deny the importance of action in morality. The association, however, conveys a point. As we have said, human action can be conceived, and has been conceived, entirely as a foray by the acting moral self into a world that does not yet involve the moral. With its action the self in effect initiates (or "creates") the moral in the world that previously lacked it. To begin, of course, this implies a view about the world. As well, it implies an understanding of the self: self as maker. Action is that which mediates between this self and this world. It is the means by which an individual person morally inserts himself into the human world. In my action I make my moral statement, I communicate my privately formed and held moral

17. Stanley Hauerwas, *Vision and Virtue* (Notre Dame, Ind.: Fides/Claretian, 1974), p. 30.

18. Hauerwas, p. 36.

19. Hauerwas, p. 35.

20. Hauerwas, pp. 37-38.

values, much as I might stand up at the end of a free-for-all school board meeting and "have my say."

Were this someone's understanding of how self and world interact, omissions provide a counter. Omissions depend on our already being beholden, already responsible. While some omissions might involve a direct willfulness (someone considers doing a particular act and then decides not to), many do not, as Aquinas pointed out. Omissions are marked not just by a conscious refusal to do something, but by a failure to notice that something should be done. And while human actions can fall on broader ground than omissions — e.g., an omission is necessarily a sin while an action is not — we have seen that their difference is not necessarily one of kind. This essential (and moral) connection between commission and omission implies that it is a mistake to think of actions as self-creations, as moral self-expressions by a self who, at various points, chooses to do this or that in or to the world by moving it about with his action. Rather, actions, like omissions, take place in an already moral world.

I want to say that this moral world is the *real* world, as Hauerwas implies when he says "actions must be based on our vision of what is most real and valuable." It is this real, moral world that we must "see" as we act or refrain from acting — to which the nimble man was particularly blind as he hopped so blithely over the corpse. Thus Hauerwas uses the term "vision" to identify the faculty by which we see this real moral world we inhabit. It may be necessary to emphasize such a term over the more typical "agency" when we forget, as generally we seem to have, that human actions are actions as they fit within this real world. If, as Hauerwas intuits, "agency" or "action" now mean for us the sallying forth on various moral (or immoral or nonmoral) forays by the self into an amoral world, perhaps guided by some foundational principle, such as the categorical imperative or the principle of utility, then we may need to find another term to point toward that which the term "agency" no longer points.

For Hauerwas, what we must do is "really look"; if we do not, we will be consigned to these forms of self-deceit. Art or aesthetics is helpful for Hauerwas[21] as he works at breaking the stranglehold "man

21. This writing from Hauerwas is early in his long and productive career. Given his subsequent intellectual and theological development (as well as Murdoch's, particu-

as maker/actor" has on us, for art holds objects up before us and asks us to see them differently than we normally do. For instance, Hauerwas goes on in his essay to discuss how we can be changed by seeing, say, a tree or a rock as alien — a thing not for us. Somewhat ironically, in the "makings" that are art we can be forced to see that the world is not of our making. Short of this "vision," we take consolation in self-pity or resentment; we love and are held captive by our own deceptions, particularly those that claim we can remake the world as we choose.[22]

Charles Taylor has emphasized the power of the aesthetic to confront our deceptions, particularly in our modern world. That it is aesthetic power is key for us moderns, since we live in a desacralized world.[23] What the power produces morally is *epiphany*, a sudden and

---

larly displayed by *Metaphysics as a Guide to Morals* [New York: Penguin Books, 1994]), Murdoch's move to aesthetic categories is likely now less attractive to Hauerwas. Yet we are concerned here with a discovery that pulls us from one way of thinking to another one. The freshness of this discovery in Hauerwas's early writings is more helpful to us here than his subsequent, more theologically involved critiques.

22. In his *Confessions* Augustine adds a fascinating suggestion regarding not only why we rest in lies but why we violently defend them. "Why does truth call forth hatred? Why is Your servant treated as an enemy by those to whom he preaches the truth, if happiness is loved, which is simply joy in truth? Simply because truth is loved in such a way that those who love some other thing want it to be the truth, and, precisely because they do not wish to be deceived, are unwilling to be convinced that they are deceived. Thus they hate the truth for the sake of the other thing which they love because they take it for the truth" (*Confessions*, trans. F. J. Sheed [Indianapolis: Hackett, 1993], bk. 10, chap. 23, pp. 190-91).

23. See Charles Taylor, *Sources of the Self* (Cambridge: Harvard University Press, 1989), especially pp. 456-521. To understand the impact of Taylor's work it is important to note that his hero is Dostoyevsky: he is the modern Christian. I do not mean to deny the power of Dostoyevsky, nor detract from his heroism, by noting that his novels must pull us *within ourselves* to expose our self-deceptions. This is because, for Taylor, "We are now in an age in which a publicly accessible cosmic order of meanings is an impossibility. The only way we can explore the order in which we are set with an aim to defining moral sources is through this part of personal resonance. . . . The great epiphanic work [e.g., of Dostoyevsky] actually can put us in contact with the sources it taps. It can *realize* the contact" (p. 512). As I believe Christians must hold, however, this contact with the sources we might have when reading Dostoyevsky must serve as an *introduction* to a new moral world that contains true things more fixed and, importantly, habitual and bodily, than what is initially made available to us in the epiphany. The bearer of this world, despite her great modern failings, is still God's church.

unexpected vision of the truth. And Taylor is surely in one sense correct: with the diminished power of the church, epiphany occasioned by great art may be the strongest power to truth now available to Westerners. Yet there is a difficulty in this: by itself, aesthetically occasioned epiphany is incapable of sustaining the world to which it points. In fact, as Taylor himself notes, the power it carries is primarily negative. "Modern art has an emancipatory potential because it involves a 'negation of objectively obligating meaning.'" Its negative power resides in its pointing out that, in fact, "we have lost the power truly to name things."[24] We must be freed from the false names that encompass us round, like the strong bulls of Bashan. Epiphany penetrates the falsity. Yet after the penetration, what then?

Tolstoy's work *The Death of Ivan Ilyich* illustrates both the power and limitation of Taylor's epiphany. Dying on his bed, Ilyich is suddenly struck by the vision of his wife, representing the utter falsity of what he and she have lived. "Her clothes, her figure, the expression of her face, the sound of her voice — all these said to him: '*Not the real thing*. Everything you lived by and still live by is a lie, a deception that blinds you from the reality of life and death.'"[25] This epiphany is replaced by another as Ilyich turns his gaze to his son at his bedside. "'But what is the real thing?' he [Ilyich] asked himself and grew quiet, listening. Just then he felt someone kissing his hand. He opened his eyes and looked at his son. He grieved for him. His wife came in and went to him. He looked at her. She gazed at him with open mouth, with unwiped tears on her nose and cheeks, with a look of despair on her face. He grieved for her."[26]

This second epiphany moves beyond seeing the false as false; rather, it opens Ilyich to some new truth. Yet the truth receives no form in Tolstoy's treatment. Ilyich dies and Tolstoy's novella is finished on the next page. This is a necessity for epiphanic art. By genre it is able to point beyond Ilyich's self-deceptive world to another one, but it cannot enter that world and begin to name what is found within it. Yet — and this is where the Christian faith must continue beyond

24. Taylor, p. 478.
25. Leo Tolstoy, *The Death of Ivan Ilyich*, trans. Lynn Solotsaroff (New York: Bantam Books, 1981), p. 128.
26. Tolstoy, p. 132.

the kiss of the son — with the true grief that enters Ilyich's soul on the last page of Tolstoy's story comes a language, a set of practices and habits into which we must be formed and trained. If, as Christians say, truth has come to live among us, it cannot be relegated to the edges of life only, but must have shape and form in our midst. Contrary to the suspicious mood of postmodernism, the power of naming remains among us, even if partly choked at its source. Moreover, the power resides, is there to be tapped, in the activity of the everyday, whose rigors, if they do not defeat us, can train us to live life to its fullest, and with Christ.

After epiphany, where then do we turn to describe our moral lives? Plainly for Christians it is to Lent and then to Easter, and afterward to Pentecost and the settled descriptions of the Christian church that has lived through time guided by the everyday practices and commitments that form its life. If the Christian faith opens us to truth, there must be something to say. The claims of the Christian faith, beginning particularly with the Incarnation, require more from us than pointing past the falsities of our lived world to a truth that is glimpsed beyond it; epiphanic art is in this sense not enough. For once again the power of naming remains among us, even if diminished by our self-deceptions. This is because the created world is not a charade; the objects of our world do not stand, in themselves, as deceptions.[27] Rather it is we who deceive ourselves, regarding them as we have come to see them for other than what they are. The Christian faith, in this way, presents a corrected "vision" (to return to Hauerwas's terms) of "the substance of the world." This is why the "ethics of vision is the ethics of realism."

Two caveats apply here, supplementing and clarifying the meta-

27. There is implied in this a response to Platonism, which Murdoch in her work is increasingly given over to, even if it is never clear that she believes in the god that is required if Platonism is to be finally coherent. As Augustine sees in the Platonists, even if he does not always act or think in terms of them: "I found that the Word, God, was *born not of flesh nor of blood, nor of the evil of man nor of the will of the flesh, but of God;* but I did not find that *the Word became flesh*" (*Confessions* 7.9). Platonism pulls us, finally, beyond this world to a god above it. Christianity, while terribly attracted by this upward motion, must resist it. It must reenter the world — which it can never see as in some sense "unreal." I do not know if there is such a thing as distinctly Christian art, but if there is it must include this return. Great art must always challenge our lived perceptions of what is real. In addition to this challenge, Christian art may need to include a re-representation of the lived world, as real.

187

phor of vision that Hauerwas employs. First, it is noteworthy that Saint Paul employs it as well, in an oft-quoted passage at the end of 1 Corinthians 13: "At present we see indistinctly, as in a mirror, but then face to face. At present I know partially; then I shall know fully, as I am fully known. So faith, hope, love remain, these three; but the greatest of these is love." The obvious point that follows from this passage regarding our vision is that it is yet, and will remain until the end, *indistinct*. Confession of this indistinctness need not bring theology, whose key task is to know (see) and study God and God's world as it is, to a dead stop. However, it implies that practices of revision and dispute must never be set aside in theology and, moreover, that any response to the call to name must be seasoned with humility.

The second point suggested by the passage from 1 Corinthians and in our extended discussion of human action is that the task of truthfully naming things in the real, human world can be carried out only as we act within it. Indeed, acting, or refraining from action, is part of the naming. Wittgenstein's adage that we "think at the end of a pencil" reminds us that thinking is an activity not merely of mind; mind cannot be divided from body. "Vision," then, cannot be abstracted from virtue, understood in the sense implied by the simplest definition given by Aquinas of that term, namely, as "good habit." Vision of real things in the world cannot be correct unless it is trained; and it is trained as well as made manifest in action.

1 Corinthians 13 implies this as it links knowledge with faith, hope, and love. Contrary to how they are frequently understood in the contemporary world, faith, hope, and love are *virtues,* good habits to act. As Paul suggests, knowledge, which he links to "seeing," requires the theological virtues; without love, knowledge, along with tongues or prophetic powers, is empty — and surely empty knowledge is false knowledge. Indeed, knowledge will finally pass away. For the present it is vital; we must know (see) the world rightly to act rightly within it. But its support is not in itself but rather in these enduring virtues, faith, hope, and love. The greatest of these, love, or *caritas,* orders knowledge, not by feeding it a generous diet of facts but by forming the knowers, the see-ers, and, for our purposes, the moral describers and actors, in fellowship with God. The god here is, for Christians, the embodied God whose love led to suffering and death at the hands of God's creatures. If this, then, is the nature of love that forms knowl-

edge, and so provides for right naming, it is not just philosophically but also theologically clear that proper naming and action cannot be undertaken from a distance, as the phrase "God's-eye view" implies, but rather in the midst of the activities of the human life. Indeed, if Christians claim they see as God sees, the Incarnation requires that this view be from within human life rather than above or beyond it. What is required for seeing rightly, then, is living within the world as God lived. This requires a great deal of practice and training that can only be gotten as the story Christians tell of God's entry into the world is enfolded in their moral lives.

## 4. Living into the Truth: Prudence in Action

The sublimity of Saint Paul's reflections on faith, hope, and love is balanced by the methodical and detailed exposition of Aquinas as he moves from act to passion to virtue. We have treated the treatise on acts, questions 1 to 21 of the *Prima Segunda*. It is followed immediately by the treatise on the passions, which are the springs of action. "Passion" reminds us both that we are creatures who receive and are affected by the world and, as well, creatures of desire, who move actively into the world, stretching toward what we love.

Of course, the passions need guidance, for we can be both rightly and wrongly affected. The significance of being rightly affected in connection to what we have been calling "vision" is illustrated by the example of the nimble man with which this chapter began. The man is presented with the dead body of a fellow human being, but he is indifferent, seeing it as little more than an old tire or a fallen tree. He chills us not because what he did or did not do is, as act or omission, horribly damaging to anyone in particular, but rather because he is not rightly affected. Not being rightly affected in this case leads to an omission — the man doesn't stop, doesn't notice, doesn't seem to care. But his improper affection might just as well have led to an action. For instance, suppose a second man passing along the path some minutes behind the nimble man stops just long enough to remove the dead man's watch and place it in his pocket. This man does something illegal, and later we might find him guilty of theft in a court of law. But the way in which we regard the two men is not much changed by the addition of theft. In fact, we might prefer the second man, since his action demonstrates that he at least cares about something.

We can combine our concerns about what people do, or don't do, or don't think of doing, or see, or don't see, or feel, or don't feel, when we say that the man traversing the mountain path (either man) inhabits a frighteningly false moral world. And this world is not just around him but *in* him insofar as it has come to reside in his passions. Another way of saying this is simply that the nimble man lacks prudence, which sounds rather mild, or curious. However, it is helpful in this context to serve as a reminder of how Aquinas thought, and we might again think, about the relation between moral failure and lack of reason and vision. Modern notions of prudence typically do not carry us in this direction. As Josef Pieper remarks,

> To the contemporary mind, prudence seems less a prerequisite to goodness than an evasion of it . . . for we think of prudence as far more akin to the idea of mere utility, the *bonum utile,* than to the ideal of nobility, the *bonum honestum.* . . . To the contemporary mind, then, the concept of the good rather excludes than includes prudence. Modern man cannot conceive of a good act which might not be imprudent, nor of a bad act which might not be prudent. He will often call lies and cowardice prudent, truthfulness and courageous sacrifice imprudent.
>
> Classical Christian ethics, on the contrary, maintains that man can be prudent and good only simultaneously; that prudence is part and parcel of the definition of goodness; that there is no sort of justice and fortitude which runs counter to the virtue of prudence; and that the unjust man has been imprudent before and is imprudent at the moment he is unjust. *Omnis virtus moralis debet esse prudens* — All virtue is necessarily prudent.[28]

Following Aquinas, Pieper accents the essential correspondence in prudence between what is true of the world and the recognition within a person of that truth. As he says, "the intrinsic goodness of man — and this is the same as saying his true humanness — consists in this, that 'reason perfected in the cognition of truth' shall inwardly

28. Josef Pieper, *The Four Cardinal Virtues* (Notre Dame, Ind.: University of Notre Dame Press, 1966), pp. 4-5.

shape and imprint his volition and action." Pieper quotes here from Aquinas, who plainly is also using the term "reason" in another way than moderns typically use it. As Pieper explains, "'Reason' means nothing to [Aquinas] other than 'regard for and openness to reality,' and 'acceptance of reality.' And 'truth' is to him nothing other than the unveiling and revelation of reality, of both natural and supernatural reality. Reason 'perfected in the cognition of truth' is therefore the receptivity of the human spirit, to which the revelation of reality, both natural and supernatural reality, have given substance."[29]

Note that the truth about what is, is received by us. The receptive side of prudence for Pieper involves coming to see or take in the world as it truly is. This right receiving forms the basis both for how we act and how we react. And clearly, this mode of reception, the capacity to be properly affected, is inseparable from these actions and reactions, since they are formed based upon it. This interconnection between the affections of the soul and its human actions or omissions displays, once again, why one cannot set apart a special sphere of "the moral" from the larger sphere of "the human." Pieper notes this and decries it as a special error to which Christians have been drawn. "There is a type of moral preaching closely akin to voluntarism, but held by many to be particularly 'Christian,' which interprets man's moral activity as the sum of isolated usages, practices of virtue and omissions. This misinterpretation has as its unfortunate result the separation of moral action from its roots in the cognition of reality and from the living existences of living human beings."[30] Moralism begins, thinks Pieper, precisely in this delimitation. Rather than being open to all the realities surrounding human action, the *quasi infinitae diversitatis*, the marking out of a special moral sphere allows the good, or, as is preferred in contemporary language, the right, to be severed from the true. So the

29. Pieper, pp. 8-9.

30. Pieper, p. 24. To be clear about what Pieper is criticizing, we can link it to the moralistic tale that is told only for its "moral" point, or, perhaps better, the mode of interpretation that reads stories only for their moral point. William Bennett's widely distributed work *The Book of Virtues* (New York: Simon & Schuster, 1993) is an example. It contains many good stories, but the presumption of the book, its arrangement, seems to be that the tales are to function to teach particular moral lessons or virtues — and that the point of the reading is to learn the lesson. All good stories, of course, are about human life in some way or another, and *as such*, they are moral.

moral sphere becomes governable with principles, casuistically applied.

A difficulty, of course, for the modern mind will be that without this distinction between the moral and the nonmoral, we will need to give an account of moral epistemology, of what and how we know what is true about the moral/human world, that is inseparable from epistemologies of how we otherwise know what we know about the world, even in areas of inquiry such as natural science.[31] And, it might be supposed, this must all be done before we can begin to be moral.[32] As well, it might be objected that without the distinction be-

31. There has been a move of late among certain modern Christian analytic philosophers to reorient epistemology in something like this direction, i.e., actually to fit how we know what we know morally in relation to how we have knowledge otherwise of our world. Specifically, this has meant a return to the intellectual virtues so prominent in Aristotle or Aquinas. Linda Zagzebski's *Virtues of the Mind: An Inquiry into the Nature of Virtue and the Ethical Foundations of Knowledge* (New York: Cambridge University Press, 1996) is perhaps the most thorough attempt to do this to date. However, trained as Zagzebski is in the standard analytic understanding of problems such as Gettier's problem, the reorientation of epistemological inquiry toward a genuinely new view proves difficult. See my review of Zagzebski's book in the *Journal of the American Academy of Religion* 66, no. 4 (1998): 975-78.

32. The epistemological turn that created modern philosophy, particularly in its father Descartes, can be intuited here. Of course, the turn with Descartes was not merely about "morality" but about anything at all that might be thought to be known. It became possible to separate the moral from the human, and so the prospect of doing moral epistemology was initially less daunting. After all, the supposition was that we needed some one foundational principle such as the categorical imperative to root morality. Of course, as time went on, whatever epistemological rooting was proposed seemed less and less secure, until the project was entirely given up by those advocating "noncognitivism" (i.e., the view that moral assertions have no cognitive content, that they assert nothing about the world), and a particular view of "morality" was simply asserted, in hopes that it might prove "ultimately preferable" or "emotionally attractive" to at least some people. (See, for instance, J. J. C. Smart's discussion of his project to state utilitarianism clearly. J. J. C. Smart and Bernard Williams, *Utilitarianism: For and Against* [New York: Cambridge University Press, 1973], pp. 3-9.)

Intriguingly, for this trend to be reversed, and for the moral to be recovered, it may be necessary to reconnect biology and ethics. This notion is the fruit of MacIntyre's most recent reflection in *Dependent Rational Animals: Why Human Beings Need the Virtues* (Chicago: Open Court, 1999). See especially MacIntyre's recanting of his earlier repudiation of Aristotle's "metaphysical biology" in the book's preface, p. x. I take this move, and the book itself, as MacIntyre's final response to the emotivism with which *After Virtue* begins.

tween moral and other kinds of knowledge we fall back into Socratic intellectualism, in which all moral failure is a sort of lack of intelligence.

In response to the first concern, we must note that it presumes that the sort of knowledge we want or need, moral or otherwise, must be rooted in a theory, and the theory must be independently justified. Postmodernism has taught us something about the impossibility of this. But we do not need to wait for postmodernism to see in Aristotle and Aquinas how knowledge is had about contingent matters (those matters that could have been other). Without imagining that these questions can be settled quickly or summarily by it, a turn to the Aristotelian virtue of practical wisdom (in Aquinas called prudence) reminds us that it is both a moral and an intellectual virtue. The crossover is not merely a double duty for prudence, but actually indicates a key difference between Aquinas's view and Socrates' or, for that matter, a modern thinker like Descartes's. As Daniel Westberg points out, for Aquinas "the basis of truth and opinion about reality applies [not only to the intellect but also] to desire and appetite. The act of an appetitive power is an inclination towards some actual thing, though it is directed according to a representation of the thing, which may be more or less true."[33] The moral world, in other words, is the real world, a world that contains "actual things." Lacking complete prudence, we misrepresent that world as we name it and move toward it in our actions and desires. Importantly, it is not by mind alone (as if there were such a thing) that moral realities are accessed and judged, but also by will and appetite. As Westberg goes on to say, philosophers such as Descartes

> tended to stress the luminosity of knowledge, and the direct apprehension of ideas by the intellect; but in Cartesian theory the act of judgment was an act of will, not of the intellect. The great difference in Thomas' account of truth is indicated for us in his treatment of wisdom, *sapientia*. Wisdom is essentially in the intellect, because its act is to judge rightly, but it has its cause in the will and thus is treated under the framework of charity. Its opposing vice, *stultitia*, is

---

33. Westberg, *Right Practical Reason: Aristotle, Action, and Prudence in Aquinas* (Oxford: Clarendon, 1994), p. 200.

regarded as a sin when it is not capable of judging spiritual things. Dullness of spirit, caused by preoccupation with pleasure, for example, results in an inability to judge. Thus it is not only in actions but in awareness of reality itself that a person can have erroneous judgments that are sinful.[34]

Westberg's account of prudence in Aquinas is rooted in the complex Thomistic psychology that refuses to grant independence to practical intellect from will or from appetite. As he notes, it is our modern tendency, rooted in a voluntarism about action, that envisions the interaction between intellect and will in act to be one of sequential presentation, i.e., that the intellect investigates first what is to be done and then passes its conclusion over to the will that subsequently moves or doesn't move toward it. This division leads to a highly unfortunate consequence in subsequent (since Aquinas) reflection about prudence and action — both within Thomistic interpretation and among those philosophers, such as Descartes, who left it behind. "Within the model of human action splitting intellect from will, the perfection of the will by love becomes more important than prudence. Proper specification of action is assumed to be a rational matter; the real problem is the agent's desire, whether to obey conscience or not."[35] What Westberg calls here "desire" really might be better termed "motivation," to match so many modern accounts of the moral life in which moral knowledge is had by comprehending and rightly using some moral principle(s), and subsequently either successfully or unsuccessfully carrying the apprehension into the actual action, depending on the strength of one's "motivation." "Motivation" is the preferred term precisely because it implies self-movement, and the "love" to which Westberg refers is more easily understood as springing up within the self, as what we have come to call an "emotion" might be thought to do.[36]

34. Westberg, p. 201.
35. Westberg, p. 225.
36. Here a point noted frequently by MacIntyre rises to the surface. Absolutism and relativism in moral thinking are brothers under the skin. A prudence that splits will from intellect, as we have just seen, gives the human moral agent two tasks: first, knowing what is correct according to the true principles of morality, and second, conforming, bending, his will to these principles in his action. These true principles, of course, quickly co-

Socrates' trouble, then, was not so much that he linked knowing with morality, but that he imagined knowing to be an exclusive function of the intellect, and that intellect was distinct, indeed, it needed to be divorced, from passion.[37] The modern distinction between knowing what is right and then moving oneself by will to do it, what we have come to call having "motivation," participates in the same division of practical intellect from will and desire that Aquinas's understanding of the reciprocal dependency of prudence upon the moral virtues and the moral virtues upon prudence disallows.

Conversely, and as the many-sided view of action presented in this book implies, how persons act or fail to act expresses more than what motivates them subjectively toward some fixed set of objects in the world. What Westberg's analysis allows us to see is that the actions or omissions and refrainings of a person indicate that person's world — and this not first as known and subsequently as willed or chosen, but as containing certain desired ends and related chosen means.[38] As the unity of the moral virtues (prudence included) in Aquinas demonstrates, passion cannot but be involved both in vision and choice. Knowing the truth about our world depends on correctly desiring what is truly in it, since

> prudence, "unlike any other intellectual virtue, depends on right appetite, and therefore requires moral virtue which perfects the appe-

---

agulate into "deontological norms" (in effect, absolutes), enhancing the function of will separate from intellect as it moves the agent to act by what he knows through them. Given this bipartite structure, should one determine that the absolutes are false or undependable, what was given by intellect topples, and one is left only with will.

37. We receive Socrates through Plato, and Plato's Socrates changes as Plato himself changes. A very good case can be made that Plato changes precisely on this point, i.e., the relation between practical reasoning and passion or love. I know of no better treatment on this matter than Martha Nussbaum's *The Fragility of Goodness* (New York: Cambridge University Press, 1986), especially pp. 85-234. In this part of the book where she treats Plato, Nussbaum attends particularly to the changes in the Socrates of the *Protagoras* or the *Republic* who sets about in effect to save the moral life from the tragedians by *techne* to the Socrates of the *Phaedrus* who, according to Nussbaum, has come to see that passion is an essential ingredient in the good life. For an engagement with Nussbaum on this and other issues, see my and Stanley Hauerwas's "Friendship and Fragility," in *Christians among the Virtues* (Notre Dame, Ind.: University of Notre Dame Press, 1997), pp. 70-88.

38. See Westberg, p. 235.

tite." This sets up a sort of circle, of course, since prudence cannot be had without the moral virtues, nor they without prudence. Yet this is fitting. For Aquinas the operation of the practical intellect is moved by the appetite to action, and the appetite of the agent of action is guided all along by the practical intellect. The perfecting of the whole process by virtues involves right reason depending on the right disposition of the appetite, and right appetite depending on prudence.[39]

The relation of the practical intellect to will and appetite opens another key door for Aquinas, namely, his ultimate rooting of prudence in charity. Charity is a kind of friendship with God that transforms us completely, opening us to the realities that are, as Pieper maintains, not merely natural. Indeed, the "natural" is reoriented in the light of charity (nature is transformed by grace) such that our vision of "what is" is not merely the next larger view after natural prudence, but rather may appear in significant discontinuity to it. The discontinuity is in one sense only apparent, for prudence transformed by charity does not see a different world entirely than what is seen or "known" by natural prudence alone. The world that contains foxes or murders does not disappear, being replaced by a new set of objects under other names. Rather, the transformation of our minds and hearts in the love of God moves us further from the vision of these things, indeed all things, than one simple step. As Pieper comments,

> [T]he accord of the natural order with the new life of friendship with God must not be construed in the sense that it is immediately "given" or realizable in smooth and "harmonious" development. We do, to be sure, incline to think in terms of such harmonies from long habit. But the writings of the great friends of God make plain, on almost every page, that the actual life of the Christian is ruled by a different kind of structural law; that life on earth, which has "not yet" attained the peace of concord, the concrete combination of the natural and supernatural, is subjected to all sorts of liabilities to contradiction and disharmony.[40]

39. Westberg, pp. 218-19.
40. Pieper, p. 36.

The consequences of this discontinuity are striking. In the first place, it is plain that the in-breaking of charity into the moral life, the fruit of a friendship with God, may be quite unexpected and surprising. We cannot know in advance just what sorts of things about our known and lived world charity will require that we radically re-vision. Further, and relatedly, we cannot suppose that the descriptions of the world now open to the person in whom the virtue of charity has been infused (Aquinas holds that, as a theological virtue, charity is infused in us directly by God — we do not gain it by steady habit), and the judgments and actions this charity-transformed prudence yields, will be more like the descriptions carried proudly by the person of natural prudence than those used by the person who lacks it. In a word, the Christian cannot suppose that the naturally prudent, the morally sensible ones, will be her allies in describing and acting in the world. As Augustine draws out the contrast, he had more to learn from (and, perhaps later as a Christian, more in common with), the drunken beggar he meets along the way to deliver his speech in praise of the emperor than from the refined and educated audience that would applaud his lies.[41] As Pieper goes on to say, "It is not the 'sinners' but the 'prudent ones' who are more liable to close themselves off from the new life which has been given by grace, and to oppose it. Typically, natural prudence courts this danger by tending to restrict the realm of determinative factors of our actions to naturally experienceable realities. Christian prudence, however, means precisely the throwing open of this realm and (in faith informed by love) the inclusion of new and invisible realities within the determinants of our decisions."[42]

Similarities between Christian prudence and prudence based on another vision of the world may remain structurally or formally. For example, "prudent" people of all sorts can be expected to reason that, because we know the world to be so-and-so, so we should act or refrain from acting in such and such a way.[43] But materially, this similar-

41. *Confessions* 6.6.
42. Pieper, p. 37.
43. "Prudence" in this sentence is importantly placed in scare quotes since we do not hold that there are a variety of kinds of prudence. Rather, as Aquinas holds, there is one true prudence, and other traits of character that resemble prudence. Lee Yearley develops Aquinas's notion that the virtues have "semblances" of the virtues in his *Mencius and Aquinas,* particularly with reference to the virtue of courage. Prudence similarly can

ity may not go very far at all. And what happens materially is plainly determinative in matters relating to morality. For the Christian, what the world is, its reality, is inseparable from the story of the God who created and redeemed the world by the power of the Word become flesh in the first-century Jew called Jesus. Moreover, this (true) world is opened to us not just as we add in certain supernatural facts about it to what facts we already naturally know, but as we are transformed in our passions and actions by charity, faith, and hope to see it as it is.

---

have semblances. In the case of prudence, this especially shades in the direction of convention. As Yearley notes: "The person embracing virtue and the person embracing semblances of virtue, then, dispute not about means to an end they both pursue but about the components of the human good. . . . The outline and implication of such conflicts is developed well in Terence Irwin's analysis of Plato's account of how different is the mad love of the truly virtuous from the slavish love of the 'prudent.' Normal, prudent people consider the truly virtuous to be imprudent, even mad, because their idea of humanity's ultimate end differs so markedly from that of the virtuous" (*Mencius and Aquinas: Theories of Virtue and Conceptions of Courage* [Albany: State University of New York Press, 1990], p. 21). Since charity transforms us with respect to the end, so a prudence transformed by charity cannot but differ from the conventional "prudence" to which Yearley, following Irwin, here refers.

# 8. Theology, Narrative, and Social Criticism

## 1. Bentham's Sympathies and Antipathies

Reading through Jeremy Bentham's *Introduction to the Principles of Morals and Legislation,* particularly chapter 2, "Of Principles Adverse to That of Utility," elicits feelings of high exhilaration simultaneously with deep dismay. Earlier we spoke metaphorically of the buzz-sawing moral theorists; in Bentham's case the metaphor is replaced with a vision of a great and finely tuned machine moving through the forest of our moral notions with amazing power and rapidity, a veritable moving sawmill, rooting up trees by the dozens and sending them flying through its spinning blades. In short order lumber emerges at its rear end, dropped neatly on the bare landscape in the form of the most useful and uniform boards, all of equal size and shape.

Arguably Bentham had even more to do than his well-known contemporary, Immanuel Kant, with the formation of our current moral landscape, or, perhaps better, with the way that landscape is typically perceived by professional ethicists. The temperament and concerns the two thinkers brought to this moral world were widely divergent: while Kant was a true philosopher interested in grounding the principles of morality in reason, Bentham is best understood as a reformer who most wanted to effect a change in what was said and done in British politics. It was this reformist instinct that led him to attack so vigorously what he called the "principle of sympathy and antipathy," by which he meant "that principle which approves or disapproves of certain actions, not on account of their tending to augment the happiness, nor yet on account of their tending to diminish the happiness of the party whose interest is in question, but merely because a man finds himself disposed to approve or disapprove of them: holding up that approbation or disapprobation as a sufficient reason for itself, and disclaiming the necessity of looking out for any extrinsic ground."[1]

In contrast to his Prussian contemporary, Bentham's moral arguments in themselves are neither particularly interesting nor subtle. In this second chapter, where Bentham seems to want to provide something of a theoretical grounding for the principle of utility, he argues merely by reduction, gathering all imaginable views that resist the principle of utility under this principle of sympathy and antipathy. Bentham's key accusation, just quoted, is that the principle lacks "extrinsic ground." Yet he quickly notes that the principle of sympathy and antipathy in fact "is not a positive principle of itself, so much as a term employed to signify the negation of all principles. [For] what one expects to find in a principle is something that points out some external consideration, as a means of warranting and guiding the internal sentiments of approbation and disapprobation."[2] Since all other "principles" Bentham can imagine that oppose utility either collapse into the principle of sympathy, as does the "theological principle," or amount to a direct opposition to the principle of utility (i.e., the ascetic principle, which is nothing more than the view that pleasure is everywhere and always bad), then there is simply no other way to appeal to extrinsic ground than through the principle of utility. In effect, Bentham's argument against other moral principles adverse to that of utility is no argument at all but simply an assertion that the principle of utility is the only imaginable legitimate principle.

1. Jeremy Bentham, *An Introduction to the Principles of Morals and Legislation* (Oxford: Clarendon, 1996), p. 25.

2. Bentham, p. 25. Bentham is in an interesting way correct about this. As I have been arguing in this book, one cannot have the sort of principle Bentham wants and also have the great variety of moral nuance and particularity that is present in our inherited moral notions. The starkness with which Bentham presents his moral reformation is actually very helpful, and accounts for the exhilaration one feels in reading him.

Yet we must not allow this lack of subtlety and argument to blind us to the great challenge Bentham presents. Understood as a political reformer and not as a philosopher, he can be taken to be saying: the great difficulty with all other grounds for morality or law that are routinely presented is that they are inherently politically conservative. By extension we can suppose that the arguments in preceding chapters of this book which defend the subtlety and irreducible variety of moral notions and action descriptions would be regarded by Bentham as little more than an attempt to preserve the moral status quo. We inherit moral notions and practices from the past, not only in the form of a particular moral term or action description, but in the web of beliefs and practices that give actions sense and context. For instance, "adultery" assumes a larger set of notions or ideas about bodily intimacy, the institution of monogamous marriage, and so on. Preserved, these will mutually reinforce and justify one another, providing a kind of moral edifice that resists radical moral rethinking of the sort Bentham hopes for. Against such a preservation of moral convention and assumption, Bentham presses for reform, and this is exactly why he goes to the principle of utility and uses it as a kind of moral fighting machine, capable of felling so many conventional notions at once.

In a footnote Bentham demonstrates an awareness of how support is given or withdrawn from certain practices by the way in which a people regard the practices. He seizes on a particularly fascinating example: the euthanasia (or exposure) of young children.

> It is upon the principle of antipathy that such and such acts are often reprobated on the score of their being unnatural: the practice of exposing children, established among the Greeks and Romans, was an unnatural practice. But here . . . ["unnatural"] means nothing; nothing, I mean which there is in the act itself. All it serves to express is the disposition of the person who is talking of it: the disposition he is in to be angry of the thoughts of it. Does it merit his anger? Very likely it may: but whether it does or no is a question, which, to be answered rightly, can only be answered upon the principle of utility. . . .
>
> The mischief common to all these ways of thinking and arguing (which, in truth, as we have seen, are but one and the same

method, couched in different forms of words) is their serving as a cloak, and pretense, and aliment, to despotism.[3]

Bentham suggests that while the Greek and Roman practice of exposure of children was rightly criticized, criticism rooted in some social group's perception of what is "natural" is invariably inadequate since it merely expresses conventional sentiments. Something more substantial (namely, of course, the principle of utility) was needed if the shared conceptions that underwrote exposure were to be overturned.

Bentham's reformist concern is detectable as well in other views discussed in this book, for example, in Joseph Fletcher's "new morality" or the proportionalists' evident dissatisfaction with a perceived Catholic traditionalism. As Bernard Haring confesses, all John Paul II's words in *Veritatis Splendor,* seem "directed above all towards one goal: to endorse total assent and submission to all utterances of the Pope, and above all on one crucial point: that the use of any artificial means for regulating birth is intrinsically evil and sinful."[4] Indeed, for his part Haring seems less concerned with the actual arguments the pope gives than with what he perceives as the outcome in terms of practice, namely, the ongoing opposition by the pope to the use of artificial birth control. As Bentham might put it, the encyclical in all its assertions and arguments amounts to a "mischief" that serves "as a cloak, and pretense, and aliment, to despotism."

I have suggested that in a variety of ways Fletcher, Haring, and now Bentham radically misperceive human actions. Consequently, however genuine their zeal for moral reform, it will become snarled and ineffectual when it comes to describing and making judgments about particular human actions. (In the above quotation from Bentham, this blindness is helpfully illustrated by how he employs the phrase "in the act itself.") Yet despite the evident weakness of his arguments and his failure to understand human action, if we are to learn from Bentham's admirable concern for moral reform, we will need to ask whether a morality rooted in such a complex web of notions and descriptions is anything other than a conservatory of conventional-

---

3. Bentham, pp. 27-28.

4. Bernard Haring, "A Distrust That Wounds," in *Considering "Veritatis Splendor,"* ed. John Wilkins (Cleveland: Pilgrim, 1994), p. 9.

ism, a perpetuation of the moral and political status quo. Why is it not one more form of oppression, authoritarianism, or despotism, made all the more frightening by its ubiquity in every little description we apply, every little thing we do?

It is to be noted that if what has been argued in this book about actions and moral descriptions is even partly correct, then the issue that opens to us here is not just whether the position outlined is inherently conservative but whether moral criticism is possible at all. Reformers like Bentham, Haring, and Fletcher have come upon moral practices they believe to be oppressive, and so have set about to reform them. Yet we have held that their reforms fail because of their endemic blindness to how moral actions and practices are rooted in our lives and language. This leads, then, to a question of what otherwise they might have done or argued to effect moral reform — or, for that matter, whether there are any other options at all. Whatever one makes of the particular moral views these men held, surely they were correct to hold that some moral practices intricately woven into the fabric of a people's form of life have been oppressive and desperately in need of reform. If one holds, in other words, to the truth that (sometimes) there is pressing need for moral reform at the same time one grants that this reform cannot come in the way Fletcher or Bentham might have hoped, then something else needs to be suggested about how it might be brought about. Otherwise we seem consigned to a moral world that is tied to the history it carries in its moral descriptions, including those descriptions that oppress those formed by them.

To begin to offer a response to this challenge, it is important to put the point concretely. The reform called for is of a common practice, or set of practices, well rooted in a particular way of life or society as to be immediately and as a matter of course intelligible to its people. "Reform" in this sense does not float free; before we can imagine it, we shall need some specification of a moral practice that might be rethought, changed, or abandoned. Taking Bentham's cue, consider the ancient practice of exposing babies. Calling this a "practice" means at least that it holds a commonly acknowledged place in the human world. For exposure, we might imagine a man walking through the hills surrounding Rome in the second century of the common era who comes upon the body of a dead human infant. What would he think? Clearly, he would presume that the infant had been exposed. By contrast, were a man walking on the same path near Rome today and also came upon a dead human infant, he would have no such ready framework of understanding and interpretation — which simply points out that exposure once was but is now no longer a practice.[5]

A full historical inquiry might be pursued to discover how this change in practice came about — one beyond the scope of this book.[6] Yet clearly this inquiry would focus on one quite specific historical point. This is that there arose in this time within the Roman Empire a new community that refused to engage in the practice of exposure; indeed, the community roundly criticized the standard practice of exposure, redescribing it as murder. The community was able to do this not because it had hold of some radically new moral idea such as the principle of utility, but rather because its members had been trained in a set of practices and a language rooted outside the dominant Roman world. These, of course, were the Christians.

## 2. And God Called Abram

*Now the LORD said to Abram, "Go forth from your country and your kindred and your father's house to the land that I will show you. I will make*

---

5. I do not mean to define "practice" in any precise way. Rather, I mean simply to propose a quick test that indicates when there is no doubt that a certain practice is firmly in place, namely, that we routinely describe human actions or situations in relation to it. This broadens the notion of "practice" as MacIntyre has used the notion, and makes clearer that the "virtues" related to it (i.e., those needed to sustain it) may be evil. (See the discussion of what is or is not a practice in Alasdair MacIntyre's *After Virtue*, 2nd ed. [Notre Dame, Ind.: University of Notre Dame Press, 1984], p. 273.) Slavery, for instance, was a practice, as we can mark by the fact that were a black man seen working in the field in the American south in the 1840s, he would be assumed to be a slave. As a practice, slavery requires certain human attitudes, capacities, and "virtues" if it is to be sustained. We can judge these as evil insofar as the descriptions that relate to and sustain the practice are false.

6. For an account that expands this point, see Darrel W. Amundsen, "Medicine and the Birth of Defective Children: Approaches of the Ancient World," in *On Moral Medicine: Theological Perspectives in Medical Ethics,* ed. Stephen Lammers and Alan Verhey, 2nd ed. (Grand Rapids: Eerdmans, 1998), pp. 681-92.

*of you a great nation, and I will bless you, and make your name great, so that you will be a blessing. And I will bless those who bless you, and the one who curses you I will curse; and in you all the families of the earth shall be blessed." So Abram went, as the* LORD *had told him; and Lot went with him. (Gen. 12:1-4)*

This is the beginning of the story of God in the human world. It is also the beginning of social and moral criticism.

God was not absent from the human world before calling Abram. There were, we can safely say, many times before Abram's call in which God spoke through and acted among God's human creatures, perhaps even in social criticism. Yet we know of this, can speak of it, only because of the beginning in Abram. In that beginning God picks one person from among many, Abram, and begins a work that will create a people who carry a story by which the stories of all peoples (even their own[7]) can be criticized.

Precisely what is meant here by social criticism and how it relates to Abram's calling will become clearer as we follow Abram along in the text from Genesis. To begin, we must attend closely to the conditions that apply as the call of Abram is extended into the human world. First, Abram is told to "go forth from . . . [his] father's house." There is a great deal of significance in this, for it is in our fathers' houses that we learn to speak, and so to describe the world we inhabit. While it is true that we acquire it as babies on our parents' or (in Augustine's case) our nurses' laps, the language we learn in our first house does not come to us quite as Augustine imagines — our elders pointing to particular objects and emitting certain sounds, which we, their children, imitate. For the sounds we learn to emit cannot for us refer to, point to, "objects" unless those objects have a meaningful place in a set of practices into which we simultaneously are being

7. I teach a course that introduces modern students to the Bible, many of whom have had little or no exposure to it. Virtually to a person, these new students of the Bible marvel at the constant refrain of the unfaithfulness of the Jewish people. "Why don't these people ever get it?" they say. But what must be said in reply, of course, is that this is a story told by Jews. This, I believe, is a key feature of being God's chosen people, namely, to be a people who carry and are carried by a story that is critical of this very same people. (Nietzsche has great disdain for the Jews exactly on this point. See *The Anti-Christ* [New York: Penguin Books, 1968], ##25-26.)

formed. A parent as a teacher of language does not mediate between the infant and the world as if pointing with a finger to a star for the infant to follow with her eyes. Rather, a parent gives an infant a world by sharing it.[8]

Any human world in this sense is a human gift, both in that it is given by human beings one to the other and in that it is itself a kind of bestowal of the human upon the human infant. Following Aquinas's equivalence, in virtue of its humanness the gift is also moral. For, quite simply, the human world we receive as we learn to speak and act is our moral world. In our father's house we learn to be within a "moral we." We are taken up into a people that sees and acts in the world in a characteristic way, and we come to share this.

A man like all other men, Abram (we can assume) lived within the moral world passed to him in his father's house. But on God's command he leaves this world, and a new possibility opens for him, and ultimately for us: the possibility of social criticism. Yet we cannot say that leaving in itself accomplishes this possibility. In our own time, in civilizations like America, men and women leave their fathers' or mothers' houses as a matter of course. The house, however, such as it is, travels with them on their back, like a tent that can be pitched in a five-bedroom, four-bath Colonial just outside the Beltway or in a six-bedroom rambling ranch house between Dallas and Fort

---

8. I refer to Augustine's discussion of the acquisition of language in the household in *Confessions* 1.8. The passage is the focus of Ludwig Wittgenstein's discussion in the *Philosophical Investigations* (New York: Macmillan, 1968), pp. 2-3. Wittgenstein improves on Augustine's view of language; however, what is perhaps clearer in Augustine is that this acquisition of language in the household is the beginning of what Augustine calls the "torrent of established custom" (*Confessions* 1.16). Once words are passed on in this form, the direction of subsequent training in descriptions is set: a particular human being comes to inhabit a particular culture. As Augustine concludes the section, "thus I learnt to convey what I meant to those about me: and so took another step along the stormy way of human life in society, while I was still subject to the authority of my parents and at the beck and call of my elders" (1.8). This might be the young Abram in his father's house — which of course he leaves. (Wittgenstein himself may very well understand the force of Augustine's discussion, despite its mistakes about language, concerning acquisition of a customary view of the world in the acquisition of language in the nursery — for it is the first matter he takes up in the *Investigations*. In a sense, everything follows for Wittgenstein from the fact that with the acquisition of language we are passed a set of descriptions about the world.)

Worth. These men of today, as with those others in the biblical story, sometimes have deeply felt motivation to leave; they run from their fathers' houses frightened or in a rage, or perhaps they are driven off, like the biblical Cain, cursed to become a "restless wanderer on the earth."

Abram's leaving suggests none of these dramatic elements. The text tells us nothing about the dark conditions of Abram's father Terah's household; nothing is intimated about abuse or jealousy or even disagreement. Rather, what is distinctive about Abram's leaving is simply that he was called by God. To be sure, Abram seems to have been the sort of man who was prepared to hear, which is why we speak of him as a person of great faith. Yet, nothing in the biblical account makes us believe there was anything so special about Abram that forced God's hand. That is, we have no reason to believe that someone else couldn't have been called. But God called Abram.

Yet the calling added to the leaving is insufficient to establish the beginning of social criticism. As the story goes, after a variety of adventures out on his own with Sarai, Abram becomes concerned, like any man would, about the continuance of his household: "'O LORD God, what will you give me for I continue childless, and the heir of my house is Eliezer of Damascus?' And Abram said, 'You have given me no offspring, and so a slave born in my house is to be my heir'" (Gen. 15:2-3). Abram is complaining — and wouldn't we all? But of course, his complaint is rooted in the only moral world he knows: that learned in his father's house. Accordingly, like his fathers before him, for Abram the descriptions "slave" and "heir" cannot match.

God does not respond by pointing this out. This will come much later in the story that begins with Abram but continues on. For instance, one day the apostle Paul will be able to say to Philemon about his slave Onesimus: "Perhaps this is the reason he was separated from you for a while, so that you might have him back forever, no longer as a slave but more than a slave, a beloved brother — especially to me but how much more to you, both in the flesh and in the Lord" (Philem. 15-16).[9] Instead, after quickly reassuring Abram by saying

___

9. The reader may note a structural connection to Augustine's *City of God*. Typically when we treat that massive work, we move quickly to book 19, where the theoretical work is most concentrated. Plainly book 19 is a capstone. However, Augustine is deeply

"this man shall not be your heir," God invites him outside, a point made all the more intriguing since the text has not previously indicated an inside. Abram's earlier remarks, his worries about heirs, fit best within the house he left, namely, his father's.

In a way God's invitation to Abram to step outside simply repeats the previous calling — but now we can see more clearly that the leaving in chapter 12 involves more for Abram than simply walking out the door, saddling the camels, and striking out on his own. Once outside, God does three things to Abram. First, God directs Abram's gaze to the heavens. Count the stars, Abram; "so shall your descendants be." Second, God gives Abram a bit of work: he needs to ritually prepare for the covenant that is struck at the end of the day. For this he must procure a three-year-old heifer, a three-year-old female goat, and so on. Third, after the work, and as the sun goes down, God causes Abram to fall into a "deep and terrifying darkness" and tells him for the first time — indeed, the only time — that "your offspring shall be aliens in a land that is not theirs, and shall be slaves there, and they shall be oppressed for four hundred years" (Gen. 15:13).

It is important to note that God had already addressed Abram's worries about Eliezer *before* he invited him outside, so we have room to interpret what is now said outside in a different light. Abram's complaint about having no biological heir makes sense inside the house of Abram's father. Once outside, however, the concerns change. The stargazing the two do signals something new; indeed, the immensity of the heavens supports the new vision God directs Abram toward. Uttered in this context, the promise for what is to come is not about Eliezer or even the soon-to-be-born Ishmael and Isaac, but about descendants so far-flung it is hard to imagine why Abram son of

---

concerned with the full narration of the heavenly city in the biblical narrative. This has at least two important functions. First, it embeds the heavenly city in human history. Or, better put, it establishes an alternative human history told by those who belong to the heavenly city that is tangled within human life as intricately as is the human history, or story, told by those of the earthly city. Second, it requires that Augustine and other Christians continue to reread and retell this narrative. This is an ongoing task, and the retellings, we can assume, will continue to bear new fruit. Paul's retelling of the story of Abraham in Gal. 4 plainly brings something new to the old text, and as such redirects it. (In our own case, the connection between Paul's remarks to Philemon and Gen. 15:4 functions in the same way.)

Terah should care about them. Perhaps God means to direct Abram's eyes beyond the immediate concern about who in the next generation will be his heir.

Yet, as he gazes at the stars, Abram's attention is not directed to his great-grandchildren, so many times times removed. Rather, what is contemplated is a new future that is both connected to the present Abram just now inhabits but also transforms it. The oft-quoted phrase in the next verse, that Abram "believed the Lord; and the Lord reckoned it to him as righteousness" (15:6), refers not so much to Abram believing that God would grant him a son. That point had already been made and, we can assume, believed inside the house. What Abram believed here under the stars is that the God who stood next to him had intentions for the human world which God would someday bring to pass, and that the glorious future briefly glimpsed had intrinsic connection to what was going on right now between God and Abram. At this moment *the biblical world becomes eschatological*, and so it remains throughout.

Eschatology, as John Yoder repeatedly stressed, has everything to do with social criticism. In fact, according to Yoder, it is only in an eschatological framework that genuine critique of a particular historical situation is possible. "We must admit that only a clearly eschatological viewpoint permits a valid critique of the present historical situation and the choice of action which can be effective. Noneschatological analysis of history is unprotected against the dangers of subjectivism and opportunism, and finishes by letting the sinful present situation be its own norm. History, from Abraham to Marx, demonstrates that significant action, for good or for evil, is accomplished by those whose present action is illuminated by an eschatological hope."[10] Those with an eschatological vision have lifted up their eyes; the furniture of their world is no longer limited to what filled their fathers' houses. Theirs is a revolutionary view — and social criticism without the possibility of revolution is, in the sense we have been using it, not social criticism at all but merely extends and further defends the present regime.

In this context Jacques Ellul has noted how so many modern "revolutions" are misnamed. In his view, what grips our own age is an un-

---

10. John Yoder, *The Original Revolution* (Scottdale, Pa.: Herald, 1977), p. 71.

questioned acquiescence to the power of the "facts." Facts in Ellul's sense are necessarily generated by this world as we know it. Change in this world is therefore limited to this world — which, for Ellul, is no real change at all.[11] So Ellul holds that Marx, the quintessential "revolutionary," is actually an antirevolutionary.

> Marx, who explains that inevitably, by the evolution of facts (including the simple fact of man), by the play of dialectical materialism, socialist society will emerge from capitalist society, is antirevolutionary. Socialism, in becoming scientific — that is to say, in submitting to fact, and in following the development of facts — has become anti-revolutionary.
>
> . . . For ever since society came into existence, the revolutionary spirit, which is a necessary part of social life, has always been the affirmation of a spiritual truth against the error of the moment: a truth which is called to incarnate itself in society, not in any automatic, mechanical way, but by the desperate, sacrificial effort of man.[12]

Ellul's reference to the notion that Marx's imagined political reform is actually antirevolutionary casts light back on the previous discussion of Bentham. Despite Bentham's admirable concern for reform, it is plain enough in retrospect that he did little more than restate the assumptions of his age. In restating them, and so clearly, he actually strengthened them, making the ascendancy of Ellul's facts complete. Utilitarianism places such "values" as efficiency and organization in full control. In contrast to Marx's or Bentham's antirevolutionary, fact-saturated, this-worldly visions, Ellul insists that the Christian "is a

---

11. This point relates to comments made regarding prudence in the previous chapter. The visions of this world yield a prudence of this world — one that sees what is only in terms of what otherwise is — and so it is "the 'prudent ones' who are most liable to close themselves off from the new life given by grace." See Josef Pieper, *The Four Cardinal Virtues* (Notre Dame, Ind.: University of Notre Dame Press, 1966), p. 37. The continuing story of Abraham illustrates this well. Once he has received his new name and his faith has had time to grow, at the command of God Abraham ends up going off to offer his only son Isaac on the altar at Mount Moriah — hardly a prudent move as Pieper's "prudent ones" would see it.

12. Jacques Ellul, *The Presence of the Kingdom,* 2nd ed., trans. Olive Wyon (Colorado Springs: Helmers & Howard, 1989), p. 29.

man of the future, not of a temporal and logical future, but of the *eschaton*, of the coming break with this present world. Thus he looks forward to this moment, and for him all facts acquire their value in the light of the coming Kingdom of God, in the light of the Judgment, and the victory of God."[13] This is precisely the position that God puts Abram in as he directs his gaze to the stars; he must learn now to see the present, including present problems about matters such as who will be his heir, in the light of the coming kingdom, which even now, in the exchange between God and Abram, is beginning to appear.

The heavenward gaze, however, means little if it is not turned back to the earth. So Abram is directed by God to a second set of actions, those specifically involving the ritual work of ratifying the covenant. This work is reoriented by the eschatological vision just mentioned. As well, it is bracketed on the other side by the third set of actions or occurrences chronicled in Genesis 15:13-16, which also reorient and deepen Abram's work with the covenant rituals: namely, Abram's descent by dream into a terrifying darkness.

Turning first to the dream, we can see that what God tells Abram in it is not all bad news. The dream ends with the good news that the oppressors of Abram's descendants will receive their recompense, that Abram himself will die a peaceful death in old age and find rest, and so on. Yet the "terrifying darkness" into which Abram falls to receive news of the future is clearly linked with the dark forecast that begins the dream: "that your offspring shall be aliens in a land that is not theirs, and shall be slaves there, and they shall be oppressed for four hundred years" (15:13). What is striking here is that just as the covenant of the Hebrew people with God is to be struck, the text sends a clear signal that being the covenanted people of God will not be all triumph; indeed, it will be laced through with terrible sufferings. This is one of the rare points in Genesis where Exodus intrudes, but as such it functions all the more significantly; namely, it destabilizes any reading of Genesis as a set of triumphalist etiologies or "origin stories" that the Israelites can carry forward to bolster their power, as might any people.

The intrusion of the prediction of coming suffering for Abram's descendants functions much like the passion predictions in the center section of the Gospel of Mark. There Christ's passion intrudes into the

13. Ellul, p. 37.

breathless story of Messiah's arrival, subverting it. Mark the Evangelist plainly meant to head off interpreters prone to greet the Christ in the conventional mode they had learned in their fathers' houses, namely, that Messiah would come and by force oust the Roman oppressors. Similarly, the expectations of Abram, stitched into his mind in the patterns of inherited descriptions of a successful life, are reoriented in his sleep. The terrifying dream introduces Abram (and us) to a new and surprising notion: the hope of the promise actually includes deep suffering. Were he awake, we could imagine his response: What sort of promise is this if it involves such darkness and suffering? My father would have called such a promise a "threat." To which God might have responded: You are no longer in your father's house. Here, under the stars (the text gives no indication that Abram has gone back inside for this little nap), you are in my house. And in my house you and your descendants must come to learn a whole new set of descriptions.[14]

In this context we can return fruitfully to the second set of items on God's agenda in the series of three in Genesis 15: Abram's ritual preparations with heifers, goats, and the like. What Abram must do is partake in the ratification of the covenant itself by laying out some dead birds, chopping up some animals, etc. At the end of the chapter God passes through these creatures in a fiery form when the text tells us that "the Lord made a covenant with Abram" (Gen. 15:18). The acts commanded are thoroughly saturated with ancient ritual. There

---

14. The moral work done by terms such as "threat" and "promise" is particularly interesting given that "promise keeping" has been so central a focus in recent moral philosophy. It has been frequently noted, for instance, that we are bound to keep a promise but not a threat. Yet this opens the question of what is a threat and what is a promise, and consequently the question of what is for the good of a particular person who might have been promised or threatened. Christians and Jews need not hold that God *causes* their suffering to nonetheless deviate significantly from the growing opinion in Western culture that suffering is always only bad, and therefore can never be included in a promise. Here in this text, God's promise to Abraham and his descendants includes that they will suffer. The inclusion of suffering with blessing, and the fact that the promise comes from God, therefore keeps Abraham's descendants from automatically redescribing a promise of suffering as a threat. (Note that there is no explanation in the biblical text of this suffering that links it to the disobedience of the children of Abraham.) For the people who carry such a promise, it cannot but force a continual reexamination of what suffering means. Historically, of course, this people becomes capable of describing and bearing suffering in a way the world has never otherwise seen.

arc specifications regarding what animals to bring (15:9), and descriptions of which to cut in half (15:10) as well as of Abram afterwards standing guard over the whole bloody mess, shooing the scavenging birds away (15:11) — details sure to bring a reader up short were he in search of a pious nugget or even an eternal theological truth.

Asking about these ritual details — why, for instance, Abram is told to bring three animals that are three years old, why he is to select from among the birds a pigeon and a turtledove — is, I suggest, both exactly the wrong and also exactly the right way to treat the text. It is the wrong way if the question sends us looking for ancient cultic rituals that might match the practices of Abram. Speculation of this sort has a way of turning study of the biblical text into a kind of pseudoscientific probabilism: "Maybe *that* was the reason the ancient Near Eastern, nomadic Abram cut his cows but not his pigeons. Or, on the other hand, maybe it was *this*."[15] In another sense, however, it is

15. This comment and the preceding discussion of the texts from Genesis, which proceeds without the aid of modern scripture scholarship, may appear dismissive of "scripture scholarship" per se. However, as subsequent comments in the text indicate, a detailed investigation of, say, ancient cultic practices surrounding the sacrifice of animals is invaluable if the practice of Bible reading in the church is yet to challenge our contemporary "moral" descriptions. As opposed to explaining a puzzling ancient text in contemporary terms, a crucial task of the scripture scholar is rather to suggest to us how puzzling practices or action descriptions in the text are rightly contextualized in terms of another world of practices and actions than those with which we are familiar.

Scripture scholars sometimes fulfill the latter function while seemingly attempting the former. For instance, Claus Westermann comments on the text before us that "the two doves are not divided, i.e., they cannot have been an original part of the ritual of the cutting of the animals. This is a certain demonstration that the list in v. 9 has been subsequently filled out by naming all sacrificial animals in the sacrificial laws." *Genesis 12-36: A Continental Commentary*, trans. John J. Scullion, S. J. (Minneapolis: Fortress Press, 1995), p. 225. Here Westermann "explains" the text by referring us to how it was redacted in relation to subsequent Hebrew laws of sacrifice. This is the sort of explanation I believe we neither can have nor need. Contrary to Westermann's confident "certain demonstration," we simply cannot know precisely why Abram — or why *the text says* Abram (two frequently distinguished matters that I have been careful not to distinguish) — split his cows but not his pigeons. However, if we take Westermann's comments less as an assertion about the earlier forms of this text and more as a reminder that biblical texts, here and elsewhere, bring to us a complicated world of sacrificial practice that needs to be investigated in order for the texts to be understood, then we will not be able to appropriate this about Abram, or other texts in which the sacrificial practices are central, as if they are not strange (and challenging) to our contemporary practices and descriptions.

exactly the right question if we allow it to open us in this time to another time — not speculatively, but as something that might now be a genuine option for us — so that the other time might now enter our own. Here, as elsewhere, God is in the details. A theologian interested in "universal" or "fundamental" ideas might come to such a text as Genesis 15 with the attitude that the really important thing is that God and Abram struck a covenant and honored its terms, and so ought we. What this forgets, however, is that the text emerges from an ancient cultic world that confronts our own. It is strange in its details, but this strangeness is crucial in our reading it as God's word. For what comes to a world as strange is also what originates in a place beyond that world, and therefore has the power to challenge it essentially.

Ellul maintains that a characteristic of our technical and consumerist world is its conservatism: despite constant talk of "revolutionary" this or "deep cultural shift" that, in fact genuine revolution has become nearly impossible since everything is judged in terms of the technical facts of our times, measured in terms of efficiency or of progress, and thus shielded from any genuine spiritual change.[16] As he holds, spiritual revolutions, the only genuine revolutions, have their origin outside this enclosed world, presenting themselves to the human spirit as all-inspiring and all-encompassing, worthy of the greatest sacrifice. The root of such a revolution of spirit might be thought to be an idea, yet ideas come cheap, particularly in the modern world. Better understood, revolutions of spirit come with what Ellul calls a distinctive style of life built in relation to an allegiance to another country, for Christians the kingdom or reign of God. For

16. As Ellul's discussion of revolutions points out, worlds such as our own Western world become factories of themselves: they produce progeny that differ in detail but not in genuine substance from their parents, giving the illusion of change when everything in fact remains the same. "Now, in spite of the conviction that our epoch is revolutionary, that people are revolutionary, we are forced to assert that beneath all its apparent movement, and apparent development, we are not moving at all. . . . In point of fact there are a certain number of values and forces which are of decisive importance in our world civilization: the primacy of production, the continual growth of the power of the State and the formation of the national State, the autonomous development of technics, etc. These, among others far more than the ownership of the means of production, or any totalitarian doctrine — are the constitutive elements of the modern world. So long as these elements continue to be taken for granted, the world is standing still" (Ellul, p. 24).

214

Christians the reign of God is not yet upon us; it is in the future, but also already among us in Christ. This means it is possible for us to live in it now, which we do by pointing in our lives and action to the kingdom that is yet to come.

All actions point beyond themselves, but none so clearly as ritual or cultic actions. Moreover, they have the power to bring the strange, the other, into our midst. This pointing beyond as well as the transportation of the strange into our midst rightly provoke questions such as "Why did Abram cut his cows but not his pigeons?" Moreover, in ongoing cultic practice and the repeated questions concerning the significance of the practice, a moral world, a peculiar human world, can survive amidst and within another human world of a different order.

Another biblical reference to the cultic illustrates how such an alternative world might be preserved. Here the question of why we do it this way is at the center of the text.

> Then Moses called all the elders of Israel and said to them, "Go, select lambs for your families, and slaughter the Passover lamb. Take a bunch of hyssop, dip it into the blood that is in the basin. None of you shall go outside the door of your house until morning. For the LORD will pass through to strike down the Egyptians; when he sees the blood on the lintel and on the two doorposts, the LORD will pass over that door and will not allow the destroyer to enter your houses to strike you down. You shall observe this rite as a perpetual ordinance for you and your children. When you come to the land that the LORD will give you, as he has promised, you shall keep this observance. And when your children ask you, 'What do you mean by this observance?' you shall say, 'It is the Passover sacrifice to the LORD, for he passed over the houses of the Israelites in Egypt, when he struck down the Egyptians but spared our houses.'" And the people bowed down and worshiped. (Exod. 12:21-27)

The ritual practice of splitting cows did not continue, and its "why's" are lost to us. Yet it is precisely by standing in continuity with the man or the people who once engaged in these rituals that it becomes possible that a particular people can arise, as did Abraham and his children, from among the nations, and not only arise but also remain distinct from them. The roots of the ritual action that give it sense and meaning are not unlike what we have suggested roots all human action: namely, the narrative in which it fits.[17] So the correct answer to the child's question "What do you mean by this observance?" is a recounting of the story. The ritual in this sense calls forth the story and the explanation, offered from one generation to the next. The memory of the action of Moses or of Abram is carried on within a people who come to understand human life in relation to the ritual acts, and to the story they retell.

One wonders if the covenant rituals of Genesis 15 are left behind because they were more akin to the rituals of Abram's father's house. Abram, after all, was surely a man trained in rituals of some sort, and as God breaks in with something new for this man and his descendants, God may also need to confirm what is new by means that are old. Intriguingly, when the giving of the covenant is replayed two chapters later, the animal division ritual gives way to circumcision (17:9-14), which remains. By it the covenant is carried forth in a way that indelibly marks men in their own bodies rather than in the bodies of their animals. And, as with the Passover, this ritual celebration and mark is later the basis of key moral and theological disputes both within Judaism and between Judaism and the emerging Christianity of Saint Paul. Importantly, while essential to these two faiths, the debate about the significance of the ritual of circumcision remains for those outside them very strange indeed. But Jews and Christians on their own account are called out by God to be quite peculiar people. And, as we have been arguing, it is the extension of this peculiarity through time, in the manner of Augustine's heavenly city that lives within the earthly city but also looks eschatologically beyond, that the possibility of genuine moral and social criticism hinges.

17. This suggests that all human action is in one sense ritualistic. For any human action loses meaning when the set of practices and the way of life and belief that upholds the practices disappear. Absent this way of life, the "why" cannot be accessed, and, as noted earlier, without the "why" we lose also the "what." That said, however, it continues to make good sense to reserve room for a distinction. A ritual action's "usefulness" relates to and almost entirely depends upon the cult and the beliefs that sustain it. Hence, it is very difficult to fit ritual actions within a new frame of reference, and therefore we are quicker to see them as something of the past — an artifact that has lost its meaning. We assume people once had reason to engage in a specific ritual action, but without full knowledge of their cult, we cannot now tell what that reason was.

## 3. Theology and Narrative

At the end of his brief treatment of human action in *After Virtue* (which we rehearsed earlier), Alasdair MacIntyre moves directly to a discussion of narrative. He is clear about why he is drawn in this direction.

> [Earlier] I argued that in successfully identifying and understanding what someone else is doing we always move towards placing a particular episode in the context of a set of narrative histories, histories both of the individuals concerned and of the settings in which they act and suffer. It is now becoming clear that we render the actions of others intelligible in this way because action itself has a basically historical character. It is because we all live out narratives in our lives and because we understand our own lives in terms of the narratives we live out that the form of narrative is appropriate for understanding the actions of others. Stories are lived before they are told.[18]

This drift in MacIntyre's discussion informs our own. Stories, not just told but lived, place any action in its rightful context, which includes its complex relation to circumstance and character. Or, put another way, the moral concern that is rooted in the very nature of human action has nowhere to go with a description of a human action, for instance, that "Sue sat on Sam," unless that action is related by narrative to who Sam and Sue are, and what circumstances contextualize this particular. The same thing can be said of the omissions discussed in the previous chapter, such as, for example, that "Sam did not attend the meeting." Actions and omissions are perfectly united in their relation to narrative.[19]

---

18. MacIntyre, p. 197.

19. We are able at this juncture to review in quick form the debate swirling around *Veritatis Splendor (VS)*, confirming why, despite appearances, and notwithstanding the cumbersome use of terms such as "intrinsically evil acts," the pope has a much clearer grasp of human action than his Catholic critics. In relation to the need for narrative mentioned in the text, it is plain that of the action "Sue sat on Sam," nothing can be said about its being good or bad (or right or wrong) of Sue to do until we hear something further from the narrative of Sue, Sam, and this particular sitting. If, however, the action is changed to "Sue murdered Sam," we do not need to turn to the narrative to make the

Borrowing from Paul Ricoeur, Gerard Loughlin uses the term "emplotment" to refer to this coalescence of action and narrative, showing how the latter draws the former further along in meaning. "[E]mplotment synthesises character, action and circumstance. It emplots together different sorts of incident and event, in particular the intentional with the accidental. Narrative relates both natural occurrences and human actions, as well as their consequences, both intended and unintended."[20] As Loughlin rightly sees, the "intentional," which relates to human actions and omissions, must be positioned in

---

judgment that it was evil, even though we will need to do so to reach more subtle judgments about just how evil it is or, as Aquinas would have it, what is its type and degree of sin. It is in this sense that we can say that "murder" is intrinsically evil. Namely, murder is an intrinsically evil act because we do not need further situational details (a fuller narrative) about a particular murder to know already and with certainty that it is wrong. Or, put another way, whatever other situational details are true of a particular murder, we can know already that they are insufficient to make this act that Sue committed right for her to do. Of course, as mentioned in chapter 3, more astute Catholic moralists such as Porter and Gaffney have argued in response to *VS* that the question is not so much whether there are intrinsically evil acts such as murder (they concede that there are) but whether a particular act of killing, say, counts as murder. They are correct; we must indeed consider whether a particular act of killing counts as a murder. And to see will require locating the act of killing in terms of a narrative. But — and here is the twist — *any* act, in virtue of being a human act, already has a narrative home, which means that any description of a human action already has begun the process of embedding the thing done in a narrative. The reason this point needs to be made is that neither "Sue sat on Sam" nor "Sue murdered Sam" stands out as an act that needs embedding in a narrative for the first time since, as we have argued, all acts *qua* acts require a narrative. In receiving them as human acts, we presume this narrative already. In this sense they are on an equal narrative footing just insofar as they are both human acts. This is because the narrative that embeds these particular acts is not just the narrative of Sam and Sue as Sam and Sue, but it is of Sam and Sue as human beings. Put another way, I can be in precisely the same epistemic position about Sam and Sue but know that Sue's murdering Sam was wrong while knowing only that Sue's sitting on Sam could have been either right or wrong. Porter's or Gaffney's point that what really matters is whether a particular killing counts as murder therefore sets up a smoke screen. For it makes it appear as if we need to go through the description killing first, and then, as a next step that involves a new and different sort of moral analysis and judgment, reach toward the "moral" description murder. This is but another way of separating judgment from description, or the human from the moral, or, relatedly, of extracting some actions from a narrative while maintaining that others require it.

20. Gerard Loughlin, *Telling God's Story: Bible, Church, and Narrative Theology* (New York: Cambridge University Press, 1996), p. 141.

relation both to the unintentional and to natural occurrences. This is so because we act in relation to the world, not only to bring certain things about in it but also in response to it.[21] The modern tendency to extract choice from the context of the world that presents us with itself shows a misunderstanding of this relation. It is a relation that must be reestablished in narrative.

21. H. Richard Niebuhr has drawn out the characteristic of responsiveness in human thought and action in terms of the very nature of the human self. The self-initiated, freely choosing self of the modern era is in this sense an illusion. As Niebuhr points out, that the self is constituted in its response rather than in its self-creation is key to a theological account of the self. "Man responsive and responsible before nature, fitting his actions into those of nature; man responsive in political or economic or cultural society as responsible citizen; responsible businessman, responsible educator, responsible scientist, responsible churchman — such men we know and understand. But what ties all these responsitivities and responsibilities together and where is the responsible *self* among all these roles played by the individual being? Can it be located within the self, as though by some mighty act of self-making it brought itself into being and the one 'I' among these many systems of interpretation and response? The self as one self among all the systematized reactions in which it engages seems to be the counterpart of a unity that lies beyond, yet expresses itself in, all the manifold systems of actions upon it. In religious language, the soul and God belong together; or otherwise stated, I am the one within myself as I encounter the One in all that acts upon me" (*The Responsible Self* [New York: Harper & Row, 1978], p. 122).

Niebuhr's treatment in this his final (and unfinished) work is both suggestive and disappointing. While Niebuhr was rare among mid-twentieth-century American Protestant theologians in the degree to which his theological reflection was tied to the church, in this last work the connection is almost entirely lacking. "Responsibility" or "responsiveness" remains for Niebuhr a kind of existential category. It rightly combats the dominant understanding of the human self as the disconnected chooser who moves the (inert) world about in its acts. However, it fails to attend to the necessarily narrative or communal presentation of the world to the self who lives and acts responsively within this world. Ironically, Niebuhr's own book *The Meaning of Revelation* (New York: Macmillan, 1960), written some twenty years before *The Responsible Self*, is one of the classic theological texts that begin to turn theological attention to the significance of narrative and community. (For a text that concentrates specifically on the arising of the category of narrative in theological reflection, see Stanley Hauerwas and L. Gregory Jones, *Why Narrative? Readings on Narrative Theology* [Grand Rapids: Eerdmans, 1989]. An excerpt from Niebuhr's book *The Meaning of Revelation* appropriately opens Hauerwas and Jones's collection.) It is difficult to say why Niebuhr's thought developed in the way it did, although the most likely explanation lies in the primacy of the category of experience or encounter, detectable even in the earlier book's explication of revelation in terms of a "moment" or "occasion." (See, for instance, *The Meaning of Revelation*, pp. 96-99.)

When this occurs, that is, when we can tell a story that relates a person's action to the world, only then are we able to see how what this person did or didn't do is intelligible in relation to human life, or, as Loughlin says, is humanly significant. "[N]arrative or emplotment is that work which draws out of multiplicity, discordance and succession, a configured and concordant unity: a story. It is the means by which life is rendered humanly significant."[22] Here Loughlin's language of "rendering" is appropriate — surely any story renders. But it must also be qualified by what MacIntyre points out above, namely, that "stories are lived before they are told." Human actions, in this sense, never stand apart from narrative. They are not there first, later to be rendered humanly significant as they are emplotted by some storyteller. Human actions *qua* human actions necessarily imply a narrative, not just in their telling but in their doing. Moreover, there is not a narrative in which the act is first done and later a narrative in which it is told of or described. Rather, the doing and the telling narratives themselves are intertwined precisely because when we tell (describe), we hope to say what actually was done.

This is why the telling and retelling of a particular human action is not simply a playful reimagining, as if the narrative of the action was already settled when it is done, subsequently to be manipulated or spun by the retellers. Rather it is the extremely serious business of continuing to discover what was done. For any story, even the first-person story in which the one who acted understood himself to be acting, needs constant reexamination in relation to the truth. This is always done narratively, and in some cases can be done indefinitely into the future. As actors we know this even as we act. For we often sense that the description under which I am now acting might turn out to be wrong, or at least not fully right, for I (or some others) might discover in the future that it may be better placed within a different narrative than the one I am right now able to tell. We sense this not just because we sometimes are unsure of what we are now doing, but also because we know that the narrative under which we are living and acting may change dramatically as it is drawn forward into some previously unimagined future.

Precisely at this point we can see how a new narrative such as

22. Loughlin, p. 142.

God's call of Abram might reconfigure the world as it breaks upon it. This is not to say that the reconfiguration must come all at once. Indeed, as story, it will stretch out over time, as well as grow and change as we learn to tell it better. Moreover, as the story unfolds, its initiation will grow in meaning. This is true not only because the new narrative must grow, but also because the in-breaking of the new narrative necessarily is contextualized, especially at first, by the older narratives it reconfigures. As the story is told, the force and meaning of the in-breaking will become clearer. This is what happens with Abraham at the point in time we have called the beginning of social criticism. At the juncture of the old and the new, a description is placed on an act that assumes and borrows upon a received meaning in the old story but is subverted in the telling of the new story. The new story borrows on the old in the sense that it continues to "refer" to events or things or acts in that story, but in a new way — which of course changes these actions, events, and things. What has begun (and did begin with Abraham) is a new pattern of description that will give rise to novel descriptions or infuse older terms with new meanings. At the point of the deviation of the narratives, a new moral world is born, or, perhaps better, discovered. Importantly, this occurs not by word only, but also by deed. The new moral world unfolds as a people acts into it. To do so it must always be directed by a story and not a principle. At best a principle will reduce, cut out, and also literalize (and so impoverish) the story it "reforms."

This relation between narrative and action extends and reiterates two key points we have been trying to illustrate. First, we now can see the interrelation between morality, human action, and narrative. As we have argued following Aquinas, human action is necessarily moral action. Further, following MacIntyre, we have suggested that human action presumes a human narrative. It follows, then, that a morality can only be adequately carried by a narrative. Second, we can see in what way the eschatological claims of Christians are worth considering: namely, as these claims about what is yet to come pass concretely through act and story into the present, human actions done or omitted today are not placed in relation to the conservative (and dominant) moral understanding of this time, but rather in relation to the eschaton. The calling for the church now, as it always has been, is for this generation of Christians to live "in the world (of today) but not of

221

the world (of today)." Faithfulness to this calling depends on the community's capacity to carry forward a set of stories and descriptions that are not of this world precisely because they are of the world to come — with the key claim added that this world, the world of today, is not self-interpreting. Rather, this world is rightly understood in terms of the world to come. If this latter claim is to be sustained, Christians must set about the task of showing that, and how, the kingdom of God is among us even now.

Sustaining the story and action descriptions related to it is a task that can be done in no other way except according to the pattern noted above. By their ritual acts the Jews continue to reenact the Passover, fielding their children's questions by telling once again its full story. For Christians, who evangelize, the questions will need to be solicited not only from their children but also from inquiring strangers. As one might ask: "Just what are you Christians doing when you eat the bread and drink the wine? And what could it all possibly mean?"

Christians hope, of course, that these strangers will consider joining them, and so the church will continue in the world. But they cannot see the perpetuation of their community and its story as self-justifying. Ultimately the justification for the perpetuation of the story told and of the related descriptions acted within must lie in the story's and descriptions' truthfulness about the world. Of course, the determination of the truthfulness of what sometimes has been called a "grand narrative" is a notoriously difficult affair.[23] However, one point that follows from the above analysis is that the question of the truthfulness of a particular narrative and its related descriptions is really the same question as the truthfulness of a morality, since, as we have seen, moral action is human action and human action presumes a narrative. Conceived in terms of action, this point leads to another, namely, that any narrative laying claim to the truth must be able to be lived and acted within. Extended for Christians, whose story is eschatological, if the Christian story is true, there must now be a people who is faithfully living and acting in it.

This means the criteria for the truthfulness of the Christian narra-

---

23. See Michael Goldberg's extended discussion in *Theology and Narrative* (Philadelphia: Trinity Press International, 1991), especially pp. 146-93.

tive are actually more stringent than if truth criteria are conceived in a more general form. If a "morality" is taken merely as the set of descriptions of acting and not acting that flows from a narrative about human life in the world, it is entirely possible that we might have not yet discovered true moral action and descriptions, for we have not yet discovered the true narrative of the human and natural world.[24] Or, in another direction, it might be that we once had it but lost it — and now need to go looking to reclaim it. However, Christians are tied by their theology to the notion that the story they tell, and its related descriptions, must now be in the world — for if it were not yet, or if it was and then wasn't, God would be neither provident nor faithful. Put bluntly, for Christians the existence of the church, the true church, in any age is a necessary criterion for the truth of their eschatological narrative.

The ongoing story of God's providence and faithfulness begins with Abraham when, as we have said, social criticism entered the world. If Christianity is to have a claim on the truth, then the beginning must be extended to the end, and these and the various points in between must be connected by a people living God's life in the world. Christian theology, as the handmaid to the community that carries this truth, serves the community as a pointer to the truth. In this way theology calls the community to see itself in terms of the long and unbroken line that stretches back to Abraham.[25] As the

24. There is an important analogy between the key role played by teleology in Aquinas's (as well as Aristotle's) understanding of human action and the eschatological structure of Christian theology. Eschatology, however, implies community, and therefore politics, whereas teleology does not. Of course, Aristotle's teleology, and Aquinas's following him, leads to the political since he holds that human beings are by nature political animals. But one could break that connection and still have a teleology. The eschatological structure, however, of Christian theology implies community in that it points not to my end as a creature of so-and-so features (including the political) but to our mutual and shared end in the kingdom of God.

25. Augustine, upon whose account of the city of God many of our reflections in this section are patterned, takes the story back further to the Garden of Eden, specifically to Cain and Abel. "Now, the first man born of the two parents of the human race was Cain. He belonged to the city of man. The nextborn was Abel, and he was of the City of God" (*City of God* 15.1). The reading of the first family in this way is figurative, particularly for us, but I believe also for Augustine. The story of Abraham's leaving can be similarly read — and used interpretively in construing how social criticism arises and

223

community does this, it must recognize that the line is (and must remain) a tracing of an ongoing critique of how the world sees itself: the history of God's people in the world is a connected history of social critique. Relatedly, the church cannot but also recognize that its line is not the only line. A people called the Jews (at the least)[26] also traces out such a line.[27] The dots along these lines are myriad, and of a variety of types. Typically these dots are thought of as events, understood as God's faithful acts within the narrative: God's calling of Abraham, the Israelites' crossing of the Red Sea, Jesus' calling of the disciples, or the church's formulation of the Nicene Creed. However, Paul Ramsey's suggestive phrasing of action descriptions (such as "adultery") as "ancient landmarks" clears a way for us to see that these dots also include descriptions of actions or omissions by which the people formed by the narrative have acted out God's life in the world. If one were to set about to articulate a task for Christian ethics that extends the theological task just mentioned, far from consolidating these many and various descriptions into some one fundamental moral principle, Christian ethics must critically investigate the great variety of human actions or omissions available through the storied theological description of the human world in the light of God's calling of his people Israel and the sending of his Son to live and die among us.

---

functions within a society. It is important, however, not to move to such a reading until the historical tie from Abraham to the Jewish people is made. Any reading that ignores this threatens God's embodied presence in human history. For the Christian church to understand itself in relation to the city of God, it must begin by understanding itself in relation to Israel. While it may allow it, I do not believe Augustine's account entails this. This is why the call of Abraham is the appropriate first term.

26. It is intriguing that the covenant of Gen. 15 is immediately prior to the birth described in chapter 16 of Ishmael, whose story is extended in Islam. The relation of the story of Christians with Jews is so tight, not only in its earlier times but even now as Christians are being forced by the Holocaust to recognize their own deep unfaithfulness to the God of Abraham. Christian theology cannot now continue without recognizing that Christians are not the only peculiar people God brought forth from Abraham. The question of whether this must also be said of Muslims is less quickly answered, but it remains a key matter Christian theologians will need to address more explicitly in the future.

27. For an insightful attempt to mark Jewish and Christian narratives in relation one to the other, see Michael Goldberg, *Jews and Christians: Getting Our Stories Straight* (Philadelphia: Trinity Press International, 1991).

224

## 4. Reading and Living the Gospel

The fact that two lines can be drawn back to Abraham should function for Christians as a double sign of God's care. As well, it should remind theologians these descriptions must also be open to criticism and challenge from other communities carried by other stories. Christians cannot presume, in other words, that the only place to find true descriptions of the human (moral) world is inside their own story. However, it must be their first concern to know the meaning and use of their own descriptions as they arise out of and relate to the ongoing story they tell of God's coming kingdom, even now present in Christ Jesus.

In this regard we should expect various moral descriptions of things done that will be tied to different narratives.[28] While in some cases the difference between these descriptions will not necessarily produce a quarrel since the stories and their peoples may (we hope)

---

28. Recently I received a forwarded e-mail from a Jewish colleague, Rabbi Marc Shapiro, that had circulated among Jews. It was entitled "An Easy Mitzvah" and urged us to visit a certain Internet site, which would result in a meal being served to a poor person. My inquiry to him for a further explanation about what exactly qualified as a mitzvah yielded the following e-mail reply: "A mitzvah is a good deed. There are obligatory mitzvahs, such as sitting in a sukkah or fasting on Yom Kippur, and then there are mitzvahs which are more vague, e.g., it is a mitzvah to give charity, but obviously, the more you give the better, but there is no command for me to give the dollar in my pocket at present. It is a mitzvah to help people, but I am not commanded to go down to the soup kitchen every Thursday night. These type of mitzvahs are left to individual judgment and discretion. An easy mitzvah is one in which all you have to do is press a button — it's a lot harder, and thus a lot more meritorious, to work at the soup kitchen. The Talmud says that you are rewarded for your efforts to do a mitzvah even if you don't succeed in carrying it out (your car breaks down on the way to the soup kitchen) but the rabbis say that all these mitzvahs should be done for their own sake, not in order to achieve a heavenly reward, and certainly not to be honored in this world."

The moral world of a Jew includes the possibility of a mitzvah, even an easy one, while this is not so clearly available to me as a Christian. Put more concretely, I may visit my friend Rabbi Shapiro in his sukkah, but as I sit with him I will not be, like him, performing the obligatory mitzvah of "sitting in a sukkah." However, plainly both of us can work side by side in a soup kitchen, as well as share an interpretation of what we are doing together. An investigation of the way such action descriptions merge and split apart, merge and split apart, is also appropriate work for those Christian theologians sometimes referred to as Christian ethicists.

find ways to live side by side, we should not imagine that genuine moral conflict and disagreement will never ensue. In fact, the church expects to be in disagreement with the world, both in its story and its descriptions. When there is a contest, however, it is important to see that what is being contested is the truth about the human world and about the narratives through which human life is rightly lived.

Questions about morality are questions about how to live the human life well, a point that may seem obvious. Yet the analysis undertaken in this book suggests it is less obvious than we might guess. In fact, if we have been even close to correct about the action theorists who classify actions as a species of events; or about the physicalism that underlies proportionalism; or about the buzz sawing of Enlightenment moral theorists or reformers such as Bentham; then a good bit of what has happened in the modern moral discussion is rightly characterized by an emptying out of the human from the moral. I suggest that one of the gravest dangers of our own time is the supposition that we can speak of the moral without speaking of the human. Since this is impossible to do, i.e., whenever one speaks about the moral, one necessarily speaks about the human, we have been brought by our deceptions to having public discussions of the human that pretend to be about something else much more limited and (some imagine) more scientific: discussions about such things as "the moral," or "the social," or "the political," or "the psychological." In such a context, essentially human questions are given inhuman answers, although it is virtually impossible to show them as inhuman, since no one imagines that such a thing is at stake in the questions. It is easier, in such a context, to suppose either that we all agree about morality or that we all disagree, and it really doesn't matter. For if essentially human questions are given inhuman answers and these are widely agreed upon, then those who give the questions human answers will appear to be holding things up unnecessarily, particularly when they squabble among themselves. Genuine religious disagreement of the sort that stands between Christians and Jews may turn out to be among those most precious gifts of God we must carefully preserve.

Theologically there is another important wrinkle in this. For the full coupling of the moral and the human implies that genuine moral action requires the entry, foursquare, into some essentially human story that we do not just read or examine but rather live. For Christians this should be an easy thing to grasp since their key texts, the Gospel stories of Jesus, refuse to allow their readers to survey them from a distance. They do not let us hold the world they tell of separate from our own human world. In Mark, for instance, we do not read well if we do not see ourselves in the disciples, who in their slowness of understanding are nonetheless repeatedly presented with the question "Who do you say that I am?"

This has implications with regard to those who enter the world of the Gospels with the working notion that truth about the Gospels' world can and should be first described in the form of a more or less well substantiated hypothesis of past events from which certain tentative conclusions can be drawn and applied to the human life of action, thought, and passion as we now know it.[29] In contrast, and as Loughlin notes, "The [Gospel] narratives may not, or not in all their parts, be literal descriptions of past events — almost certainly many of them are not. They do however render the true identity of an actual person — Jesus of Nazareth. They show us what no merely descriptive story can show us, that he was and is the Christ of God. In this sense they are more profoundly referential than any historian's account, which is always hypothetical. The gospels are not hypotheses but poetic and faithful narratives."[30]

Apart from his use of the oxymoronic "merely descriptive story"

---

29. Reading the Gospel of Mark carefully is one of the best antidotes for those who like to read the Bible as a source for the problems of today — as if we could control the text sufficiently to gather from it nuggets from the world back then to apply to our world of today. Mark refuses us this distance; instead his Gospel draws us up into the story of Jesus, in effect demanding that we become participants rather than readers from afar as we see ourselves as Jesus' disciples. Of course, modern readers put up a significant resistance, for we are used to standing aloof, particularly in our scholarly reading. Indeed, even a text such as David Rhoads, Joanna Dewey, and Donald Michie's *Mark as Story* (Minneapolis: Fortress, 1999), which makes this point about what Mark demands of his readers, cannot resist in its final turns a return to a more comfortable distance. "Having experienced this story world, contemporary readers may be able to think anew about the meaning of life, its purpose, its possibilities, and its outcome — to see and struggle with the real world in new ways and perhaps be better prepared to live more faithful and humane lives" (p. 146). I find it difficult to imagine that this — leading more humane lives — is the sort of thing Mark (or God) had in mind with his Gospel.

30. Loughlin, p. 156.

(there is no such thing) Loughlin here rightly seizes on the key point that the Gospels never let loose the tight embrace that holds together the story of Jesus as told and as acted or reenacted by the tellers and hearers. The claim, indeed, that Jesus of Nazareth is the Christ of God requires that the claim not be merely a literal description of past events, but also one that comes into our present. It is about us, and our lives, as much as it is about the disciples'.

In a reverse direction, it also follows that what has come to stand in the Christian tradition as acts that mark its truth can and should govern how we understand what is imagined by some actor or claimant to be true. As Bruce Marshal notes, statements regarding Christ's Lordship coupled with actions that deviate a great deal from the practical sense Christians have given that Lordship become meaning orphans or, strictly, false.

> The problem with the crusader's use of the sentence, *"Christus est Dominus,"* is simply that, uttered as a warrant for splitting people's heads open, it lacks the meaning which the religion insists it must have, if it is to be a true proposition, one which corresponds to reality. By using *"Dominus"* in this context, the crusader shows that what he means by the term is a medieval knight errant, much like himself. But according to the normative patterns of Christian speech and action, Christ is not that kind of Lord; when the predicate *"Dominus"* has that meaning, it is not applicable to the subject *"Christus,"* that is, *"Christus est Dominus"* becomes intrasystematically false.[31]

Marshal is not implying that the crusader's claim that *Christus est Dominus* cannot be understood or lacks meaning when he makes it. Indeed, his claim has meaning precisely in the action he takes that follows upon it. But so rendered meaningful, it becomes "intrasystematically" false, that is to say, in the action it becomes, or is shown to be, another claim than the Christian claim *Christus est Dominus*, such as "Christ is a medieval knight-errant." And this latter claim is false according to Christians.

To be understood as false in this way, however, the context or nar-

---

31. Bruce Marshal, "Aquinas as Postliberal Theologian," *Thomist* 53 (1989): 353-402, quoted in Loughlin, p. 160.

rative in which *Christus est Dominus* otherwise has meaning — and against which the crusader's action must be checked — must be embodied. That is, if we are to say that the crusader's action of killing the infidel is not consonant with what Christians mean by *Christus est Dominus*, then we shall need another set of practices which differently show forth or embody that claim. There are a great host of these practices, and their numbers must continue to increase, since Christians are charged in each generation to be Christ to the world. But the list surely includes: feeding the hungry, sharing the Eucharist, remaining faithful in marriage, comforting the sick, venerating the cross, succoring the dying, seeking the truth. Insofar as Christians have over time engaged in these practices, a set of action descriptions that describe the practices has arisen to hold them in place, a vocabulary of action or omission. By this vocabulary Christians fill out their claim of Christ's Lordship and all it entails about the human world.

The action vocabulary of Christians flowing from their affirmation that Jesus is Lord will include a contrasting set of descriptions: acts contrary to Christ's Lordship. This vocabulary is not in opposition to the descriptions of acts of Christ's Lordship; rather it is complementary to it logically, in the same way that the vocabulary and meaning of sins is understood by Aquinas in the *Summa* to relate to the virtues. It is in this sense, for instance, that marital fidelity is not contradicted but rather complemented by the notion of adultery, since adultery as a description is premised on there being (and people acting out) faithfulness in marriage.[32]

32. Plainly descriptions such as "adultery" will be carried by others besides Christians. We need not hold that the vocabulary of action or omission Christians carry will necessarily diverge from that of other communities who carry other stories. This is partly true because the Christian church has already given many of its descriptions to the world. To be sure, some descriptions, such as "sharing the Eucharist," have meaning only to the extent that there is a Christian community that carries with it the story of Christ's last meal with his disciples and his subsequent death and resurrection. Yet other descriptions like "adultery" will have broader connection since the practice is broader than the church. This should be expected, both because God's kingdom on earth, while represented by the church, is far broader than it, and because we are all subject to the natural law. (See John Bowlin's *Contingency and Fortune in Aquinas's Ethics* [New York: Cambridge University Press, 1999], particularly chap. 3, in which Aquinas's understanding of natural law is properly distinguished from modern interpretations of it.) Hence Christians should expect that at least some of the descriptions of the moral

It is in this context that Pope John Paul II's quotation of Vatican II's lists of acts that he calls "intrinsically evil" is best fit.

> Whatever is hostile to life itself, such as any kind of homicide, genocide, abortion, euthanasia, and voluntary suicide; whatever violates the integrity of the human person, such as mutilation, physical and mental torture and attempts to coerce the spirit; whatever is offensive to human dignity, such as subhuman living conditions, arbitrary imprisonment, deportation, slavery, prostitution and trafficking in women and children; degrading conditions of work which treat laborers as mere instruments of profit, and not as free responsible persons: all these and the like are a disgrace, and so long as they infect human civilization they contaminate those who inflict them more than those who suffer injustice, and they are a negation of the honor due to the Creator.[33]

One might quarrel with this list, adding some descriptions and subtracting others. Quarreling like this remains an important task of Christian theologians. As Aquinas notes, "the theologian considers human acts under the aspect of merit and demerit, which is proper to human acts,"[34] and such consideration will of course include disputation. But that there are such actions, i.e., actions contrary to the Lordship of Christ, seems indisputable. Otherwise the disjunction between what the crusader mentioned above does and what he says could not be identified.

The claim *Christus est Dominus* therefore both implies certain actions and excludes certain others. There is good reason, however, to think that it cannot be spelled out precisely or exhaustively in terms of them. The virtue of prudence resists this full specification since, as Pieper notes, prudence takes account of the

> realities which surround man's concrete activity [which] are of an almost infinite variety, [from Aquinas] *quasi infinitae deversitatis.*

world they carry will link with others' descriptions at a variety of points, each to be discovered in its particularity. One of the key ongoing tasks of ecumenical discussion as well as "intrareligious dialogue" will be to discover what different Christian or religious communities mean by their descriptions.

33. *Veritatis Splendor*, para. #80.

34. Aquinas, *Summa Theologiae* I-II.7.2.

And above all man himself — in this distinguishing himself from animals — is [from Aquinas] "a being of manifold and diverse activities; precisely by virtue of its rank in the order of being is the soul of man directed toward infinite variety." Since this is so, [from Aquinas] "the good of man changes in multifold fashion, according to the various conditions of men and the times and places, and similar factors." However, the goals of human action do not change, nor do man's basic directions. For every "condition" of man, at all times and places, he is under the obligation to be just and brave and temperate.[35]

Exactly which act from among a number of possible acts is the prudent one can never be prespecified, for it must respond to the great variety of truths about the world that apply to a particular person at a particular time. This is not to say that a prudent act might be any act at all — the pope has already given us a list of exclusions, which is by no means exhaustive. Moreover, as Pieper's comments imply, those who act prudently are those who have already been trained in the cardinal virtues of temperance, fortitude, and justice — and for Christians these are true virtues as they have been transformed by charity.[36] As we have seen in this final chapter, this transformation includes that prudence be attuned eschatologically, formed critically in the coming kingdom, that is even now living among us. The prudent community that carries and is carried by the story of the God of Abraham

35. Pieper, p. 25.

36. Here we can see, once again, the tight connection between virtue and act, in this case the futility of speaking of act independent from virtue. Earlier we argued that act cannot be shoved aside by virtue designations, as if all good acts could be sufficiently redescribed as "acts of virtue" (e.g., just acts, temperate acts, etc.) and all evil acts as "acts of vice." Following the analysis of this chapter, this is doubly true for Christians since they learn their virtue from the stories of a Jewish man in the first century who "went about doing good," from the subsequent stories of the saints who followed this man as well as earlier ones, like Abram. Hence, even such a grand term as the virtue "faith" must be tied for Christians to the specific action of the man Abram who left his father's house.

The tight connection between act and virtue is displayed in magnificent detail in the second part of the *Summa*, as we have noted. For a contemporary theological treatment of virtue that is (I trust) consonant with the themes of this book on action, see my and Stanley Hauerwas's *Christians among the Virtues* (Notre Dame, Ind.: University of Notre Dame Press, 1997).

and of Jesus of Nazareth does not set about to assemble a list of good or bad acts, but rather to form a people in the story — a people sufficiently in tune with the realities of the world revealed in the story so as to be able to live it in any age. This is the charge of Christians in all times and places: to act within the human world according to the revolutionary truth that it is not only our human world, but also God's.

# Index

abandonment, 155, 157, 159, 162-63. *See also* moral notions

Abraham, 204-16, 221, 223-24, 231

act classification, 95-96, 105-18, 134-36. *See also* Aquinas on species classification of human acts

action theory, 4, 18-19, 21-28, 33, 71, 159, 226

action tree, 23, 25-27, 29, 31

adultery, 40, 51, 118-19, 159, 161, 201, 229. *See also* moral notions

aesthetics. *See* art

agape, 43-44, 47, 49, 57

almsgiving, 117, 127

analogy, 163-64

Anscombe, G. E. M., ix-x, 28-33, 73, 92-93, 101, 112, 140, 150

Aquinas, St. Thomas, 2, 6, 8, 9, 67-68, 80, 83-84, 87, 137-38, 141, 145-55, 160, 166, 176, 178-79, 188, 192-97, 206, 218, 221, 223, 230-31; on acts of a man, 89, 94-95, 98, 101, 112-13; on counsel, 104, 105, 108; on individual act, 116-18, 128, 130, 137; on internal act of will and external act, 109, 121-30, 132, 134, 150, 174; on last end, 88, 90-91, 93-94, 106-7; on minutiae, 102-5; on omission and commission, 170-73, 184; on moral acts as human acts, 88-92; on reason, 117, 125, 131, 132, 150, 190-91; on species classification of human acts, 92, 96, 103, 105, 112-20, 122, 126-27, 130, 132-36, 155, 170

Aristotle, 8, 13, 83, 87, 89, 98-99, 108, 192-93, 223, 229

art, 93, 183-87

Audi, Robert, 145

Augustine, Saint, 185, 187, 197, 205-8, 216, 223-24

Austin, J. L., ix, 85

Bader-Saye, Scott, x, 165

Bennett, William, 191

Bentham, Jeremy, 43, 48, 52, 144, 199-203, 210, 226

Bolt, Robert, 138-39, 158